UNRAVELLING CRIMINAL JUSTICE

Unravelling Criminal Justice

Eleven British Studies

Edited by

DAVID DOWNES
Professor of Social Administration
London School of Economics

palgrave

First published 1992 by
THE MACMILLAN PRESS LTD
Houndmills, Basingstoke, Hampshire RG21 2XS
and London
Companies and representatives
throughout the world

ISBN 0–333–54056–5 hardcover 2/37/92X
ISBN 0–333–54057–3 paperback

A catalogue record for this book is available
from the British Library.
**Printed and bound by Antony Rowe Ltd,
Eastbourne**
Transferred to digital printing 2001

Contents

Notes on the Editor and the Contributors

Michael Adler is a Senior Lecturer in Social Policy and a Research Member of the Centre of Criminology and the Social and Philosophical Study of Law at the University of Edinburgh. He is the author (with Alison Petch and Jack Tweedie) of *Parental Choice and Educational Policy* (1989), as well as numerous articles on the socio-legal aspects of consumer indebtedness, education, housing and social security, and (with Brian Longhurst) on imprisonment in Scotland.

Harry Blagg is Lecturer in Social Policy at the University of Lancaster, currently on secondment to the State Government Advisory Committee on Young Offenders in Western Australia. He is co-author (with David Smith) of *Crime, Penal Policy and Social Work* (1989).

Anthony E. Bottoms is Wolfson Professor of Criminology and Director of the Institute of Criminology at the University of Cambridge. His main research interests lie in the fields of criminal justice policy and environmental criminology. He has conducted empirical research on a variety of topics, including penal institutions, community penalties, crime prevention, the relationship between housing policy and crime, and defendants' views of the criminal process.

Pat Carlen is Professor of Criminology at Keele University, and has published ten books, foremost amongst them being: *Magistrates' Justice*; *Women's Imprisonment*; *Women, Crime and Poverty*; and *Alternatives to Women's Imprisonment*. She is the co-author of a book on law, education and social control.

David Downes is Professor of Social Administration at the London School of Economics, where he has taught since 1963. His books include: *The Delinquent Solution* (1966); *Gambling, Work and Leisure* (1976); (with Paul Rock) *Understanding Deviance* (2nd edn, 1988); and *Contrasts in Tolerance* (1988). He edited *Crime and the City: Essays in Memory of John Mays* (1989), and he was editor of the *British Journal of Criminology* from 1985 to 1990.

Tony Jefferson is Reader in Criminology at the Centre for Criminological and Legal Research, University of Sheffield. He has written widely on questions relating to policing, race, crime, the media and youth culture, including several co-authored books: *Introducing Police Work* (with Mike Brogden and Sandra Walklate); *Interpreting Policework* and *Controlling the Constable* (both with Roger Grimshaw); *Policing the Crisis* (with Stuart Hall *et al.*) and *Resistance through Rituals* (co-edited with Stuart Hall). His latest book is *The Case against Paramilitary Policing*. He is currently working on aspects of masculinity.

Roy D. King is currently Professor of Social Theory and Institutions and Head of the School of Sociology and Social Policy at University College of North Wales, where he is also joint Director of the Centre for Social Policy Research and Development. He has researched widely on prisons in Britain and the United States and has been an adviser to both the Home Office Prison Department and the US Federal Bureau of Prisons. He is the co-author of several books, including *A Taste of Prison* (1976); *Albany: Birth of a Prison – End of an Era* (1978); and *The Future of the Prison System* (1980); as well as numerous articles on prisons and imprisonment.

Roger Leng has been a lecturer in the School of Law, University of Birmingham, since 1976. He has written widely in the fields of criminal law and company law and has acted as a consultant to the Law Reform Commission of Canada.

Michael Levi is Professor of Criminology in the School of Social and Administrative Studies at the University of Wales College of Cardiff. He has written many articles on white-collar crime and policing and two books, *The Phantom Capitalists* (1981) and *Regulating Fraud: White-Collar Crime and the Criminal Process* (1987). Recent work includes *Customer Confidentiality, Money Laundering and Police–Bank Relationships* (1991), and a new book on *Victims of Fraud* (forthcoming).

Brian Longhurst is Lecturer in Sociology at the University of Salford. He was previously Research Fellow in the Department of Social Policy and Social Work at the University of Edinburgh. He is author of *Karl Mannheim and the Contemporary Sociology of Knowledge* (1989), as well as articles on imprisonment (with M. Adler), the sociology of knowledge and the sociology of culture.

Doreen McBarnet is Senior Research Fellow at the Centre for Socio-Legal Studies, Wolfson College, Oxford, which she joined in 1977 after lecturing for several years in the Sociology Department at Glasgow University. Her past research has included work on criminal justice, and she is currently engaged on research on tax avoidance and on European corporate finance. She is the author of *Conviction* (1981), co-editor of *Law, State and Society* (1981), and has contributed to books and journals in sociology, law, criminology and accounting.

Michael McConville is Professor of Law and Director of the Legal Research Institute at the University of Warwick. He has written widely on criminology, criminal justice and evidence, both in England and the United States of America. His co-authored books include: *Negotiated Justice* (1977); *Jury Trials* (1979); *Courts, Prosecution and Conviction* (1981); and *Defense of the Poor* (1985). He has just completed a book on policing communities and is writing a book on the work of defence solicitors in criminal cases.

Kathleen McDermott is now Assistant Dean of Students at Columbia University in New York City. Previously she was a Senior Research Fellow at the Centre for Social Policy Research and Development, University College of North Wales. Together with Professor Roy King, she has conducted extensive research on prisons in England and Wales, and most recently on the impact of imprisonment on prisoners' families. She is also the author of many articles on prisons and imprisonment.

Rod Morgan is Professor of Criminal Justice at the University of Bristol. In addition to his work on police consultative groups he has recently completed research and publications on lay visitors to police stations and those aspects of the Police and Criminal Evidence Act 1984 relating to detention in police custody. He has recently published (with D. Smith) *Coming to Terms with Policing* (1989), and he is co-editor of *Policing and Society*. He is currently doing research on prison disciplinary hearings and complaints against the Customs and Excise and Immigration Departments. At the time of writing he was full-time assessor to Lord Justice Woolf's Inquiry into the disturbance at Strangeways Prison, Manchester.

Geoffrey Pearson is Wates Professor of Social Work at the University of London, Goldsmiths' College. He has held teaching posts at University College, Cardiff, the University of Bradford, and Middlesex Polytechnic. He is a member of the council of the British Society of Criminology, and associate editor of the *British Journal of Criminology*. He is the author of *The Deviant Imagination* (1975); *Hooligan: A History of Respectable Fears* (1983); *Young People and Heroin* (1986); and *The New Heroin Users* (1987).

Andrew Pithouse is Lecturer in Social Work in the School of Social and Administrative Studies at the University of Wales College of Cardiff. He has written on the socialisation of social workers, on mental handicap and on the Children Act 1989.

Alice Sampson, formerly Research Fellow at Middlesex Polytechnic, is Research Officer at the Home Office Crime Prevention Unit.

Andrew Sanders is a Senior Lecturer in the School of Law at Birmingham University. His teaching and research are primarily in criminology and criminal justice. His research on the prosecution process and on access to legal advice for suspects in police custody has been published widely. He is currently writing a criminal justice text, and is a member of the Parole Board.

Philip Schlesinger is Professor of Film and Media Studies at the University of Stirling. Relevant current research includes a qualitative study of women's interpretations of televised violence funded by the Broadcasting Standards Council, and related past work has focused on terrorism and the media, part-funded by the Nuffield Foundation. He is currently engaged in work on culture and national identity, and is the author of *Putting 'Reality' Together* (2nd edn, 1987), and of *Media, State and Nation* (1991); and is co-author of *Televising 'Terrorism'* (1983) and of *Los Intelectuales en la Sociedad de la Información* (1987). An editor of the journal *Media, Culture and Society*, he has co-edited *Communicating Politics* (1986) and *Media, Culture and Society: A Critical Reader* (1986).

Mary Seneviratne is a Principal Lecturer in Law at Sheffield City Polytechnic where she teaches criminal law and family law. For a number of years she was a Research Fellow at the Centre for Criminological and Socio-Legal Studies, University of Sheffield, where she undertook research into local government complaints procedures and into the criminal justice system. She has also worked as a solicitor in local government, and has recently submitted her PhD thesis on 'Complaints Procedure in Local Authorities'.

David Smith is Lecturer in Social Work at the University of Lancaster. He is co-author with Harry Blagg of *Crime, Penal Policy and Social Work* (1989).

Simon Stevenson is Lecturer in British and European History in the Division of Humanities, Griffith University, Brisbane, Australia, and was formerly a Research Associate at the Institute of Criminology, University of Cambridge. He has published a number of articles on aspects of the history of criminal justice in sixteenth-, nineteenth- and twentieth-century England.

Paul Stubbs, formerly Visiting Research Fellow at the University of Lancaster, is Lecturer in Social Work at the University of Bradford.

Howard Tumber is a Lecturer in Sociology at the City University where he is currently Director of Communication Policy Studies. He has worked as a research analyst and consultant and researched on an ERSC-funded project on foreign correspondents, and on a Broadcasting Research Unit-supported study of the media and the Falklands War. Related work was conducted for the Broadcasting Research Unit on the media and the inner city riots of 1982. He is the author of *Television and the Riots* (1982), and co-author of *Journalists at War* (1988). He is currently engaged on research into business and the media.

Monica Walker is a Research Fellow at the Centre for Criminological and Legal Research, University of Sheffield, where she teaches research methods and statistics. She has written a book on crime statistics and has published several articles in this field. She has been a statistical adviser in the Faculty of Law for many years and has assisted in many research projects. She is also the statistical adviser to the *International Journal for the Sociology of Law* and the *British Journal of Criminology*.

Introduction[*]

DAVID DOWNES

The criminal justice system in Britain is in deep trouble. The crime rate has risen eight-fold since 1950 and, though the bulk of even so-called serious offences are relatively petty and small-scale in their immediate effects, the signs are that the resulting decline in the quality of life in the worst-hit areas is cumulatively severe. The causes of this marked deterioration arguably lie in deep-seated social, economic and cultural trends beyond the reach of, though in their turn affecting, criminal justice processes. It is a truism that much the same picture can be drawn for most societies across the industrial world, more starkly for the United States, less so for Japan. Differences do obtain, however, in the extent to which the criminal justice responses of different societies have adapted to these changes, not least to the emergence of especially damaging phenomena, of the kind with which our system did not have to cope 30 years ago, such as terrorism, hard-drug trafficking and certain forms of corporate crime.

In Britain the combination of new forms of deviance and a greatly swollen rate of standard crimes has brought a sense of endemic crisis and at times actual breakdown to key pressure points in the criminal justice system. Indeed, to use the term 'system' for so ill co-ordinated a set of processes is itself problematic. Despite some striking successes at local level, crime prevention initiatives have yet to be translated into coherent national practice. Levels of public trust in police effectiveness have declined throughout the 1980s. Reforms in the prosecution system have yet to make significant inroads into the large volume of cases which are either non-prosecutable or divertible. The rules of evidence and their judicial interpretation have facilitated a series of miscarriages of justice – most notoriously in the cases of the Guildford Four and the Birmingham Six – which must have damaged the high reputation generally claimed for British justice around the world (though the system specifically at fault in these cases was English justice). Not least, levels of sentencing to custody have been unwarrantedly high by Western European standards, and standards of conditions of imprisonment correspondingly low, trends which culminated in the disturbances at Strangeways prison in April 1990. Welcome as recent falls in the prison population have been, it is too soon to say whether they offer merely temporary respite or a sea-change in judicial thinking. On all counts, the 'system' is over-ripe for radical reform and, while the chapters that follow have not been shaped by a reformist agenda, they arose from a research initiative intended to bring criminological work to bear on key issues related to crime and the criminal justice system. This book draws together the most salient findings from the projects involved.

In addition, for reasons outlined below, the book is aimed at an elusive audience: the so-called general reader or educated layperson who usually avoids sociology like the plague. So much is this the case that the very idea of a sociological best-seller sounds a non-starter, though some authors, such as Erving Goffman and Howard Becker, undoubtedly achieved that status in the USA. Even in Britain, a book such as *Images of Deviance*, edited by Stan Cohen, sold over 60,000 copies between 1971 and 1985, and Cohen and Laurie Taylor's study of maximum security imprisonment, *Psychological Survival*, achieved a sale of almost 25,000, hardly derisory figures. Yet in general, even criminology's superficially exciting subject matter fails to draw the crowds. Why should this be so? It is no real defence to cite the complaint as afflicting all academic fields. History found its popular voice in A. J. P. Taylor, philosophy in Bertrand Russell, and even the seemingly impenetrable field of physics has Steven Hawking. Among the social sciences, John Maynard Keynes in economics and Sigmund Freud in psychology are embedded in at least middle-class popular consciousness. Perhaps the closest figures in sociology to such 'household names' are Ralf Dahrendorf and A. H. 'Chelly' Halsey, both of whom take prominent roles in public-policy debate. However, there is no real sociological counterpart to Russell and Keynes, a fact of life which did not worry sociologists unduly until, in the early 1980s, a frontal assault was launched against the social sciences in general, and sociology in particular, which exposed their institutional vulnerability and lack of political clout.

The main symbol of the successful expansion of the social sciences in Britain, from their foundation in the early years of this century at the London School of Economics, had been the creation of the Social Science Research Council by the Labour government in 1965. Though the SSRC dispensed funding for post-graduate teaching and research which was minuscule by comparison with the American foundations, or those of science and medicine, it none the less presided over a flourishing field. The general expansion of higher education following the Robbins Report of 1964 and the announcement of Crosland's binary policy in 1965 fuelled a heady rate of growth of sociology departments: from one only in the immediate post-war period – at the LSE – to 50 or more by 1970. In the process, false as well as great expectations were generated about what might flow from such expansion.

One excessive, if not false, expectation was that the social sciences could automatically be turned to for the technically precise diagnosis of and solution to urgent social problems. The return of a Conservative administration in 1970 saw the beginnings of a more hostile relationship between government (though not their officials, among whom interest and support were growing) and the social sciences than had been the case under Labour. The thorniest problem of the day in social terms was the growing awareness that poverty, newly defined in terms of relative deprivation by Abel-Smith and Townsend (1965), was not only stubbornly ineradicable but actually growing. The same issues had been hotly debated for a decade in the USA, and the terms of the debate in both countries had merged to become a contest between those, usually on the Left, who saw the issue in structural terms, as the outcome of socially wrought inequalities of wealth and income, and those, usually on the Right, who saw it as the outcome of the 'culture of poverty' entrapping individuals and their families into self-perpetuating and unnecessary 'cycles of deprivation'. The Secretary of State for Health and Social Services, Sir Keith Joseph, adhered to the second view and launched a research programme under SSRC auspices to investigate the subject. Its findings challenged the 'cycles of deprivation' thesis (see Rutter and Madge, 1976) but the whole process revealed starkly how resistant were the social science practitioners to agenda-setting by the government.

The return of a doctrinally much harsher Conservative government in 1979 gave Sir Keith Joseph direct control over the SSRC, as Secretary of State for Education. In the context of economic crisis, the expansion of higher education in general, and the social sciences in particular, had lost their lustre. Combined with the phenomenon of student unrest, which had come to be associated on the Right with the social sciences – usually wrongly – but which had singled out Conservative politicians, not least Sir Keith Joseph, for attack or exclusion from campus debates, government hostility to such targets was increased. Joseph's first inclination had been simply to close the SSRC down but he instead appointed Lord Rothschild to head an enquiry into the 'scale and nature' of its work, expecting him to recommend its dissolution. Instead, Rothschild mounted a spirited defence of the social sciences and the SSRC, whose 'dismemberment or liquidation ... would not only be an act of intellectual vandalism ...; it would also have damaging consequences for the whole country – and ones from which it would take a long time to recover' (1982, p. 89). The Rothschild Report effectively saved the day for the social sciences, particularly sociology, but there was a price: more policy relevance, more effective dissemination and clearer English should be much higher priorities. Such 'corrective action' was overdue: in particular, 'the most serious weakness of the SSRC is its failure to make known to the general public – the man in the street – its own work and that of the social scientists it finances' (Rothschild, p. 88). In the event, Joseph contented himself with changing the name of the Social Science Research Council to the Economic and Social Research Council, a prelude to a decade of shifting priorities and administrative changes. (For a full account of the saga, see Flather, 1987.)

The SSRC had now been put on its mettle to show that it could commission and disseminate widely research of relevance to pressing social problems. With a sharply rising crime rate and the widespread inner-city disturbances of the early 1980s, 'law and order' was clearly a strong contender for priority funding. Rather than waiting to see what applications for funding under that heading happened to come in, the SSRC chose to back it as one of several initiatives encouraging researchers to explore certain designated fields. The methods used to define key topics, invite bids and choose between them were unusually exhaustive. First, a day conference was held to thrash out the very broad outline of research priorities in the 'law and order' field. Secondly, a working party was set up to determine more precisely specific topics for which researchers could submit their proposals. Thirdly, a sub-committee was convened to choose the best combination of projects to be funded from the amount available, £730,000. The fourth stage, dissemination, was to be dealt with by means of a conference at which findings and policy implications would be the major topics.

The immense amount of work that went into launching this initiative is worth spelling out a little, if only to counter the view that vast sums are thrown at research projects which consume them with little regard for value for money or public accountability. The first stage of drawing up a research programme consisted of three phrases. First, a meeting was held at the SSRC (on 25 October 1982) which brought together academics from relevant disciplines and key funding agencies, both governmental and voluntary. Themes emerging from this meeting gave emphasis to the need for an SSRC initiative to offset the drift towards Home Office dominance over funding, and to the potential contributions other disciplines could make to standard criminological questions. Gaps in research, such as the lack of knowledge about how policies in the criminal justice field were actually made, were broadly identified. Secondly, the Secretary of the SSRC, Cyril Smith, gathered the views of academics with research interests in the field. Thirdly, a day conference on 11 March 1983 debated research priorities. Particularly telling was Leslie Wilkins's contrast between the strong support for criminological research in the United States and the hostile climate it faced in Britain (Wilkins, 1984). In this country, finance was difficult to obtain; a research career structure outside teaching in higher education was lacking; cutbacks meant decreasing time or opportunity for research; and access to key sources of data, such as the judiciary, was fraught with difficulties. The case for such an initiative was therefore strengthened. It was also agreed that an exclusive focus on either crime or the criminal justice system failed to match the extent of public concern over both. However, there was little point in the initiative simply duplicating existing work, or reinforcing what had been the dominant tendency in criminology: a near-exclusive focus on 'one-off' studies of largely working-class forms of crime and delinquency. As a result, the five priority areas for research that emerged were:

1. the nature of the criminal justice system and its boundaries; the change it is undergoing, resource allocation within the system, and the impact of other agencies upon the system;
2. the study of the exercise of discretion within the system, principally by the police, the courts, and in the exercise of parole;
3. the study of police accountability;
4. the role of the media in shaping public attitudes to crime and sentencing;
5. the study of crime and the criminal in a broader sense, to include the hidden economy and longitudinal studies.

The second stage of the initiative was to appoint a working party to set out in more detail the main tasks for research within these 'priority areas'. Chaired by Professor Gordon Trasler of Southampton University, the group met on four occasions between October 1983 and January 1984. A key question was how far funds should be concentrated or dispersed. For example, it was argued by Michael Zander that much could be achieved in terms of 1 to 3 above by devoting a substantial part of the funding to a single project, which would follow a sample of defendants through from initial police contact to sentence or other outcome. A model for such a project had been provided by the work of Richard Ericson and his team at Toronto (Ericson, 1981 and 1982; Ericson and Baranek, 1982). After much discussion, including consultation with the Canadian team, the idea was reluctantly dropped, largely because too large a share of the resources would be taken up by this single project. Other aspects of the concentration vs. dispersal question concerned regional coverage (ideally, some projects would be mounted in Scotland, Wales and Northern Ireland); institutional balance (again, no single institution should take too large a share without exceptional justification); and disciplinary spread (similarly, funding should not be confined to 'criminologists': it was hoped that other disciplines would enter bids for research funding).

The following programme of research into ten projects was finally agreed, bids for which should assume an average cost of £70,000:

1. A policy analysis of changes in both theory and practice in the criminal justice system since 1945;
2. Managing criminal justice: a study of the interactions between principal agencies within the criminal justice system;
3. Studies of prison regimes;
4. Ethnic-minority young people and the criminal justice systems;
5. The exercise of discretion within the criminal justice system;
6. Police accountability and the Scarman Report proposals;
7. Media production, crime and criminal justice agencies;
8. Criminal careers;
9. Crime and urban decline;
10. Crime and the 'hidden economy'.

So bald a summary does little justice to the range of discussion about priorities in the field that actually took place at the meetings. For example, research into the extent to which control measures of various sorts serve to displace crime from one site or form to others was keenly defended as a top priority. In the event, this topic was listed as an option to be funded if possible in conjunction with one or more of the priorities set out above. No such possibility arose, and it remains a key under-explored question for criminological inquiry. The example shows, however, the pressure of competing priorities on all too scarce resources.

The third stage of the initiative involved publicising the programme, inviting bids for funding and selecting the best combination of projects within the limits of financial resources. By this stage, the £650,000 made available by the now renamed Economic and Social Research Council (ESRC) had been increased to £730,000 by the addition of £40,000 from the Home Office and £40,000 from the Department of Health and Social Security. This stage fell to a sub-committee chaired by the late Sir Arthur Peterson, a former Head of the Prison Department. The programme stimulated a healthy response: 147 research proposals were received, very few of them of poor quality, so that the task of whittling them down to a dozen or so fundable projects proved exacting. Many excellent proposals were inevitably turned down in the process – though that did not necessarily mean they were lost for good. They could always be funded by the regular ESRC programmes, other initiatives or other sources, and in some cases this has happened.

The final choice of 13 projects related to the original scheme as follows:

(a)   *The Nature of the Criminal Justice System and its Boundaries*

1.   'The criminal justice system since 1945: a review of theory and practice'. Anthony Bottoms and Simon Stevenson (Institute of Criminology, Cambridge University). £49,649.[1]
2.   'Crime, community and the inter-agency dimension'. Geoffrey Pearson (Bradford University), Harry Blagg and David Smith (Lancaster University). £84,063.
3.   'Discretionary decision-making within the Scottish prison system'. Michael Adler and Alison Petch (Edinburgh University). £58,675.
4.   'Security, control and humane containment in the English prison system'. Roy King (University College of North Wales at Bangor). £111,527.

(b)   *The Exercise of Discretion within the System*

5.   'Discretion to charge and to prosecute'. Michael McConville, Roger Leng and Andrew Sanders (Birmingham University). £51,749.
6.   'Ethnic minorities, young people and the criminal justice system'. Monica Walker and Tony Jefferson (Sheffield University). £73,143.

(c)   *Police Accountability*

7.   'Police accountability and the development of police–community liaison arrangements'. Rod Morgan and Christopher Maggs (Bath University). £78,109.

(d)   *The Role of the Media*

8.   'Crime, law and justice in the media: production and content'. Philip Schlesinger and Howard Tumber (Thames Polytechnic). £78,376.

(e)   *The Broader Study of Crime and Criminal Careers*

9.   'Criminal and penal careers of British women offenders'. Pat Carlen (Keele University). £13,787.
10.   'Insolvency frauds by companies'. Leonard Leigh (London School of Economics). £7,000.

11. 'The victims of fraud'. Michael Levi (University College, Cardiff).
    £35,290.
12. 'Tax evasion and avoidance: boundaries of crime and the control of
    white-collar violation'. Doreen McBarnet (Centre for Socio-legal
    Studies, Oxford University). £34,980.
13. 'Girls in the transition from school to crime: a pilot study'. Paul Wiles
    and Jacqueline Dunn (Sheffield University). £35,103.

Of these thirteen projects, all but two have been or are all but completed in
ways that break new ground, and highly successfully. The Cambridge study
of criminal justice policy since 1945 has some way to go, due to the
unexpectedly large amount of material unearthed, though analysis is well
advanced. The LSE study, the smallest in the programme, was not initiated
at all due to work commitments arising after the award. The Sheffield study
of girls was halted by the tragically early death of Jacqueline Dunn.

In general, however, a complex and exacting research programme has
been carried through with great effectiveness, to a high standard and with
what would count as 'value for money' by international if not Treasury
criteria. Ultimately, the quality and point of the projects must speak for
themselves, and make up the text of this book. Normally, the editorial
matter could rest with the appeal to readers to judge for themselves, and the
hope that the reports would make their appropriate impact on public policy
in the future. To those ends, Rothschild's cues have been taken, and authors
have done their best, with often difficult technical subject matter, to write
in plain English, for a wide audience, keeping references to the minimum
and spelling out clearly what is at stake in their project, why they were
drawn to it, what led to their choice of methods, their major findings and
what policy inferences should be drawn. Each chapter is an attempt to
convey the major point, substance and conclusions of each project, with
references for readers to the fuller and more exhaustive specialist books and
articles which have flowed from them. Before introducing each chapter in
turn, however, a myth must be challenged and a question posed about what
this collection tells us about the state of the art.

The first point refers to the damaging fiction that academic research
remains an ivory-tower pursuit with little connection with the 'real world'
of wealth-creation and practical affairs, at best a form of intellectual nit-
picking and at worst sheer self-indulgence. The damage wrought by this
myth to higher education in the 1980s is incalculable, for it fuelled a
contraction of the necessary public investment in this sector which has
yet to be realised in its long-term consequences. Between 1979–80 and

1985–6, per capita volume spending on higher education fell by over 25 per cent (Glennerster and Low, 1990). The experience of criminology embodies this trend all too well (Rock, 1988). The research on which this book is based was carried out by academics whose careers have been built on foundations laid in the expansionary days of the 1960s and 1970s. Now in their forties and fifties, they and their colleagues are working at full tilt and have brought British criminology to a new maturity. A much smaller number, in their thirties, have managed to produce excellent work despite being tied to the treadmill of short-term contract research. Following this group, however, is a void, a missing generation in what should be a vigorous progression. While a few subjects have grown, in one of which – law – criminologists have found a foothold in the 1980s, this is the exception to the rule. Unless something drastic is done to repair the demographic fault which has opened up in higher education in Britain over the past decade, the next century will soon find our institutions of higher education bereft of high-calibre successors.

The reason for this demographic time-bomb at the heart of British higher education is only partly to do with the remains of the *Brideshead Revisited* day, the preferred media image of the university. It is also the result of a growing tendency for academic work to be marginalised or hidden in media presentations of urgent public-policy debate. There can be few academics who have not experienced their expertise being tapped by researchers for current-affairs programmes or newspaper coverage of their specialist field. Only rarely, however, largely for obvious reasons of space and flow, is such help explicitly acknowledged. By contrast, academics by convention will cite in full acknowledgement those who have assisted them in their research. The result of this lack of acknowledgement of background assistance, which ranges from key contacts, that may have taken the academic months or even years to make, to condensed summaries of evidence that may have taken a decade to assemble, is a massive ignorance of the role played by academic research in constructing the very bases of public-policy debate and inquiry. In part, as Rothschild stressed, the wounds may be self-inflicted, by the overuse of technical or pseudo-scientific language, by the reticence of academics to engage in public forums, and so on. However, such self-denial is greatly outweighed by the lack of outlets for social scientific writing in popular form. The only substantial weekly of this sort, *New Society*, has gone, merged with the *New Statesman*. Since scholarly self-effacement in the Thatcher era was about as highly esteemed as chastity in a brothel, this situation leaves academics with the unenviable choice between joining what deserves to be called the 'hype-active society' or continuing to see their work misconstrued as impractical and futile. Both should be resisted, and it is to be hoped that this book offers a third alternative, the successful communication to a wider audience than the purely academic of what is at stake in one field of contemporary research.

The second point relates to the question raised most trenchantly by Jock Young in an article entitled 'The failure of criminology: the need for a radical realism' (Young, 1986). One of Young's basic arguments is that the 1980s have witnessed, if not brought about, an eclipse of theorising about the causes of crime by the rise of an 'administrative criminology' preoccupied with the sheer containment of crime through the search for greater efficiency in surveillance, policing and control. While this argument captures an important aspect of developments over the past 10–15 years, and is indeed borne out by the relatively few applications that were made for projects with a focus on, for example, the causes of inner-city crime and delinquency, it skates over the critical and realist complexion of much recent work on criminal justice processes. Another way of reading post-war criminological history is to see the causal theme as dominating three decades, from the 1950s to the 1970s, so much so that the exploration and monitoring of the institutions of criminal justice were massively neglected. Some shift in that direction was overdue, and the chapters in this book are based on analyses which transcend the narrow pursuit of greater administrative convenience and control.

The first chapter by Anthony Bottoms and Simon Stevenson is based upon research which was regarded as a linch-pin for the entire initiative. The post-war period up to 1970 in criminal justice policy and practice has until now never been the subject of analysis based upon primary source material. Only one book (Morris, 1989) has pioneered coverage of the period as a whole in introductory text form. Yet the past 45 years have seen changes of great magnitude, such as the rise and fall of hope in rehabilitative measures; the remorseless rise in the prison population which, despite recent reductions, brought about crises of conditions and management that culminated in the riot at Strangeways and the Inquiry mounted by Lord Justice Woolf; and the drift towards 'law and order' strategies in policing which helped trigger the disorders in Brixton, Toxteth and other inner-city flash-points. These themes are taken up and explored in some of the following chapters, but the lack of an overall context within which to situate their development gave impetus for the Cambridge research. The extensive nature of the archival material made available to the researchers by the Home Office has meant a longer time will be needed for their full analysis. This chapter is a preliminary review of major themes, with examples taken as case-studies to show how policy issues and often conflicting assumptions framed key specific developments. Its kaleidoscopic coverage has involved a greater length and range of reference than the other chapters.

Chapters 2 to 4 are also concerned with the nature of the criminal justice system and its boundaries. Geoffrey Pearson and his colleagues write on a topic that emerged in the 1980s as a constant recommendation for improvements in Britain's often ill-co-ordinated system: that better 'inter-agency' co-operation is needed if, for example, less-serious offenders are to be successfully diverted from custodial sentencing. The research revealed that, valuable as such initiatives at the local level can be, they stand to lose momentum or even founder if perfectly predictable conflicts, such as those arising from the power differences between the agencies, are ignored. It is far better, they argue, to take account of such conflicts at the outset, and produce a more realistic set of objectives accordingly.

Michael Adler and Brian Longhurst also found competitive struggles for power emerging as a theme, this time from their study of routine administrative decision-making in the Scottish prison system. Making sense of such crucial decisions as those governing the classification of prisoners, which then determined the kind of prison to which they were sent, led them to the analysis of the shifting nature of the 'discourse', or dominant ideas and beliefs, underlying them. Their methods enabled them to clarify much that is otherwise obscure about day-to-day routine decision-making within the prison system and to propose better, clearer and more open ways of arriving at reasonable objectives.

In the context of the current furore over the state of prisons in England and Wales, the importance of the research by Roy King and Kathleen McDermott can hardly be overestimated. They gathered exhaustive information about life and conditions in five representative prisons in the Midlands region. They then compared their findings with equivalent evidence from the early 1970s. The contrasts revealed a more or less total picture of deterioration, firm indications of the 'ever-deepening crisis' which afflicts the prison system. Their evidence has already provided the Woolf Inquiry with a documentary basis of unusual strength and objectivity for its recommendations. Given the widespread conviction that prisons are, with a few exceptions, more akin to 'holiday camps' than jails, it is vital that evidence to the contrary is seen to be as rigorously and independently gathered as this project's undoubtedly has been. The project cost just over £100,000. Properly interpreted, its findings could save the Home Office millions. More importantly, they point the way to a far more humane and less oppressive prison system.

The exercise of discretion within the system arguably affects more people at the point of prosecution than any other. Yet until the creation of the Crown Prosecution Service in 1984, that vital decision was overwhelmingly a matter for the police. As a result, England and Wales, unlike Scotland and virtually every other comparable society, combined the powers of arrest and prosecution in the same agency. Much has been hoped for from the Crown Prosecution Service as a consequence, in particular that cases based on poor evidence would be dropped before they came to court at all, and that many more less-serious cases would be diverted on public-interest grounds. The research by Roger Leng, Mike McConville and Andrew Sanders shows the disturbing extent to which the police remain prime movers in the decision to prosecute, so that less has been achieved along these lines than could reasonably have been hoped for. The potential for constructive change remains as yet largely unrealised.

Another flashpoint for discretion and its possible abuse has been seen for at least two decades as centring on ethnicity. Young black people of Afro-Caribbean background form a disproportionately large group in prison. Yet studies of sentencing do not show any discernible discrimination against them, once allowance is made for the nature of the offence and previous convictions (Reiner, 1989). As a result, it has been assumed that the bias entered in at the point of arrest and prosecution. The notable study of policing in London had documented a much higher rate of stop-and-search among black than white youths (Smith, 1983). This marked inequity was not, however, duplicated in Leeds, the setting for the study carried out by Tony Jefferson, Monica Walker and Mary Seneviratne into the policing of ethnic-minority young people. Instead, they found an inversion of that situation in certain inner-city areas. In the attempt to control for the variable of social class, they differentiated their sample on the basis of very small areas formed by census enumeration districts. Areas with a relatively high black population were found to have markedly higher white arrest rates, whereas in other areas arrest rates were at their height for black people. Their inference is that the relationship between ethnicity and policing is far more varied and complicated than the London experience suggests, and that the large proportionate differences between black and white groups in the prisons result from small but cumulative differences throughout the whole spectrum of criminal justice. This vital study adds urgency to the need for both more local studies and at least one major cohort study of the sort referred to above (p. xvi), though the latter need may be met by a study currently being conducted in the Midlands by Roger Hood at the Oxford Centre for Criminological Research.

Following the Scarman Inquiry Report on the disorders at Brixton in 1981, police accountability emerged as *the* issue in the law-and-order field until the 1987 election removed any likelihood of radical change on this front. Part of the reason for its disappearance as a leading issue is the speed with which the recommendations of Scarman were taken up and acted upon by the police, at least in principle and at most in actual practice. What stood in need of further inquiry was how far the practice matched the principle, and the research of Rod Morgan addressed that question in relation to the rapid growth of Police Consultative Committees. Work on the police had tended to be either studies of policing-on-the-ground or of the constitutional framework within which the police operated. Morgan's chapter draws these somewhat separate perspectives into closer alignment to show how the police have set the agenda for PCCs, which in turn are mainly composed of the more orthodox constituencies. In other words, only minimal moves towards greater accountability have occurred. Again, a crucial link in the criminal justice chain is exhaustively scrutinised for public-policy debate.

Media coverage of crime and its control has for the past two decades veered as a subject for analysis between the traditional 'looking-glass' image – 'We don't make the news, we simply report it' – and the malevolent but creative role – mobilising bias, setting agendas and creating 'moral panics'. But whatever version of the two is preferred, both tend to be 'media-centric', in the sense that the media are seen as playing upon a largely passive mass audience. Philip Schlesinger and Howard Tumber, in the first British study of its kind, document how such an assumption can no longer be made. The growth of sophistication among the news sources of the media has been stimulated by the growing awareness of the influential nature of media coverage. Not only powerful institutions such as the police but also relatively small-scale pressure groups, such as the Howard League for Penal Reform and the Prison Reform Trust, have succeeded in both attracting media attention and adding their own inflections to the coverage of key issues. This case-study is but one aspect of their work on this project, which also includes a content analysis of media coverage of crime, and an audience-reaction study.

The three chapters related to the topic of crime and criminal careers tackle very different themes, two of which have not, until now, been seriously addressed in this country or, for the most part, elsewhere. Pat Carlen's work on female offenders draws on a repertoire of life histories built up from extensive interviews, and forms part of a larger research programme she had pioneered for some ten years. Certain themes recur in the 'careers' of her subjects, notably the experience of having been 'in Care', the most significant of the risks facing adolescent girls by comparison with boys, even without a prior offending history. Many of her policy recommendations, such as that for the non-imprisonability of less-serious, non-violent offenders, could be applied equally to males. Yet in relation to imprisonment, differences do obtain between them, partly due to the irony that, because women are in general far less involved in criminality than men, the small minority who *are* imprisoned experience unusually severe stigmatisation, are placed in fewer prisons, further from home, and face more medicalised regimes. Such anomalies can mean that the pains of imprisonment bear more heavily on women than men, particularly when they have young children. Carlen's far-reaching recommendations for change deserve correspondingly close attention.

Though concern for victim support emerged as a core concern of the 1980s (Rock, 1990), the work of Mike Levi and Andrew Pithouse on the victims of fraud is, astonishingly, the first genuine study of the subject, as was Levi's own earlier work on long-term fraudsters. As is usually the case, searching scrutiny beneath the surface of any phenomenon – and fraud is no exception – reveals far more complexity than is commonly assumed. Typically, victims were far more likely to be organisations than private individuals, though where the latter lost large sums, running into thousands, they were most likely to have been victimised by family or close friends rather than strangers. A higher proportion of 'blue-collar' offenders received sentences of imprisonment than 'white-collar', though those who *were* imprisoned in the latter group received the longer sentences, perhaps because their 'take' was far higher. Though Levi does not press the point, complex class sympathies may be involved here, with more leniency being displayed towards those middle-class offenders whose frauds have condonable aspects, but less towards the minority whose acts can in no sense be mitigated. Overall, however, responses showed great scope for consciousness-raising about the risks, character and consequences of fraud which, by contrast with such offences as burglary and theft, generates a greater tendency to self-blame on the victims' part.

Finally, Doreen McBarnet analyses an even murkier field of white-collar crime, the grey area between tax evasion and tax avoidance. Like Mary Douglas in *Purity and Danger* (1966), she is drawn to the ways in which the need to define boundaries creates ambiguity and anomaly. The very attempt to resolve such problems in turn creates the resources for their further elaboration. A paradox unfolds in which the tax-avoider chalks up gains which can be far huger than their original base. Judicial attempts to cut through the thickets of mystification spawned by the most sophisticated avoidance schemes have recently addressed *purposes* rather than formal adherence to the law, but have been held at bay. This field is excitingly shown to have set limits to the rule of law. Moreover, as McBarnet comments, 'even in avoidance there are strata and stratified success'.

Avoidance on the upper registers of the scale is available only to the very well-heeled: the poor can only evade. The old saw that there is one law for the rich and one for the poor has seldom been more starkly borne out.

The diversity of this collection arises from the lack of thematic unity in the initiative, which in turn stemmed from the original decision to go for an array of pressing and neglected questions rather than concentrate wholly on one set of problems. I am convinced this is a strength rather than a weakness, and the very high standards of successful completion lend it support. For far too long, criminology focused on a limited field with a tunnel vision: the attempt to explain and control largely working-class forms of 'street' crime. That set of problems is still a compelling challenge, but criminology, like crime itself, is now an expanding universe, which embraces deviance and control of both formal and informal kinds and at every social level. This collection seeks to push the field forward in several crucial respects and, in the process, social knowledge, however modestly, is advanced, and with it the scope for informed public policy debate.

It is to be hoped that this initiative, and others like it, does not represent a high-point in criminological activity from which there is now to be an inexorable decline. The 1980s saw a mounting concern about 'law and order', which led to a number of fresh sources for project funding, not least a number of local authorities – Islington, Merseyside and Haringey especially spring to mind – as well as growing research budgets for such established sources as the Home Office Research and Planning Unit and the ESRC after the shock of the early part of the decade described above. This buoyant research market led to the creation of several new Centres of Criminology, largely built on existing staff, and the high levels of specialist expertise built up over the previous two decades ensured supply met demand. Sources of resilience and innovation in both teaching and research are to be found in such polytechnics as Middlesex and Liverpool, and in colleges of higher education such as Edge Hill and Ealing. Indeed, criminology provides ample evidence of the futility of such status differences in higher education. By contrast, the news about core staffing has been dismal: a seemingly endless barrage of cuts, early retirement, frozen posts, and – most damningly from the international perspective as well as our own – the phasing-out of tenure, the sole institutional guarantee that the realm of intellectual authority remains distinct from the line of political command. In the wake of these developments came the most drastic curtailment of funding for graduate research grants, not surprisingly leading to a slump in post-graduate recruitment. Yet throughout the 1980s, policy-making and public debate have been increasingly informed by criminological work in this field. Social science has shown its mettle: *it is time not only to pay its keep, but also to ensure its future survival.*

NOTE

* My thanks are extended to Martin Bulmer, Terence Morris and Paul Rock for blameless good advice on this introduction; to the Economic and Social Research Council, and especially Tim Whitaker, for their help and support throughout; and to Hannah Downes for so accomplished an index. Finally, I would like to express my deep appreciation of the encouragement of Tim Farmiloe who, at Macmillan Press, embodies all that is best in publishing.

1. Projects 1 and 12 later received smaller but substantial additional funding as more extensive sources of data became available. Original grant figures were subject to subsequent marginal adjustments. Some funding was retained to finance conferences and other ways of disseminating research findings.

REFERENCES

Abel-Smith, B. and Townsend, P. (1965), *The Poor and the Poorest* (London: Bell).

Cohen, S. (ed.) (1971), *Images of Deviance* (Harmondsworth, Middx: Penguin).

Cohen, S. and Taylor, L. (1972), *Psychological Survival* (Harmondsworth, Middx: Penguin).

Douglas, M. (1966), *Purity and Danger* (London: Routledge & Kegan Paul).

Ericson, R. V. (1981), *Making Crime: A Study of Detective Work* (Toronto: Butterworth).

Ericson, R. V. (1982), *Reproducing Order: A Study of Police Patrol Work* (Toronto: University of Toronto Press).

Ericson, R. V. and Baranek, P. M. (1982), *The Ordering of Justice: A Study of Accused Persons as Defendants in the Criminal Process* (Toronto: University of Toronto Press).

Flather, P. (1987), '"Pulling through" – conspiracies, counterplots, and how the SSRC escaped the axe in 1982', in M. Bulmer (ed.), *Social Science Research and Government: Comparative Essays on Britain and the United States* (Cambridge: Cambridge University Press).

Glennerster, H. and Low, W. (1990), 'Education and the welfare state: does it add up?', in J. Hills (ed.), *The State of Welfare* (Oxford: Oxford University Press).

Morris, T. P. (1989), *Crime and Criminal Justice in Britain since 1945* (Oxford: Basil Blackwell).

Reiner, R. (1989), 'Race and criminal justice', *New Community*, **16**(1), 5–21.

Rock, P. (1988), 'The present state of criminology in Britain', in Paul Rock (ed.), *A History of British Criminology* (Oxford: Oxford University Press).

Rock, P. (1990), *Helping Victims of Crime: The Home Office and Victim Support in England and Wales* (Oxford: Oxford University Press).

Rothschild, Lord (1982), *An Enquiry into the Social Science Research Council* (London: HMSO) Cmnd. 8554.

Rutter, M. and Madge, N. (1976), *Cycles of Deprivation* (London: Heinemann).

Smith, D. *et al.* (1983), *Police and People in London* (London: Policy Studies Institute).
Wilkins, L. T. (1984), 'U.K./U.S.A. – contrasts in criminology: a personal view', *Howard Journal of Criminal Justice*, **23**(1), 11–23.
Young, J. (1986), 'The failure of criminology: the need for a radical realism', in Roger Matthews and Jock Young (eds), *Confronting Crime* (London: Sage).

1 'What Went Wrong?': Criminal Justice Policy in England and Wales, 1945–70

ANTHONY E. BOTTOMS and SIMON STEVENSON

INTRODUCTION

The aim of this research was to carry out a detailed analysis of policy-making in the field of criminal justice in England and Wales in the quarter-century following the end of the Second World War, with a special focus on the police, the courts, penal policy and children and young persons. The research used the normal methods of empirically-oriented historians and political scientists, that is to say, it proceeded by a very thorough examination of published and available unpublished sources to build up a detailed picture of what happened, and why.[1] When this detailed picture had been assembled, it then became possible to stand back a little and try to discern and to explain some of the broad movements of policy that had taken place. The research was not expected to be of direct significance to present-day policy-makers, but it was hoped that, by throwing light on the way that policy had been shaped in an earlier (but not too remote) period, some lessons for the present could be learned.

The period 1945–70 saw many developments in criminal justice. Capital and corporal punishment were abolished; Parliament passed three Criminal Justice Acts (1948, 1961, 1967), two Police Acts (1946 and 1964), and two Children and Young Persons Acts (1963 and 1969); five Royal Commissions deliberated (though only four reported); and there was a host of relevant reports on all kinds of matters, from individual incidents to general reviews. It is naturally impossible, within the space of one chapter, to discuss all these matters, which together present an immensely complex kaleidoscope. We have, however, sought to give at least some indication of the main developments of the period by a judicious choice of examples.[2] And despite all the complexities, we have had little hesitation in selecting a title for our chapter: 'What Went Wrong?' seems easily the most appropriate question to ask, given the high hopes of the early post-war period and the many disappointments that followed (for a broader social analysis with a similar theme, see Marwick, 1982).

The structure of the chapter is as follows. After a brief reminder to readers of some of the main general features of the period under review, we

1

offer a characterisation of criminal justice in England and Wales (hereafter, for simplicity, 'England') as it appeared at the end of the war. In the following long section, we explain why many of the post-war hopes were to remain unfulfilled, and how some cherished beliefs became dented. We then, for completeness, address the rather separate but very important issue of the rapid modernisation of society in post-war Britain, and how this affected one sphere of criminal justice, namely policing; and, in order not to present a distorted picture, we also examine some threads of ideological continuity which persisted from 1945 to 1970. We conclude with a brief look at criminal justice policy in 1970 and beyond, a time at which there was substantially greater uncertainty, and more political dissensus about criminal justice, than had existed in 1945.

BRITISH SOCIETY AND RISING CRIME RATES, 1945–70

During the first quarter-century after the Second World War Britain was governed for approximately equal amounts of time by Labour (1945–51, 1964–70) and by Conservative (1951–64) administrations. In the space of this short period Britain's world role shrank considerably. In 1945 she could see herself as a major world power, partner in a great war victory and leader of a substantial colonial empire; but gradually the countries of the Empire were granted independence (beginning with India in 1947), and Britain's global significance shrank in an era dominated by the 'cold war' politics of the superpowers (the USA and the USSR).

On the domestic front, the closing years of the war saw the development of a broad cross-party consensus dedicated to the creation of a post-war 'welfare state': the state would intervene in the economy to maintain full employment, and welfarist policies for health, housing, child care, unemployment and sickness benefit, and so on, would be developed. Governments of both political persuasions pursued goals of broadly this kind throughout the period under review (though of course with differences of emphasis as between the parties); and the word 'Butskellism' was popularly coined to reflect these similarities.[3] The consensus, however, became increasingly fragile as the period wore on, and was broken decisively at a later date.

Major changes in British society during this period can be traced through the social statistics of the time (see generally, Halsey, 1988). Economically, there was a considerable growth in the Gross Domestic Product, and, after a period of austerity in the immediate post-war period, personal incomes rose and Harold Macmillan, as Prime Minister, could declare in 1957 that the people had 'never had it so good'. Unemployment rates were low (less than 5 per cent) throughout the period, in sharp contrast to the 1930s (and, later, the 1980s). However, the relative economic position of Britain *vis-à-vis* her main economic competitors weakened noticeably. Moreover, the need to control inflation produced as a series of 'stop–go' governmental interventions in the economy: these and other factors led to short-term fluctuations in personal consumption which have been shown to be related to short-term movements in recorded crime rates (Field, 1990).

In housing, there was a rapid move away from privately rented accommodation, with increases both in owner-occupation and in local-authority housing. The latter development occurred largely through the construction of new estates (and New Towns), with considerable clearance of older Victorian properties, and the destruction of many traditional communities. In education, the grammar school/secondary modern dichotomy created by the 1944 Education Act came under increasing criticism, and the movement towards comprehensive schools gathered pace, particularly in the 1960s. More children stayed on at school voluntarily beyond the official school-leaving age, and that age was itself increased from 14 to 15 in 1947. Those a little older also went on to higher education in increasing numbers, with many new universities being created in the 1960s. National service in the armed forces had occupied the time of male late-adolescents for up to two years in the earlier part of the period, but this was phased out at the end of the 1950s.

The burgeoning post-war economy produced an influx of labour from Commonwealth countries, particularly the West Indies and the Indian sub-continent, until statutory controls on immigration were introduced (from 1962). This development made Britain a multi-cultural society, but also produced significant race relations tensions in some urban areas. In the late 1960s one major politician went so far as to use the racial issue as 'a vehicle through which to articulate a definition of "Englishness", a recipe for holding England together' (Hall *et al.*, 1978, p. 246).

In family life, more married women went out to work, the rate of births to teenage mothers rose, and divorce became easier to obtain. Only one in 500 of the adult population had a television set at home in 1947; but by the mid-1960s the figure was over nine out of ten. Cars were also increasingly a feature of family life: the number of private cars licensed rose by nearly 600 per cent between 1948 and 1968, and motoring became much less the preserve of the higher social classes than it had been before the war. By contrast, membership of and attendance at all main-stream Churches (except the Roman Catholic Church) declined significantly during the period.

One social historian, Arthur Marwick, has characterised this period as falling into two distinct phases: those of 'social consensus' (from 1945 to 1957) and 'roads to freedom' (from 1957 onwards). According to Marwick, the second of these periods included a 'great release from older restraints and controls . . . release not just from post-war austerity, but from social controls going back to Victorian times' (Marwick, 1982, pp. 16, 18). Amongst other things, betting shops sprang up following the legalisation of off-course cash betting on horse- and dog-racing; theatre censorship was abolished; the film censors became more tolerant; the obscenity laws were liberalised; consenting homosexual behaviour between adult males was decriminalised, as were some abortions; and satire programmes became fashionable on television. Some saw the advent of commercial television (ITV) in 1955, and the subsequent changes in BBC television's style and content, as having had a particular social impact. This impact, it has been claimed, made is impossible to return to the 'orderly system of deference to one's betters which the traditionalists had hoped to see re-established' after the war, not least because ITV 'challenged the idea that some affairs of State were too important to be debated in public, which had been one of the strengths of the [former] system of deference' (Lloyd, 1979, p. 332).

In this economically more affluent and socially more relaxed climate, youth culture began to flourish, and the Beatles and Rolling Stones became household names. The 'Teddy Boys' of the 1950s were replaced by the 'Mods and Rockers' of the 1960s, and some strange events took place in and around the almost ritual confrontations between the police and the 'Mods and Rockers' that occurred at summer Bank Holiday weekends in the mid-1960s. From the late 1950s onwards, the police also became in-volved in other public-order tensions which were to become of much greater political significance, arising out of demonstrations by groups such as the Campaign for Nuclear Disarmament, the Committee of 100 and, from the mid-1960s, extra-parliamentary New Left groups focusing on issues such as student rights and the Vietnam War.

An examination of the recorded indictable crime figures for this quarter-century shows that there was little overall increase in crime during the first decade (1945–55) (see Figure 1.1). However, recorded crime had risen sharply during the war, and many had expected a decrease in the figures with the return to post-war normality and the advent of the welfare state. Thus, there was considerable political anxiety in the late 1940s and early 1950s as the overall rates increased a little, with a particular increase in crimes of violence and sexual offences. These anxieties multiplied as the crime rate began a wholly unexpected and indeed unprecedented rise from 1955 onwards (Figure 1.1; for further details, see McClintock and Avison,

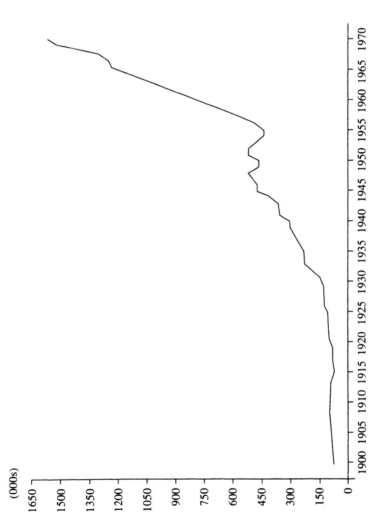

FIGURE 1.1   *Indictable offences recorded by the police, 1900–70*

1968). This rapid post-war rise, which was common to most Western countries, is probably best explained as deriving from, first, increased opportunities for property crimes, given the spread of motor vehicle use, televisions, and so on; and secondly, a growth of individualism consequent upon the post-war relaxation of traditional social controls, together with disruptions and changes to traditional community and family ties.[4] But whatever the true explanation for the rise in crime, the crucially important point for present purposes is that criminal justice policy-makers did not in any way *expect* increases of this magnitude – yet somehow, they had to cope with them.

It is very important to emphasise from the outset that criminal justice policy was not, throughout this period, much of a party-political issue. Hence, the criminal justice policy-making which we have studied in this research was largely backstage policy-making – the work of Home Office civil servants, Royal Commissions, departmental committees; lobbying from relevant professional associations, penal reform bodies and trades unions, and so on. The only really high-profile criminal justice topic on the national political agenda in the period 1945–70 was the emotive subject of capital punishment for murder, which both Conservative and Labour parties chose to make a 'free vote' or 'conscience' issue, outside the scope of the party Whips. At the beginning of the period, all convicted murderers were mandatorily sentenced to death (though some were subsequently reprieved). An abolitionist amendment to the Criminal Justice Bill of 1947–8 was successful in the Commons, but fell in the Lords. Subsequently, a Royal Commission was appointed, which reported in 1953. This was eventually followed by partial abolition of capital punishment in the Homicide Act 1957, complete abolition for an experimental period of five years in 1965, and a final confirmatory abolitionist vote in 1969 (see Christoph, 1962; Morris, 1989). But in many respects capital punishment was a *sui generis* topic, lying outside the mainstream of criminal justice policy-making; in view of this, and the fact that this subject has been well served by previous writers, we have deliberately chosen to focus our primary research attention elsewhere.

CRIMINAL JUSTICE POLICY IN 1945

What, then, did the mainstream of criminal justice policy look like in 1945?

A hypothetical Home Office civil servant in 1945, looking out on White-hall with its echoes of traditional British supremacy and pomp, could be well content. The English legal system was widely believed to be the best in the world and, even if the British Empire were soon to be dissolved, England (like Rome before her) would have left a proud legacy of law and legal institutions to her former colonies. There were, certainly, some imperfections in the legal system, such as – to take two examples topical in 1945 – insufficient legal aid and an imbalance in the political persuasions of those selected to serve as justices of the peace. But these problems could, and no doubt would, be dealt with.

As for the police, they had been set on a good course by the Desborough Committee of 1919 (Home Office, 1919). They had on the whole survived the inter-war period quite well (despite some public-order problems in the 1930s), and had particularly distinguished themselves during the 1939–45 war (Critchley, 1978, ch. 7). Thus Chuter Ede, the incoming Labour Home Secretary, was able to introduce the Police Bill 1945 in the Commons with a paean of praise for them ('The civilian police force of this country is an object of universal admiration . . . and undoubtedly some of the more recent phases of their activities [in wartime] have given them an even higher standing with the ordinary citizen than they ever had before'[5]). Indeed, a later writer, surveying the broad sweep of the history of policing in England from the nineteenth century to the 1980s, saw the early post-war years as the highpoint of perceived police legitimacy in this entire period (Reiner, 1985, ch. 2) – a legitimacy perhaps well illustrated by contemporaneous media presentations such as the film *The Blue Lamp*.[6]

If there were grounds for satisfaction and optimism as regards the courts and the police in 1945, that was also true as regards the treatment of convicted offenders. Alexander Paterson (1884–1947), a Prison Commissioner, was undoubtedly the dominant influence on the penal system of the inter-war years, a period which had seen the progressive liberalisation of prison regimes and regulations. Since the same years had also seen a proportionate decline in the courts' use of custody, and neither policy had produced disastrous results, many informed people were inclined to believe that mercy could well temper penal severity without undue risk.[7] Paterson was also the inspiration behind the inter-war Borstal system, with its emphasis on the personal influence of the housemaster on his 'lads'. His was a predominantly religious philosophy, but it had many points in common with the outlooks of groups from the Fabian and scientific–positivist traditions which emerged during the 1930s – in particular, all these groups placed a strong emphasis on the reform or rehabilitation of the offender as a primary aim of penal policy. This loose coalition of 'liberal progressives', as Victor Bailey has dubbed them,

crucially laid a framework of principle, policy and practice in the inter-
war years, which survived the wartime flux of the early forties, and was
available to the post-war Labour government, eager to inaugurate a
universal welfare state. (Bailey, 1987, p. 266)

Moreover, by 1945 many viewed the incipient welfare state legislation
on health, housing, children and so on as 'the preliminary manoeuvres in an
attack on juvenile crime', to be backed up (where necessary) by a reform-
oriented penal system. Thus, by the late 1940s,

> this larger attempt to diminish the supply of crime in the future claimed
> the allegiance of Conservative as well as Labour politicians. The injus-
> tices of the pre-war era and the wartime struggle for national survival had
> shaped a political consensus about the needs of a full social democracy,
> needs which were defined, in large part, by the 'liberal progressive'.
> (Bailey, 1987, pp. 304–5)

Amongst the particular concerns of the 'liberal progressives' was the
probation system, which was viewed as one of the most important contributions of Anglo-American legal systems to the development of a sound
criminal policy. In England probation had historically been closely associated with the work of 'police court missionaries', employed by voluntary
religious societies but also engaged as probation officers by local justices.
A departmental committee of 1936 had recommended the termination of
this system of 'dual control', and the development of a more secular
professionalism (and professional training) among probation officers, an
approach pursued with vigour by the Home Office during the war years.
Significantly, when in 1944 the Home Secretary set up a standing Advisory
Committee on the Treatment of Offenders (see below) one of the first topics
it was asked to consider was: 'What more can be done to develop the
probation service as a highly skilled profession requiring not only a missionary spirit but training and expert knowledge?'

Philosophically and in terms of public confidence, then, the English
criminal justice system seemed in fundamentally good heart at the end of
the Second World War. Administratively, too, the problems looked soluble.
There was something of a manpower problem in the police service, but this
could no doubt be solved as servicemen were demobilised. The Borstal
system had been virtually dismantled, but would be re-established. The
total population in prisons and Borstals had risen during the war, but in the
last full year of hostilities (1944) the average daily population was still less
than 13,000, as against over 20,000 in 1910 (see Figure 1.2).

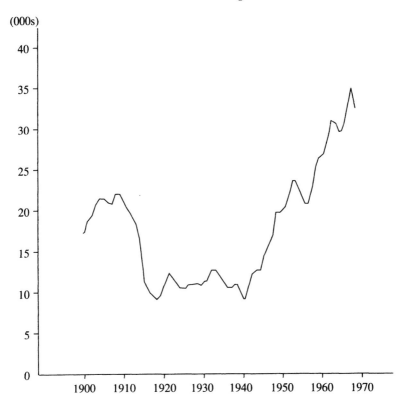

FIGURE 1.2 *Average daily prison population, 1900–70**

* Includes persons in borstals, detention centres and remand centres as well as prisons.

The incoming government also looked well-prepared to tackle the relevant policy issues. There had been a major Criminal Justice Bill in 1938–9 which had enjoyed broad cross-party support, and had been lost only because of the commencement of war. Core provisions of that Bill, which had been intended to modernise the legislative framework for both custodial and non-custodial measures, would undoubtedly constitute some of the key elements of post-war criminal justice policy. Other important policy suggestions could be expected to emerge from two important bodies which the wartime Home Secretary, Herbert Morrison, had caused to be created in 1944 – in each case, with a deliberate eye to rational post-war reconstruction. These two bodies were the Police Post-War Committee, chaired by the Permanent Secretary of the Home Office, and the Advisory Council on the Treatment of Offenders (ACTO), chaired by Mr Justice Birkett (formerly the celebrated criminal advocate Norman Birkett).

All things considered, then, the omens for the criminal justice policy-maker in 1945 looked good. So what went wrong?

PROBLEMS FOR CRIMINAL JUSTICE OPTIMISTS, 1945–70

There were perhaps five central problems which together help to explain 'what went wrong' for the optimistic hopes of the immediate post-war period. These problems were: the political climate created by, and the practical results of, the continuing growth of recorded crime; the strength of traditional values and affinities; problems of manpower for criminal justice agencies in a full employment economy; the beginnings of uncomfortable research results; and a series of individual incidents revealing underlying imperfections in the system. We shall deal with each of these in turn, using relevant examples: many of these examples come from the middle years of the period, where the main tensions can perhaps be seen most clearly.

The Rise in Crime

We shall give just one main example – though a centrally significant one – concerning the impact of the rise in crime on the criminal justice policy-making of the period. This example concerns the White Paper *Penal Practice in a Changing Society* (Home Office, 1959) presented to Parliament by Home Secretary R. A. Butler in 1959, and described by a contemporary commentator in very positive terms as 'a document which is likely to go down as a landmark in penal history' (Klare, 1962, p. 114).

Penal Practice in a Changing Society is mostly about custodial institutions, and it was to a significant extent the work of Sir Lionel Fox, Chairman of the Prison Commission for England and Wales from 1942 to 1960 – though it was also the end-product of a deliberate political decision by Butler, on becoming Home Secretary early in 1957, to heighten the political profile of penal reform, and to encourage public debate on the subject by preparing a White Paper.

Fox towered over the field of penal policymaking in the first part of the period studied in this research. He was a disciple of Paterson, though a man with very different talents: Paterson once described himself as 'a missionary, not an administrator', while Fox was excellent at deskwork and committees, but weaker on human contact with prison staff (Neale, 1983). In policy terms, during the 1950s Fox retained Paterson's liberal optimism and reformative spirit, but increasingly added to it a belief in the merits and potentiality of scientific research on offenders and their treatment. *Penal Practice in a Changing Society* clearly reflected these views:

We must through continued research learn more of [the causes of recidivism]. Through more precise methods of classification and continual search for improved techniques we must seek to reduce recidivism by more effective personal training. (para. 51)

The Commissioners wish to develop a system of classification which is based more on a study of the personalities of offenders and less on objective criteria such as previous convictions and sentences. (para. 58)

Local prisons[8] . . . are in themselves quite unfitted to modern conceptions of penal treatment, built as they were 100 years or more ago to serve the purposes of solitary confinement, treadmill hard labour and brutal repression. They stand as a monumental denial to the principles to which we are committed. (para. 54)

[By creating more training prisons] it might . . . be possible to reduce the population of the local prisons so as to allow one or more of them at a time to be emptied for reconstruction. Most of these buildings could then be turned into prisons which, while falling short of the ideal, would at least be reasonably well adapted to requirements. (para. 61)

A local prison so reorganised, with an adequate staff and enough work of suitable quality, would no longer be a place where a prisoner must be left because there is nowhere else to send him, but a training unit to which he is allocated because that is the right place for him. (para. 64)

Brave, and very optimistic, sentiments – and certainly the high point of governmental optimism in this country as regards treatment programmes in prisons. But already, as the White Paper which he had decided upon in 1957 was being drafted in 1958, the Home Secretary's perception of the political climate was shifting:

I have noted a considerable change in atmosphere. The public are very anxious about the increase in crime. . . . Later in the autumn I am to answer 28 bloodthirsty resolutions at the Conservative Conference at Blackpool. It is with the greatest difficulty that we have chosen one out of the 28 which is at least moderate. . . . [9]

This atmosphere influenced the content of the White Paper. Butler insisted, in the same memorandum, that the final drafts

> must have some reference to the present success of the police. . . . I am in doubt as to whether the idealistic portions of this document designed to chart the way into the future will appear in their proper setting unless some comfort is given at some stage in [the first] paragraphs about the efficiency of the police force and the present operation of the criminal law.

But the rise in crime did not merely affect the mood of Home Secretaries or the drafting of White Papers; it had severely practical consequences. Societies with rapidly rising recorded crime rates do not inevitably have increasing prison populations (as the experience of The Netherlands in the post-war era vividly reminds us: see Downes, 1988), but in practice they usually do, because only marked changes in relevant policies or practices (sentencing, remand, remission and so on) will in such circumstances prevent the growth of the total numbers in custody. A key element in the strategy of *Penal Practice in a Changing Society* was to reduce the prison overcrowding which had developed in post-war England by building more closed training prisons, and by acquiring more buildings suitable for conversion into open training prisons. Fox, wrote Butler in an obituary comment in *The Times* in 1961, 'was particularly pleased with the new building programme – 40 projects, of which 10 had been completed before his death'.[10] But no one in the Home Office realised the potential impact of further rises in crime on the future size of the prison population. Within a few years the whole of the extra accommodation provided by the building programme had been engulfed by the rising tide of prisoners (see Figure 1.2). Only seven years after *Penal Practice in a Changing Society*, and *despite* the extra accommodation, there was a fresh prison population crisis, leading, among other things, to a new Home Secretary, Roy Jenkins, adding a wholly new penal measure (the suspended sentence) to the 1966 Criminal Justice Bill in an attempt to stem the flow.[11] That measure also proved unsuccessful, except in the very short term (Sparks, 1971), and chronic overcrowding was to remain a feature of the English prison system for at least another twenty years. The optimistic paragraphs about the local prisons in *Penal Practice in a Changing Society* remained hopelessly unfulfilled, a text to mock the future.

Butler, in a public speech in February 1960, commented that it was

> ironic that an overdue drive to modernise our penal methods and to introduce a more redemptive character into some of our penal treatment should have coincided with a crime wave.[12]

But perhaps once the crime wave had started, the Home Office was also to blame for not adequately considering the possibility that it might continue. Arguably, too, Butler had in part contributed to his own political troubles over penal reform (see further below) by using the high-profile strategy of publishing a major White Paper.

Many other examples of the impact of the rise in crime on the criminal justice system and on policy-making could be given. One very clear case was the impact on the workloads of the courts: as Professor Jackson of Cambridge put it in the mid-1960s:

> [The pre-war] system of higher criminal courts would doubtless have sufficed if criminal work had continued at the level of 1938. What happened was that from 1945 onwards the number of criminal cases went up and up. By 1959 Assizes were dealing with about twice as many cases as in 1938, while the cases in Quarter Sessions had increased more than threefold. Criminal courts were getting through their lists, but at some cost. (Jackson, 1964, p. 102)

The Strength of Traditional Values and Affinities

As in the previous section, we begin our consideration of the strength of tradition with a single main example; this example has some close links with the issues just discussed.

An essential part of the strategy of the 1959 White Paper was to build a number of custodial 'observation and classification centres' for adults, adjacent to remand centres for young persons, which would carry out essential diagnostic work on the personalities of offenders both for the courts and at the start of a sentence (to help determine to which prison the offender should optimally be sent) (Home Office, 1959, paras 58–9).

Hugh Klare (1962, p. 138), then Secretary of the Howard League for Penal Reform, has indicated that in the original conception of the White Paper (which he called 'rather a grand design') the projected remand centres and observation and classification centres would have served five purposes:

(1) they would have produced information for the courts and they could have been so sited as to be physically near Crown Courts in permanent session. This would have reduced the time waiting for trial . . . ;

(2) they would have allowed persons remanded in custody to be kept in secure conditions but yet not in prison, a step which would have gone some way, at least, to reduce the ever-growing pressure on local prisons;

(3)   they could have acted as classification centres for borstal trainees
      and prisoners on the basis of the information already obtained;
(4)   they would have allowed medical officers in prisons for the first
      time to concentrate on treatment rather than on diagnosis;
(5)   they could have provided invaluable material for research in their
      diagnostic, classificatory, and follow-up material.

The first of these goals, as Klare noted, would have required a reorganisation of the higher courts, which then consisted of peripatetic assizes and
(in most areas) intermittent sittings of quarter sessions. It is clear that Fox
wanted, at least in the major centres of population, permanent Crown
Courts dealing exclusively with criminal cases, which would be served by
nearby remand and observation centres. Diagnosis would thus be placed
cheek by jowl with sentencing, as a way of fostering an overall treatment
vision. As long ago as 1944 Fox had asked:

> Must we not face the fact sometime – and therefore why not now? – that
> the organisation of the superior courts is still medieval in conception, and
> can hardly be reconciled with modern conceptions of penal law, admin-
> istration and treatment?[13]

A Home Office/Lord Chancellor's Office interdepartmental committee
on the business of the criminal courts was set up in 1958, to consider
amongst other things the post-war workload problems of the higher criminal courts (see Jackson, 1964, cited above); the time spent by defendants
awaiting their trials; the issue of permanent Crown Courts; and the arrangements for 'providing the courts with the information necessary to enable
them to select the most appropriate treatment for offenders'. In some
respects, the approach of the interdepartmental committee (chaired by Mr
Justice Streatfeild) was quite modern: for example, it commissioned a
statistical analysis of time spent awaiting trial, which was one of the first
pieces of Home Office research to be published (see Gibson, 1960). On the
question of most interest to Fox, however, the Streatfeild Committee's
report (Home Office and Lord Chancellor's Office, 1961) was much more
traditional: permanent Crown Courts, even in large urban areas, were not
favoured. Exclusive concentration on criminal work could, it was argued,
tend to cause staleness, and hence decreased efficiency, in judges, and
perhaps to their becoming 'prosecution-minded'; additionally, to work
continuously as a Crown Court judge in a particular city could lead to
judicial and social isolation and personal strain.[14] The evidence of the legal
profession, at all levels, was strongly against such a change (it was opposed

'by a substantial number of judges, by the bodies representing the legal professions, and by individual members of the professions, practically all of whom testified from their personal experience that they found it dangerously monotonous to take criminal work over long periods': para. 129) The possibility that one might have permanent criminal courts without permanently assigned judges was not seriously considered.

If the proposal for Crown Courts were widened beyond a few main population centres to the country as a whole, then, the Streatfeild Committee thought, further objections would come into play:

> Crown Courts on this scale, even if they were peripatetic, could hardly sit in every place in which assizes or quarter sessions are now held. . . . Our evidence has confirmed previous experience that any proposals affecting the distinctive character of assizes and quarter sessions or the existence of particular courts would be highly controversial and difficult to implement. (para. 136)

So Fox's vision for observation and assessment centres foundered on the rock of the traditionalist views of the legal profession, and traditional local loyalties. Ironically, however, only eight years after the Streatfeild Report, a new and more prestigious body, the Royal Commission on Assizes and Quarter Sessions, produced a report which took a much more favourable view of permanent Crown Courts, while accepting the principle of the rotation of judges. The Royal Commission's recommendations were to sweep away completely the 'distinctive character of assizes and quarter sessions': indeed the Commission took as its starting point.

> the shortcomings of the Assize system, the need to limit the number of Assize towns . . ., the establishment of permanent courts, the separation of civil and criminal business at High Court level . . . and the establishment of a strong, unified and mainly static administrative organisation. (Royal Commission on Assizes and Quarter Sessions, 1969, p. 17)

But by the time this report was implemented (after the Courts Act 1971), other crises and preoccupations had overtaken the prison system, and the climate of penal thought was beginning to change (see further below). No serious thought was given to the revival of Fox's observation centre vision, and the centres for adults were never built.[15]

As well as affording an excellent example of 'liberal progressivism' in penal thought being blocked initially by more traditional values and institutions, this story also illustrates very nicely the conflict, in the 1960s, between impulses of bureaucratic and managerial efficiency (as illustrated by the Royal Commission) and those of traditional professional values and local loyalties (as illustrated by the Streatfield Committee). Very similar tensions were to be found contemporaneously in debates about the amalgamations of police forces (see further below), and in the beginnings of a managerial culture in the prison service.

Traditionalism of a rather different kind also affected the 'liberal progressives' in the penal field – this time through the enduring appeal of a harsher and more retributive penal philosophy, exemplified above all in the issue of corporal punishment, especially for young offenders.[16] A departmental committee on this subject in 1938 had come down in favour of abolition, and its marshalling of the available empirical evidence on the effectiveness of corporal punishment persuaded the then Home Secretary, Sir Samuel Hoare, to include a proposal for abolition in his Criminal Justice Bill 1938 – as it turned out, the most controversial item in that abortive measure. With Labour in power after the war, abolition was achieved fairly easily in the Criminal Justice Act 1948. But the increases in crime quickly led to calls for restoration, first in the early 1950s, and then more powerfully later in the same decade (Stevenson, 1989). ACTO was asked to examine the issue, and produced a report in less than a year (Advisory Council, 1960). In opposing restoration, the Council relied on a mixture of arguments (see pp. 26f.), including the absence of evidence as to the effectiveness of corporal punishment as a general or individual deterrent; the fact that reintroduction would be against the trend internationally; a view that it would be 'out of line with modern penal methods and would militate against the success of reformative treatment'; and an argument that 'many more detention centres [were] to be made available' following the passage of the forthcoming Criminal Justice Bill 1961. The last of these arguments was a weak one, since the projected expansion of detention centres was originally designed to take place for quite other reasons than as a substitute for corporal punishment.[17] The fact that the argument was deployed (by ACTO and subsequently by politicians) illustrates, first, the ambiguity of the place of the detention centre in the penal system for young offenders throughout the period under review, and secondly, the intense political pressures produced by the corporal punishment issue at the time, so that the expansion of detention centres could be presented as a sop to the corporal punishment lobby, despite its origins elsewhere.

Reintroduction of corporal punishment was successfully resisted, but – as he revealed in a radio interview in 1971 – at some political cost to Butler within the Conservative Party, and at some personal cost also:

My life history ha[s] been one of serving the Conservative Party and the Conservative Establishments throughout the years. But I [have] had to take an awful lot of opposition. . . . India, education, Conservative reform, the new face of Conservative capitalism, *the birching and flogging at the Home Office, which haunted me almost every week of my time at the Home Office and on which I eventually won* – all these things had created a certain criticism of me in the Conservative party . . . [emphasis added][18]

But although the pressure for the restoration of corporal punishment was seen off in 1960, the retributive impulse revealed by the issue had not permanently vanished. It was to come into its own again in the 1970s, in the penal sphere exemplified above all by the revival of the idea of the 'short sharp shock' detention centre (a concept that had appeared in the 1940s and 1950s, but had been played down in the 1960s); and, in a wider political context, through a more general reaching out for authoritarian solutions to social problems (see Hall *et al.*, 1978).

Problems of Manpower

The problems of criminal justice manpower in the period under review are best assessed with special reference to the police, who of course were and are by far the largest of the criminal justice agencies.

In the period between the two World Wars, the police had enjoyed a privileged position. The pay scales created by the Desborough Committee in 1919 gave the constable a wage which was approximately 30 per cent above the national average wage for men; and, despite some subsequent fluctuations, pay remained relatively advantageous throughout the inter-war period (see Figure 1.3; also Martin and Wilson, 1969, ch. 3). Additionally, the security of employment afforded by membership of the service was a very attractive feature in an era of high unemployment.

By 1945 the inter-war pay differential had been substantially eroded (Figure 1.3), and thereafter continuing inflation in the post-war period meant that the police required periodic pay reviews to keep up with national trends in earnings. Other social changes also had an effect on the attractiveness of a police career, as Martin and Wilson (1969, p. 77) succinctly explain:

The police, or at least the substantial proportion with at least ten years service, clearly earned more than the national average when their allowances were taken into account, but equally clearly they did not earn very much more. The differential was considered by many to be too small, and was aggravated by other social changes. With full employment the

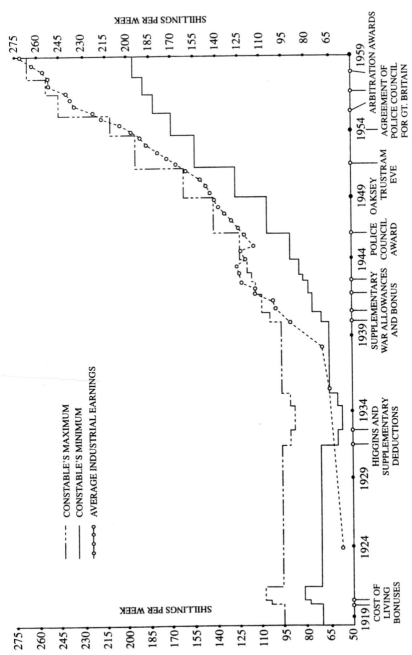

FIGURE 1.3   *A Comparison of Movements in (a) the constable's pay, and (b) average industrial earnings*

SOURCE: *Interim Report of the Royal Commission on the Police (1960).*

security of the police service no longer meant the difference between a steady job and the fear of the dole, paid holidays soon became general and the health service and national insurance soon reduced the value of free medical attention, sick pay and a pension. The disadvantages of police life, however, remained.

These 'disadvantages' were assessed, in an informal survey in 1966 (Home Office, 1967, pp. 22–7) as including especially, first, hours of work (unlike many other occupations by that date, the policeman did not enjoy a five-day working week, and he also had to put up with shift work and weekend work); and secondly, 'unsatisfactory man-management' (in particular, 'unnecessarily strict adherence to the letter of [police] . . . regulations' and 'thoughtless application of disciplinary measures' – both increasingly unfashionable in the period characterised by Arthur Marwick as one of 'a great release from older restraints and controls'). The report containing these survey results concluded that premature wastage in the police was not excessive relative to other occupations in a full-employment economy; nevertheless, mid-career wastage of trained and experienced officers was substantially higher than before the Second World War, and constituted a continuing source of difficulty for operational policing.

These various developments help to explain the fact that, in addition to periodic pay awards, there were in the period 1945–70 three major official reports on aspects of the closely related issues of police pay, conditions of service, manpower needs, and recruitment and wastage. These were the Oaksey Committee of 1949, the Interim Report of the Royal Commission on the Police in 1960, and a report of a Working Party on Manpower in 1966 (see Home Office, 1949b, 1967; Royal Commission on the Police, 1960). Both Oaksey and the Royal Commission proposed substantial pay increases; as a working paper prepared for the latter body put it:

> [the] primary purpose [was] that of giving the police a tremendous boost and proposing a substantial increase in pay so as to get the service up to strength quickly by stimulating recruitment and curtailing wastage.[19]

But the Oaksey and Royal Commission 'boosts', while having the desired effects for a time, can be seen with hindsight to have been only temporary palliatives. In large part, of course, this was because of continuing inflation and the fact that the police, as public sector employees, were potentially always in line for direct government action to curb pay increases at the (regularly recurring) times of public expenditure restraints. These factors would have created problems even with a workforce intended to be numerically stable; but in fact the police, especially in the 1960s, were working within a framework of approved increases in 'authorised establishments', given the increasing problems of crime and traffic.[20] Only six years after the Royal Commission's 'tremendous boost', the Working Party on Manpower found it necessary to put forward a further programme to assist the police to move 'as rapidly as possible to a total strength which approaches its authorised establishment'. By this date, however, the Working Party felt it necessary to add, pessimistically, that

> it is impossible to be sanguine about the prospects of complete success. The question must be asked whether, in conditions of full employment and economic restraint, the police service can ever have all the manpower it would like. (Home Office, 1967, p. 8)

By 1976 discontent in the police service reached a new peak when negotiations over pay broke down, the Police Federation (representing the lower ranks) withdrew from the Police Council of Great Britain, and subsequent secret ballots resulted in an overwhelming vote to demand the right of the police to strike (outlawed in the Police Act 1919 as part of the Desborough settlement). A new and prestigious committee, chaired by a Law Lord (Lord Edmund-Davies), was appointed (see Home Office, 1978): eloquent enough testimony to the continuing failure to solve some of the difficulties of the post-war years. Meanwhile, in 1970 the total strength of the police service in England and Wales remained at only 86 per cent of the authorised establishment.

Overall, then, the economic situation in the post-war period, coupled with the growth in crime and traffic, created an endemic problem of police manpower which successive governments attempted to tackle, but none with lasting success. Ironically, it can be seen with hindsight that among the contributors to this failure were both (a) the relative overall success (as compared with the pre-war period) of the attempt to create conditions of full employment within a welfare state society; and (b) the relative economic failures of the period (recurring high inflation, 'stop–go' economic policies, and a relatively low growth-rate as against competitor nations). Arguably, too, insufficient critical thought was given, in a rapidly changing society, to what the police were expected to achieve, and hence how many of them were really needed – we return to these issues in a later section of this paper.

Uncomfortable Research Results

The period under review was characterised by a considerable growth of investment in research relevant to criminal justice topics. *Penal Practice in a Changing Society* gave prominence to the importance of research (Home Office, 1959, pp. 5–6 and Appendix B) and mentioned both the founding of the Home Office Research Unit in 1957 and the imminent establishment of the Institute of Criminology at Cambridge University, the first fully fledged university department in the subject in this country (see Lodge, 1974; Radzinowicz, 1988). Crime and criminality, the White Paper asserted,

> cannot be dealt with effectively without more knowledge of its causes and a more accurate measurement than we have at present of the success of the various forms of treatment. (Home Office, 1959, para. 17)

Whilst the truth of this statement is undeniable, the problem not foreseen by the White Paper was that the results of research, when they came, might point in directions destructive of current and recent policy. An early example, which led to legislative change within the period under review, concerned preventive detention.

Preventive detention had first been established in 1908 as a way of providing prolonged incapacitative detention for habitual offenders, but had largely fallen into disuse by the 1930s because of what were described as 'cumbrous procedures', together with the fact that the 1908 legislation required a 'dual track' system: that is, the offender was sentenced first to a period of penal servitude, then to a separate additional period of preventive detention (PD). A departmental committee of 1932 recommended a streamlining of the system (which would *inter alia* be 'single track' rather than 'dual track'), and these reforms were incorporated both into the 1938 Criminal Justice Bill and, in a different form, the Criminal Justice Act 1948.

By the time ACTO came to review the sentence in the early 1960s, there was substantial evidence that all was not well. Research by the Home Office Research Unit showed that

> in some ways the offenders sentenced to preventive detention are *less of a danger to society than many given long term or other sentences of imprisonment*; many of the preventive detainees' current and also past offences are quite trivial and these offenders include very little violence among their offences [emphasis added]. (Hammond and Chayen, 1963, p. 185)

Contemporaneous psychiatrically based research by Donald West (1963) of the Cambridge Institute of Criminology also showed 'conclusively', as ACTO put it, that the majority of preventive detainees are of the passive–inadequate type, feckless and inadequate in every sphere, who regard the commission of crime as a means of escaping immediate difficulties rather than a part of a deliberately anti-social way of life. (Advisory Council, 1963b, p. 8)

A classic individual example of this kind of offender was 'Charlie Smith', *The Unknown Citizen* of Tony Parker's influential biographical book of the period (Parker, 1963). Clearly, the preventive detention sentence was not working as originally intended; there was therefore little opposition when ACTO recommended abolition of the measure in 1963, and this was duly enacted in the Criminal Justice Act 1967.[21]

This particular example did not cause much consternation among leading policy-makers, nor among 'liberal progressives', the latter of whom in particular had never really liked the prolonged incarceration entailed by preventive detention. But the story of negative research results was in due course to be repeated in a much more fundamental way. Two of the cornerstones of early post-war thought in English criminal justice were, first, belief in the crime-preventive effectiveness of traditional police beat work, and secondly, belief in the considerable reformative possibilities of various kinds of penal treatment (either in custodial or in non-custodial settings). Both these cornerstone beliefs were to come under very serious fire as a direct result of empirical research results. The research-based questioning of accepted doctrines about beat patrolling (by foot or by car) did not occur within our period, but when it came was of great importance (see Clarke and Hough, 1980, 1984). But questioning of the tenets of the 'rehabilitative ideal' in penology did begin to occur before 1970, though it did not have its full impact until the mid-1970s with the publication of substantial reviews of relevant research findings in both the United States and Britain (Lipton, Martinson and Wilks, 1975; Brody, 1976). Those familiar with Martinson's 'nothing works' messages of penological pessimism in the 1970s might be surprised to learn that a very similar view had been proclaimed in the British House of Commons in 1960, by a very unusual Labour MP (Sir George Benson) who had himself conducted original criminological research. Like many others, Benson had been impressed by Mannheim and Wilkins's (1955) pioneering statistical study concerning the prediction of recidivism among Borstal trainees. He carried out his own studies with male young prisoners (persons under 21 sentenced to imprisonment) as an extension of that work:

The Prison Commissioners gave me the data relating to some 300 boys who had been sentenced to prison and who had passed through Lewes.

The follow-up period was similar to that of Mannheim and Wilkins. I classified them according to the borstal predictors into the A, B, X, C and D groups[22] and got the astonishing result that imprisonment in Lewes gave results identical with borstal training.

The Prison Commissioners did not like that; they were horrified. . . . In effect, the Prison Commissioners said, 'This must be wrong. We have concentrated on reform in borstal. Borstal must give better results.'

. . . we have struck what is possibly a fundamental fact in our penal law . . . that . . . 'On a given type of individual all forms of penal treatment give identical results'. . . . This uniformity of results from penal treatment ought to have been realised many years ago. The first evidence is to be found in research by the Metropolitan Police in 1937, when they undertook a piece of research on first offenders. . . . Fine, dismissal, imprisonment gave identical results. On the other hand, curiously enough, the results from probation were worse. The reconviction rate varied with age, but sentence seemed to have little or no effect.[23]

In the light of later studies, we now know that Benson's alleged 'fundamental fact in our penal law' was oversimplified: different treatments do sometimes produce differential recidivism rates. But Benson's 'law' was much more accurate than the then beliefs of the Prison Commissioners, and many others; the fact is that even in the light of modern research revising some of Martinson's oversimplistic messages, 'no serious researcher has been willing to reassert the rehabilitationists' traditional claim that treatment can routinely be made to work for the bulk of criminal offenders' (von Hirsch, 1986, p. 4).

The negative research results concerning penal treatment produced in the 1960s by Benson and others were indeed shattering to the many adherents of a 'liberal progressive' approach in penology. They had advocated research, but they had not remotely expected research to emerge with results of this kind. It was another example of 'what went wrong'.

Incidents and Underlying Imperfections

It is a fact well known to students of social policy that reforms of the system often take place not so much because of a careful routine analysis by ministers and civil servants in the relevant Department of State, nor even because of a critique or exposé by an outside journalist or pressure group, but because one or more individual incident(s) occurs, drawing public attention to some underlying imperfections of policy in a dramatic way which seems to demand change. Very often an inquiry is set up after such incidents, and it is the report of the inquiry that sets the agenda for subsequent reforms; but the reforms would not have taken place without the public attention created by the original incident. There were a number of incidents of this kind in the field of English criminal justice in the period 1945–70. Indeed, some individual incidents strongly influenced the debate on capital punishment in the early 1950s, despite the fact that this debate was at that time also very well served by a massive Royal Commission report unrelated to the incidents in question (Royal Commission on Capital Punishment, 1953). James Christoph (1962, p. 96) detected a distinct change of the public mood on capital punishment from 1948 to 1956, paving the way for the beginnings of legislative changes; but he also noted that

> The activities of the [Royal] Commission, thorough as they may have been, could not have kept popular or Parliamentary attention focused on the question of capital punishment for long had not other events added a sense of urgency and vivid human interest to the debate that previously had raged mainly at the level of blue books and white papers. What gave the debate its uniquely compelling flavour was the impact of a handful of highly publicised murder cases in the early fifties. *Possibly more than any other factor, it was these cases that led to increased uneasiness among supporters of hanging and their previously indifferent allies in the public* [emphasis added][24]

In the 'mainstream' criminal justice topics principally studied in our research, the influence of individual incidents can be seen most vividly as regards the prisons and the police. As previously noted, in the prisons a series of inter-war liberalisations had taken place, without much in the way of apparently deleterious effects (but see note 7). In the post-war period Fox's liberal progressivism continued to emphasise treatment rather than security in closed prisons,[25] whilst a combination of population pressures, the ready availability of ex-service camps and the prevailing liberal philosophy led to a rapid growth in the number of open prisons. The overall result was a considerable escalation in the total number of escapes and attempted escapes (see Thomas, 1972, pp. 171–4, 185–7). The Prison Commissioners were forced to take note of these developments, but, as J. E. Thomas (1972, p. 188) has shrewdly noted, for them to have attempted serious ameliorative measures was, given the philosophy of (for example) *Penal Practice in a Changing Society*, 'ideologically unthinkable'.

Individual incidents forced a change in this situation, three incidents being of special importance. First, a group of men broke into Birmingham

Prison one night in August 1964 and, with illegally obtained keys, 'sprang' Charles Wilson, one of the Great Train Robbers,[26] sentenced to 30 years' imprisonment only a short time beforehand. Secondly, Ronald Biggs, another Train Robber serving 30 years, found friends who managed in July 1965, with the aid of a furniture van, a rope ladder and possibly a shotgun, to spirit him away from a routine period of exercise in the exercise yard at Wandsworth to celebrated (and non-extraditable) exile in Brazil. Thirdly, and politically of greatest significance, George Blake, convicted of spying for the Soviet Union in 1961 and sentenced to no less than 42 years imprisonment, managed in October 1966 to escape from Wormwood Scrubs during a period of 'association' (see note 25) by breaking a second-floor decayed window bar (probably with a single kick or hammer blow), dropping to ground level via a handily placed covered way, and then proceeding across the grounds to where his friends had thoughtfully draped a rope ladder over the wall for his (unnoticed) convenience.

The Prison Department (successor, from 1963, to the former Prison Commissioners) had become a public laughing-stock. After the Blake escape, the Home Secretary appointed no less a figure than Lord Mountbatten (the last Viceroy of India, and a relative of the Queen) to head an immediate inquiry, Mountbatten having established in advance that his report would be taken seriously (Morris, 1989, p. 131). Mountbatten's report (Home Office, 1966) made a large number of recommendations to improve security, including the introduction of a security classification system (A, B, C or D) for all prisoners, and the considerable strengthening of perimeter security (for example, with television surveillance and dog patrols) in appropriate prisons. The result was a sharp drop in the number of escapes, but also a definite change of priorities and mood in the Prison Service, which would never again treat the basic custodial task in as cavalier a fashion as it had begun to do in the post-war period. Indeed, so complete was the immediate change that Lord Mountbatten himself complained in 1971 that regime activities and rehabilitative programmes in higher-security prisons were being unduly restricted.[27] The policy line of the post-war Prison Commissioners and Prison Department had, unwittingly but unmistakably, been radically jolted by George Blake and his predecessors in escape.

Turning now to the police, in this sphere the relevant incidents were more numerous, and their impact on policy less obviously discernible through a single official report. But their cumulative importance was, nevertheless, considerable.

As has been well summarised elsewhere (for example, Critchley, 1978, pp. 270–4), the Royal Commission on the Police was set up in 1959 not because of direct 'concern about the [general] efficiency of the police, or about the state of crime, or the adequacy of police strength' (p. 274) but as the end-point of a series of individual incidents which caused concern in Parliament. The incidents at issue were (at least by modern standards) 'pretty small beer' (Reiner, 1985, p. 62),[28] but they did at least begin to raise awkward questions as to whether the extremely high post-war reputation of the English police was altogether justified, and they also created uncertainty among MPs about the adequacy of the Home Secretary's accountability to Parliament in police matters. As the Secretary of the Royal Commission very well expressed the matter in a letter to his Chairman in 1961:[29]

One of my principles is to think twice before burdening you and your colleagues with yet further reading matter. Even so, I now blame myself, having re-read the [debate in the House of Commons leading to the appointment of the Commission] for not bringing it to your attention earlier; I now enclose it. . . . [In the debate] many of the issues now before the Commission are brought into sharp focus in the references to a specific case. . . . Reflecting on this and on the evidence we have received, and [on other Parliamentary debates in 1958–9] . . . one is left in little doubt that the Commission was not set up because anyone directly concerned with the police thought the system was wrong or worked badly. The motive was, I think, a powerful urge from both sides of the House of Commons and from the House of Lords, combining apprehension that all was not well with frustration at Members' inability to get at the Home Secretary or anyone else: hence, I think, the great importance [of] the issue of the Home Secretary's accountability to Parliament, on the implications of which some of the witnesses might usefully be reminded.

The incidents of the 1950s, therefore, were very much indirectly instrumental in leading to the so-called 'tripartite' structure of police accountability suggested by the Royal Commission on the Police (1962) in its Final Report, and enacted (with modifications) in the Police Act 1964. That tripartite structure – defining differing roles for the Chief Constable, the local police authority and the Home Secretary – remains in force today (see further, Stevenson and Bottoms, 1990).

Later incidents were to suggest more fundamental underlying problems in the police service itself. After the Royal Commission's Final Report, but before the Police Act, came two incidents involving malpractices in the police interrogation of suspects. The first was the Sheffield 'rhino whip' affair, where Sheffield detectives were found to have committed 'brutal and sustained assaults with weapons . . . for the purpose of inducing confessions' from suspects, and police colleagues had clearly been reluctant to blow the whistle on the blatant illegalities (Home Office, 1963). The second matter concerned Detective Sergeant Challenor of the Metropolitan Police, who apparently planted false evidence on at least two dozen suspects, unnoticed by colleagues and supervisors, and was then discovered to have been seriously mentally ill whilst on duty (Home Office, 1964; Grigg, 1965). Neither incident led immediately to much other than a specific enquiry on its particular facts,[30] but in retrospect these reports can be seen as the beginnings of a path which was later to develop into a clear public realisation that the police do not always behave impeccably in the interrogation process. This path was to lead, eventually, to the work of the Royal Commission on Criminal Procedure (1981), and, beyond that, to the problems revealed by the reassessments in the late 1980s and early 1990s of the 1970s Guildford and Birmingham pub-bombing convictions, and the setting up of a further Royal Commission in 1991.

Back in the 1960s, worse was to follow. On 29 November 1969 *The Times* published a sensational story about a particular incident, for which it had incontrovertible supporting evidence, and which, in its view, was probably not an isolated matter:

> We have, we believe, proved that at least three detectives are taking large sums of money in exchange for dropping charges, for being lenient with evidence offered in court, and for allowing a criminal to work unhindered. Our investigations into the activities of these three men convince us that their cases are not isolated. We cannot prove that other officers are guilty but we believe there is enough suspicion to justify a full inquiry.

It was 'a bombshell that still reverberates' (Reiner, 1985, p. 65), but it was only the beginning of revelations about corruption in the Metropolitan Police. During the 1970s there were two more major scandals, one involving the Drug Squad and the other the Obscene Publications Squad (see Cox *et al.*, 1977), and Sir Robert Mark was appointed as Commissioner of the Metropolitan Police with a brief to root out the malaise. Obviously all was far from well in England's largest police force. It was a considerable shock to the public, and a very considerable shift from the high point of police legitimacy in the early post-war years.

ISSUES RELATED TO MODERNISATION

A number of geographers and sociologists have recently emphasised the 'shrinking' of time–space produced by modern technological developments, and the importance of this for social life (see, for example, Giddens, 1984, ch. 3). For example, motorways and fast, comfortable cars make road travel much quicker and simpler, and thus reduce the perceptual distance between, say, Bristol and London. Or again, with modern direct-dial telephones, people are able to communicate easily with one another over large distances, and across time-zones; and with the aid of satellite technology, television companies can beam events on the other side of the world into our living rooms as they happen. We all become accustomed to such developments, and in all kinds of subtle ways they affect our behaviour and social perceptions.

The period 1945–70 was, in England, one of rapid modernisation in these respects. We have already noted the growth of the private car during this period; this was accompanied by a considerable road-building programme, including most notably the beginning of the national motorway network (from 1959 onwards). As to telephones, census figures show that the number of households with a telephone rose from 1.5 million in 1951 to 4.2 million in 1966; and distance communication was immensely aided by the rapid expansion, during the 1960s, of the so-called 'STD' (subscriber trunk dialling) system, meaning that longer-distance calls no longer had to be routed through the operator.

Inevitably, the criminal justice system was required to adjust to changes of this sort. The most interesting case study is that of the police, who of course have to provide on-the-ground 24-hour cover in a way that most of the other criminal justice agencies and institutions do not. Among the obvious manifestations of police adjustment to modernisation during 1945–70 were:

> First, a complex pattern of police force amalgamations which eventually reduced the total number of separate forces in England and Wales from 159 to in 1945 to 49 in 1970 – though not without some extremely vigorous protests along the way about the way that traditional local loyalties were being trampled upon; and
> Secondly, the introduction in the 1960s of a network of 'regional crime squads', under a national co-ordinator; in each squad, several police forces would collaborate in the investigation and pursuit of major crimes and criminals. (Chappell, 1965)

However, perhaps the most interesting example of response to modernisation concerns the beat system. Immediately after the war, the Second Report of the Police Post-War Committee (completed in 1946 but not published until 1949) noted that:

In considering whether the police service of this country is fully up to date, one of the first matters for examination is the beat system, the present principles of which, generally speaking, differ little from those first instituted when police forces were established something like 100 years ago. (Home Office, 1949a, p. 4)

The traditional beat system was different in rural areas (where a constable, usually resident in the area, was responsible for covering all occurrences within his 'patch' over a 24-hour period, although only patrolling for up to a third of that time) and in town areas (where beats were patrolled throughout 24 hours by constables working on foot in shifts). We must restrict attention here to the town beats. The Second Post-War Report described various different methods that had been evolved of working a town beat (for example, the walking of fixed routes; variable routes but with fixed reporting points; working of beats at the officer's discretion, and so on), and also various methods of trying to supplement the foot beat men with support from mobile patrols, a strategy of which the Committee approved (as subsequently, though in a slightly different way, did the Oaksey Committee: Home Office 1949b). However, the Second Report rejected outright an American innovation of motorised patrols:

So far as one can judge, this method almost completely dispenses with [the traditional practice of] trying property at night, *and also diminishes that contact with the public which is so useful to the police and to the public itself.* Even if all cars used were fitted with wireless transmitting and receiving apparatus, this method would not be suitable for adoption in this country. [emphasis added]. (Home Office, 1949a, p. 7)

Adherence to the foot beat as the bedrock of day-to-day police operations remained strong for some time. The Interim Report of the Royal Commission on the Police noted that the development of New Towns and new housing estates had increased the total built-up area of Great Britain by nearly 25 per cent from 1939 to 1960, creating 'a substantial increase in the areas which the police are expected to patrol'. But there was no suggestion that forces should abandon the traditional foot beat system as the main method of operational policing. It was true, the Commission said, that

new and improved techniques, such as the extended use of patrol cars and motor cycles and developments in the use of wireless have come increasingly to [the police's] aid; but these advantages are not unaccompanied by drawbacks. *Police witnesses have repeatedly emphasised to us that it is the uniformed man on the beat who provides the most effective deter-*

rent to crime. We entirely accept this.   [emphasis added] (Royal Commission, 1960, para. 66)

Indeed, the Royal Commission considered that there was a tendency in many areas to 'resort to methods of policing which, making all allowances for the technical advances of recent years, have the appearance of an expedient rather than a policy' (para. 79). Two years later, the Association of Chief Police Officers (ACPO) similarly argued that cars 'are not, in our view, substitutes for the beat constable working on foot'; and that 'the postwar tendency to offset dwindling manpower by mechanising beats has led to a loss of communication between the public and the police' (Home Office, 1967, p. 133).

Reviewing these various reports with the benefit of hindsight, three points stand out. First, until the early 1960s attachment to the traditional urban foot beat system remained very strong, buttressed, at least in part, by sentiments of loyalty to an activity which had been practised for many years, and which was thought in its heyday to have worked very well. Secondly, the reports display a perhaps surprising, but nevertheless persistent, failure to appreciate the rapidity and likely acceleration of technological change. One usually looks in vain, for example, for any attempt to assess likely future developments in the volume or character of road traffic, and their potential impact on the beat system. But thirdly, and very interestingly, the reports do show a sensitive awareness of what was subsequently to be, for a while, all too easily forgotten: namely, that putting the police in cars can easily lead to an erosion of contact and effective two-way communication and confidence between the police and the public.

One interesting possible way of modifying the traditional beat system was noted by the ACPO committee in 1962: 'the pattern of beat duty may well be altered as soon as every officer is provided with a personal wireless set' (Home Office, 1967, p. 133). The significance of this point was that traditionally the police station had no means of contacting foot beat constables, or they the station, save by means of the telephone, fixed reporting points or messages passed through mobile patrols; obviously things might be radically different if foot beats were to continue, accompanied by personal radio as standard equipment.

That, however, never occurred on any widespread scale. Instead, the foot beat was abandoned, in most parts of the country with surprising rapidity, following the Report of the Working Party on Operational Efficiency and Management in 1966 (Home Office, 1967). The tone of this report, in its discussion of the traditional beat system, was completely different from that of its predecessors:

There is a need, so far as possible, to adjust the system of policing an area to accord more closely with the hazards of crime and road traffic with which the policeman is primarily employed to deal. . . . [T]he availability of new equipment introduced as a result of harnessing scientific efforts to police needs broadens the horizon, and the question must now be asked whether there is any longer good reason to retain a system which had its heyday in totally different conditions from those which obtain today, when populations tended to be static, crime was adequately contained, traffic problems barely existed, and the police lacked the modern resources of mobility and electronic equipment. (Home Office, 1967, p. 117)

The new system that the Working Party advocated, based on experiments by the Home Office Police Research and Planning Branch in several Lancashire towns, was known as 'unit beat policing'. It sought to maximise not only the traditional advantages of the village constable living in his area, but also the perceived strengths of motorised patrols, both linked by personal radio to a central 'collator' at the police station. In a typical urban area, the Working Party thought,

the pattern of policing might consist of foot patrols in the city centres, with the whole of the inner and outer suburban areas divided into 'beats'. . . . Each of these beats should be the particular responsibility of a single constable, who preferably . . . would live in his own area. Superimposed over this ground system would be mobile patrols operating continuously day and night. (Home Office, 1967, p. 118)

The system was thought likely to provide a better service to the public (especially through the area constable), to be more interesting for the police themselves, and to yield 'substantial economies in manpower' (probably of the order of 5 per cent of the entire police service). Early and tentative research in the Lancashire pilot projects also suggested that the scheme might both reduce crime and improve detection rates. The Working Party considered whether to await further research results before recommending the scheme, but were in no doubt that they should not hold up progress. The traditional beat system's 'inefficient use of manpower', its 'lack of appeal to the young [policeman] of today', and its failure 'to exploit to the full the advantages of modern equipment' all suggested to the Working Party that it was time to move on quickly, to a new system which would achieve objectives 'which have only recently become attainable as a result of technological advance' (Home Office, 1967, pp. 117–18).

In the longer term, of course, a much less optimistic assessment of unit beat policing had to be made. Gains in crime reduction or the improvement of detection rates became very hard to discern. Even if some manpower was saved, authorised establishments continued to increase in the 1970s despite the introduction of the new system, albeit not as rapidly as before (Home Office, 1978, p. 94). And, most importantly in the long run, police–public relations did not improve. The Working Party's assumption was that the area constable would be the core of the new system, and 'superimposed over this ground system' would be motorised patrols, to provide a fast emergency service. The reality was that the motorised patrols ('Panda cars') became the core of the system, particularly because (a) they, unlike the area constables, were on duty 24 hours a day; (b) the rank-and-file constables' 'action-centred perspective on policing was accentuated by the technology of fast cars, sirens and flashing blue lights' (Reiner, 1985, p. 64); and (c) for reasons connected with both the previous points, collators in police stations basically treated the area constables as peripheral figures. The consequence of all this was, as accurately predicted by the Police Post-War Committee in 1946, a 'diminution of that contact with the public which is so useful to the police and to the public itself' (see above); hence 'what was intended as professionalisation ended up as the politicisation of relations with the public' (Reiner, 1985, p. 64).

The reasons for the 1966 Working Party's failure to foresee all this are not hard to ascertain. The Working Party realised that the world was changing rapidly due to advancing technology, and that previous reviews of the beat system had given far too little attention to these trends. Having grasped the technological nettle, however, the Working Party made the mistake – by no means unknown at that time in wider political circles – of adopting a kind of technological Utopianism. As with some other policing issues in the 1960s, it was too easily assumed that the newly formed Home Office Police Research and Planning Branch (where scientists and policemen worked jointly in a small but influential team) could solve longstanding problems by the simple application of positive science. The earlier policy-makers' failure to appreciate the likely pace of technological change, and its societal implications, had been replaced by an over-readiness among 1960s policy-makers to believe in technological solutions. It would be left to a later generation to try to strike a better balance.

THREADS OF CONTINUITY

In emphasising in this chapter the problems created for the criminal justice system by, for example, rising crime rates and unwelcome incidents, there is inevitably a danger that we might underplay important threads of continuity in criminal justice thinking during 1945–70. To conclude this chapter, therefore, we will return to one such thread, namely the 'welfare state' emphasis with which our story began.

Two topics relevant to this theme require examination: the probation service, and children and young persons. We noted earlier that during the war the Home Office was pressing for greater professionalism, and professional training, in the probation service; and these goals were duly realised. By the late 1950s and early 1960s the probation service had united around the banner of 'social casework' (based principally on a modified version of psychoanalytic theory), and there was much talk within the service of its acquiring the status of a profession (see King, 1958, for a handbook of probation at this time). A year or two later the service gained additional duties and enhanced status when it was asked to become the principal organisation responsible for prison after-care. After-care services had been examined by ACTO (Advisory Council, 1963a), who had found an outdated structure of 'discharged prisoners' aid societies' and the like, with roots in Victorian philanthropy: it was inevitable that, in a welfare state era, these structures should be reformed, and also that the social-casework-oriented probation services should be asked to take on the relevant tasks.

The self-assurance of the service in the early 1960s was, however, to be followed, later in the same decade, by some ideological turmoil. But ironically, these tensions were themselves in large part the result of the successes of post-war social work, and of liberal-welfare thought, pressed to their logical conclusions. Two (related) issues were dominant. First, at a time when an interdepartmental committee was sitting to consider the future of the personal social services (see Home Office, Department of Education *et al.*, 1968) many within probation felt that the service had much in common with other social work agencies (all of whom were tackling related social problems, and all practising 'social casework'), and therefore that an amalgamation was desirable. This was resisted by others, keener on probation's proud heritage and unique combination of tasks, and this latter group ultimately gained the victory, aided by their friends in the government and the Home Office.[31] Secondly, the concurrent debate on future policy for children and young persons (see further below) seemed likely to remove significant elements of work from the probation service (if that service were to survive as a separate agency); thus the service began to seem less attractive to those probation officers who had joined primarily to help young offenders.[32] Both of these issues caused considerable heart-searching in the probation service of the late 1960s. In retrospect, however, both can be seen as having been inevitably raised by post-war developments. In a true welfare state, it is bound to be the case that welfare and social services of various kinds are set up to assist the disadvantaged: once they have been set up, then questions are equally likely to be raised about the relationships between the services, and whether there should be better co-ordination or even amalgamation. Also, if one has both a probation service and a separate children's service, then within a broad consensus of welfare-oriented policy, someone is sure to ask why child delinquents cannot be dealt with by the children's service, rather than having their delinquent status singled out by allocation to the probation service. Hence the tensions in the probation service in the late 1960s can legitimately be seen as the product of a continuity in, and development of, the 'liberal progressive' thought of the 1940s.

Turning then specifically to the policy area of children and young persons, here developments were exceptionally complex, especially in the 1960s. (They involved, from 1960 to 1969, a departmental committee report, a Labour Party study group, two White Papers and two statutes: see generally, Bottoms, 1974; Clarke, 1980; Stevenson, 1989.) The whole complicated story began with a letter to *The Times* on 16 March 1955, signed by, among others, the wife of the Archbishop of Canterbury (Mrs Rosamund Fisher), the eminent child psychiatrist Dr John Bowlby, the celebrated 'liberal progressive' Margery Fry, and Eileen Younghusband, a leading social-work thinker. The theme was the 'urgent need for reorientating the social services towards the maintenance of the family', not least because juvenile crime often resulted from family breakdown. A major source of difficulty was thought to be that the various welfare or social agencies set up under the umbrella of the welfare state were 'each . . . [concentrating] on its particular aspect of the case, and the family itself is lost sight of'; the pressing need was for the appointment of a committee of inquiry 'whose terms of reference would be wide enough to include all causes of family breakdown, with positive recommendations for their prevention and alleviation'.

This letter was followed up by a delegation to the Home Office by the same group (the 'Fisher group'); then, in their wake and influenced by these events, a further delegation, this time from the Magistrates' Association, pressed the Home Office for a review of 'the procedure in juvenile courts and the treatment of juveniles coming before them'. The Home Office agreed to concede a departmental committee (the Ingleby Committee) to consider both the issue posed by the Magistrates' Association and (in response to the Fisher group's concern) an examination of whether local authority children's departments 'should . . . be given new powers and duties to prevent or forestall the suffering of children through neglect in their own homes'.

The narrow drafting of the second part of the committee's brief meant, however, that the issue of a unified 'family service' (in place of the proliferation of existing social services) was outside its terms of reference; but that did not prevent the main critics of the Ingleby Committee's report (Home Office, 1960) from concentrating their attention on precisely this issue. These critics were, politically speaking, primarily from the left, and their analysis eventually paved the way – after Labour regained power in 1964 – for a complex series of developments through which, by the end of the decade, the government had under active and formal consideration the three separate but interconnected issues of (a) the future organisation of the personal social services; (b) juvenile justice procedures and treatments for young offenders; and (c) community development programmes. The Labour Government's initial proposals for juvenile justice, enshrined in a 1965 White Paper (Home Office, 1965), would have entailed the abolition of the juvenile courts and their replacement by non-judicial 'family councils', linked to a proposed unified 'family service': but concerted opposition from magistrates, lawyers and probation officers forced a climbdown on the 'family councils' issue.[33]

Revised proposals, published in a second White Paper (Home Office 1968) and enacted with modifications in the Children and Young Persons Act 1969, were generally regarded in a less hostile light, mainly because the juvenile court was retained. However, the Act's provisions, had they ever been fully implemented, would have led to a drastic reduction in the role of the court, and an enhancement of the discretionary power of social workers. The Conservative opposition therefore regarded some key clauses of the 1969 Bill as eroding the traditional safeguards and frameworks of criminal law and criminal procedure, and they formally opposed them in Parliament. On being returned to power in 1970, the Conservatives quickly announced that they would never bring into effect certain central sections of the Act.[34] Even so, the parts of the Act that were implemented caused a huge controversy in the 1970s, with the main opposition to them coming from the magistrates and the police (Harwin, 1982; Morris and Giller, 1987, ch. 4).

Victor Bailey (1987, Postscript) has correctly pointed out that there was a clear ideological continuity between the 'liberal progressives' of the 1940s and those pressing for juvenile court and related reforms in the 1960s. It is also the case, however, that the context was very different. In the 1940s the then ideas of the principal reformers posed no particular threat to central legal tenets and institutions, but merely sought greater individualisation and welfare within agreed legal structures. In the 1960s the reformers challenged the structures themselves, creating for a time, in England at least,[35] a serious political dissensus between those advocating a welfare philosophy and those more inclined to have confidence in the traditional legal apparatus. Thus, paradoxically, a strong strand of ideological continuity produced a quite new intensity of political conflict. This dissensus was made the more acute by the fact that some of the traditionalists were deeply worried about continually rising crime rates, and therefore all the more inclined to favour a firm response within existing frameworks, rather than a resort to a new and untested framework based on social work principles.

CRIMINAL JUSTICE IN 1970 – AND BEYOND

The years 1969–70 can reasonably be regarded as a watershed in English criminal justice. The Children and Young Persons Act 1969 contained the most developed application of welfare principles to criminal justice ever seen in an English statute, and as such was the culmination of a range of measures which can be traced back to the first decade of the twentieth century (Garland, 1985; Bailey, 1987). But, as we have seen, within a year significant parts of the Act were being repudiated by the new Conservative government, and they were never to be reinstated. By the early 1990s, perhaps the central and fundamental underlying principle of the 1969 Act (namely the desirability of a single set of social institutions and policies for juvenile delinquents and for children in need) was decisively reversed in a set of reforms centred around the Children Act 1989 and the Criminal Justice Act 1991.

1969 also saw *The Times* revelation on police corruption in London (see above), a key event in shifting political and public attitudes to the police, which helped to ensure that the 1970s and 1980s would find the topics of complaints against the police, and police accountability, high on the political agenda. Police operations were also being revolutionised all over the country with the adoption of the motorised patrol system, though the disadvantages of that system were not yet fully apparent.

As for the prison service, 1969–70 saw it still reeling from the hammer-blow of the escapes setback of the 1960s, and the consequent Mountbatten Report. In 1964 senior administrators in the prison service had proudly and symbolically elevated Fox's Prison Rule 6 of 1952 to the top of the mast-head as Rule 1 ('The purpose of the training and treatment of convicted prisoners shall be to encourage and assist them to lead a good and useful life'). An official prisons policy paper of 1969, while not repudiating Rule 1, stated however that the *first* task of the service was 'to hold those committed to custody and to provide conditions for their detention which are currently acceptable to society' (Home Office, 1969, p. 7). This task, which the policy paper characterised in shorthand as that of 'humane containment', was described as perhaps 'a prosaic and limited one', but it was nevertheless thought to be 'not an easy one' to accomplish. As the prison service struggled with gross overcrowding for the next two decades, and during the same period delivered declining regime standards (King and McDermott, 1989), the truth of these words was forcefully brought home.

All this, of course, was a very far cry from the high hopes of the early post-war years. The scaling-down of those original hopes, plus anxieties about how to put right the all-too-evident failures of the police service and the prison system, plus the full realisation of the implications of negative research results as regards reformative penal treatment and routine police beat work, plus a relentless continuing rise in recorded crime, all combined to create during the next two decades an atmosphere of considerable uncertainty in many spheres of criminal justice policy in England – with, often, a preference for the pragmatic solution rather than any very well-thought-through remedy (see Bottoms, 1980a).

By the late 1980s, however, it was possible to discern a new kind of overarching policy emerging from the Home Office and elsewhere, centred upon the sound application of managerial techniques, improved collaboration and shared working between the different parts of the system ('inter-agency co-operation'), and a new emphasis on crime prevention. Perhaps, as some said, one might in time discern that this approach was sufficiently coherent to justify its being regarded as a new theoretical model of criminal justice, to rank alongside classicism and positivism. If so, others warned, we should also remember that all previous dominant theoretical models of criminal justice have had their flaws – and the most obvious flaw of managerialism is that its impulses of instrumentalism and utilitarianism might be incompatible with principles of justice (see generally, Peters, 1986).

Returning to 1970, that year has also been seen by some writers as decisive in heralding the beginnings of a marked political dissensus over criminal justice issues, and a turning towards authoritarian solutions (Hall, *et al.*, 1978). It is certainly true that, as well as the dissensus on juvenile justice (see above: though that was not a high-profile topic in national political terms), 1970 did see 'law and order' (with special reference to public order) creep on to the political agenda for the General Election of that year – though not in a very prominent place on that agenda. It is also true that the late 1970s and early 1980s were to see even more marked political dissensus over issues such as police accountability and the revamped 'short sharp shock' detention centre, as well as a renewed emphasis on longer sentences (and restricted parole eligibility) for serious offenders. At the time of writing, however, it remains unclear whether or not the new stress on inter-agency co-operation, crime prevention and resource management – which has resulted at the end of the 1980s in a Conservative government pressing for an increased use of non-custodial penalties by the courts – will succeed again in uniting the political parties around a broadly agreed political programme on criminal justice.

These issues take us well beyond the scope of our ESRC research. We have raised them briefly because our research does perhaps help to set some recent and current criminal justice topics into a broader historical context, and thus assist with a fuller understanding of them. In that sense, perhaps this chapter may not only be of interest in its own right, but may serve as an extended preface to some of the current policy topics addressed by a number of the other research projects in the ESRC Initiative, as summarised in subsequent chapters of this book.

NOTES

1. The authors are deeply grateful to the Home Office for allowing exceptional access to unpublished Home Office Papers for the period being studied. This access greatly enriched the source material for the research.
2. Nevertheless, it is not been possible to cover all developments; to give only two examples, there is no mention in this chapter of the moves towards the establishment, in 1964, of the Criminal Inquiries Compensation Scheme (granting state compensation for victims of violent crime); nor of the genesis and subsequent dissolution of the Royal Commission on the Penal System in the mid-1960s.
3. The word refers to successive Chancellors of the Exchequer from different parties: Hugh Gaitskell, Labour (Chancellor, 1950–1, subsequently Leader of the Labour Party, 1955–63) and R. A. Butler, Conservative (Chancellor, 1951–5; subsequently Home Secretary, 1957–62, and Foreign Secretary, 1963–4).
4. This explanation largely follows that suggested in a Dutch criminal policy paper of 1985. It is quite possible that some of the increase in recorded crime was artificial, the product of increased public reporting of crime and/or increased police recording. Criminological research tools were not well-enough developed in the period under study to be able to test this suggestion rigorously: however, for various reasons it is most unlikely that all or most of the increase was artificial.
5. *House of Commons Debates (Hansard)*, vol. 415, col. 641 (1 November 1945).
6. That is not to say, of course, that legitimacy was high in every local area in

the country. See, for example, Roach Family Support Committee (1989, ch. 7) on police–public relations in Hackney, London, in the immediate post-war period, following the activities of various Fascist organisations in the area.

7. See, however, Figure 1.1 on the rise in recorded crime in the 1930s; also Thomas (1972, ch. 8) on the Dartmoor Prison mutiny of 1932 and the increasing number of escapes from English prisons in the 1930s.

8. 'Local prisons', in England, are the closed prisons serving local courts (for male prisoners). Their populations normally comprise a mixture of (a) remand prisoners; (b) sentenced prisoners serving shorter terms (who during the period under study usually served the whole of their sentence in the local prison); (c) longer-term sentenced prisoners at the beginning of their sentences, awaiting transfer to a so-called 'training prison' (where they would serve the greater part of their time). In 1959, and for three decades thereafter, all local prisons dated from the Victorian era.

9. Home Office Papers CRI. 15/1/42 (R. A. Butler to Sir Charles Cunningham, 27 August 1958).

10. *The Times*, 10 October 1961.

11. This proposal was made despite the rejection of the suspended sentence by ACTO in both 1952 and 1957. For a brief account of the genesis and early development of the suspended sentence in England, see Bottoms (1980b). The Criminal Justice Bill 1966 additionally contained a proposal for the creation of a parole scheme, which was also clearly of potential importance for reducing the prison population – however, this proposal had rather different origins, unconnected with prison population pressures.

12. R. A. Butler, speech to New Bridge AGM, 22 February 1960 (Home Office Papers CRI. 15/1/81).

13. Home Office Papers 884, 452/File 1A, in PRO series HO 45/21, 948. Fox's views in 1957 were very similar: 'we shall never get a rational sentencing policy, especially in the superior courts, till our whole medieval system of assizes and quarter sessions is swept away, and a system of permanent courts of criminal justice in a few selected centres takes its place' (Home Office Papers, CRI. 15/1/14: L. W. Fox to R. A. Butler, 13 February 1957).

14. This view was, for the Streatfeild Committee, confirmed by the personal experiences of the judges serving the then permanent Crown Courts in Liverpool and Manchester: see Home Office and Lord Chancellor's Office (1961, para. 129), also *The Sunday Times*, 15 and 22 January 1961. These Crown Courts, the only ones in the country, were set up under the Criminal Justice Administration Act 1956 owing to a very difficult higher court workload situation in South Lancashire. The subsequent Royal Commission on Assizes and Quarter Sessions (1969, p. 45) evaluated the Liverpool and Manchester Crown Courts much more positively than had the Streatfeild Committee, partly because after Streatfeild reported an element of judge rotation was introduced.

15. The only such adult centre to be opened was in fact Risley Remand Centre, which had been planned by the Prison Commissioners because of its proximity to the permanent Crown Courts at Liverpool and Manchester (see note 14 above). Ironically, Risley in later years suffered from a trouble-strewn history, and became widely known as 'Grisly Risley'.

16. Before its abolition in 1948, judicial corporal punishment was available for a

range of offences for juveniles, but (in practice) only for robbery with violence for adults (for details see Advisory Council, 1960, p. 2). The campaigns for restoration in the 1950s also centred on young offenders, and were not unconnected with phenomena such as the rise of the Teddy Boys.

17. See Advisory Council (1959): the objective was to expand the senior detention centre system (for 17–21-year-olds) so as to allow the abolition of short-term imprisonment for persons under 21. This change was legislated for in the Criminal Justice Act 1961, but the section abolishing short-term imprisonment was not in fact brought into force.

18. 'A Lifetime in the Jungle – Lord Butler in conversation with Robert McKenzie', *The Listener*, vol. 86, no. 2208 (22 July 1971) p. 110

19. Royal Commission Papers, 1/6/1, in PRO series HO 272/4 (T. A. Critchley to Sir Henry Willink, 22 September 1960).

20. In the 1950s there had been a policy of holding authorised establishments at an artificially low level, in order not to 'alarm the public' when actual manpower was below the authorised establishment. The policy was abandoned following adverse comment by the Royal Commission on the Police (1960, para. 64ff.): see Stevenson and Bottoms (1990).

21. Preventive detention was replaced in 1967 (on ACTO's recommendation) by the 'extended sentence of imprisonment', but this power has been very little used, and is formally abolished in the Criminal Justice Act 1991.

22. These letters refer to Mannheim and Wilkins's (1955) prediction categories: 'A' were inmates judged (by the statistical prediction formula) to be those with a very low risk of reconviction; 'X' those with a middling risk; 'D' those with a very high risk.

23. *House of Commons Debates (Hansard)*, vol. 630, cols 598–9 (17 November 1960).

24. The main cases were (a) Derek Bentley (a 19-year-old youth executed in 1953 after a rooftop murder of a policeman, despite the fact that Bentley was only a secondary party, the fatal shot having been fired by his 16-year-old companion, too young to be hanged); (b) Ruth Ellis (hanged in 1955 for a *crime passionel* in which she killed a former lover who had, she claimed, three days beforehand caused her to miscarry by striking her in the abdomen); and (c) the Evans–Christie case (two men, both living in the same house, and both convicted for murder within the space of four years, the second (Christie) being revealed as a serial killer of women: strong doubts were inevitably raised about the justice of Evans's conviction).

25. In this connection it is important to note that at that date almost all the closed prisons in existence were built in the Victorian era, at a time when the 'separate system' was in operation (prisoners were kept separate from one another, and spent most of their time, including working time, in their cells). A prison run along such lines does not require elaborate perimeter security; but the perimeter security of the closed prisons was not strengthened when, following penal liberalisation, the authorities introduced such things as workshops, sporting activities and 'evening association' (i.e., the opportunity to associate with other prisoners, play games, watch television and so on).

26. The 'Great Train Robbery' took place in August 1963: a group of men held up a mail train carrying £2,500,000 in old banknotes by stopping it at a red

signal. It has been described as 'the most audacious robbery in the annals of British crime' (Morris, 1989, p. 129).

27. Speech at York University, April 1971: see *The Times*, 5 April 1971, and *Prison Officers' Magazine*, May 1971.

28. The incidents are described briefly in Critchley (1978, pp. 270–4): they included three cases of criminal or disciplinary proceedings against Chief Constables, two cases of alleged assault by policemen, and a dispute between the Chief Constable and the Watch Committee in the Nottingham police area.

29. Royal Commission Papers 1/6/1, in PRO series HO 272/4 (T. A. Critchley to Sir Henry Willink, 2 February 1961).

30. The Sheffield report did, however, directly lead to an amendment to the Police Bill, requiring a Chief Constable to cause a complaint which was not already the subject of a criminal charge to be investigated, and giving him a discretion (and, where so directed by the Home Secretary, a duty) to obtain the services of an officer of another police force to carry out the investigation. This clause became s. 49 of the Police Act 1964.

31. The question as to whether the probation service should form part of the new 'family service' (or 'local authority social services departments' as they became known) was outside the terms of reference of the interdepartmental committee considering the future of personal social services. However, a number of bodies offered evidence on this issue, and the committee felt 'bound to record . . . concern about the relation of the probation and aftercare service to the unified local authority social service department', especially in view of 'the danger of unplanned overlapping' (Home Office, Department of Education *et al.*, 1968, para. 704).

32. These particular fears were compounded by the probation service's assumption of responsibility for the after-care of adult prisoners (from 1966), and the introduction of parole by the Criminal Justice Act 1967 (under which probation officers were required to supervise released parolees). These developments seemed to be pushing the probation service in the direction of adult offenders, just at the same time as the developments in policy for children and young persons seemed likely to offer a diminishing role for probation officers in that sphere.

33. The Ingleby Report (Home Office, 1960, ch. 3) had considered whether the juvenile court should be replaced by a non-judicial or quasi-judicial tribunal, but had concluded that the court should be retained, though with revised procedures.

34. Speech by Mr Mark Carlisle (Minister of State, Home Office) to the annual conference of the British Association of Social Workers, 1 October 1970 (Home Office Papers CHN/71 78/1/13).

35. In Scotland there was a very different situation: the traditional juvenile court was abolished, and the 'children's hearing' substituted (see Cowperthwaite, 1988), an outcome that was achieved with relatively little political dissensus. This intriguing Anglo-Scottish contrast is too complex to pursue in detail here.

REFERENCES

Advisory Council on the Treatment of Offenders (1959), *The Treatment of Young Offenders* (London: Her Majesty's Stationery Office).

Advisory Council on the Treatment of Offenders (1960), *Corporal Punishment* (London: Her Majesty's Stationery Office) Cmnd. 1213.

Advisory Council on the Treatment of Offenders (1963a), *The Organisation of After-Care* (London: Her Majesty's Stationery Office).

Advisory Council on the Treatment of Offenders (1963b), *Preventive Detention* (London: Her Majesty's Stationery Office).

Bailey, V. (1987), *Delinquency and Citizenship: Reclaiming the Young Offender, 1914–1948* (Oxford: Clarendon Press).

Bottoms, A. E. (1974), 'On the decriminalisation of English juvenile courts', in R. Hood (ed.), *Crime, Criminology and Public Policy* (London: Heinemann Educational Books).

Bottoms, A. E. (1980a), 'An introduction to "The Coming Crisis"', in A. E. Bottoms and R. H. Preston (eds), *The Coming Penal Crisis* (Edinburgh: Scottish Academic Press).

Bottoms, A. E. (1980b), *The Suspended Sentence after Ten Years: A Review and Reassessment* (Leeds: University of Leeds Centre for Social Work and Applied Social Studies) Occasional Paper no. 2.

Brody, S. R. (1976), *The Effectiveness of Sentencing: A Review of the Literature*, Home Office Research Study no. 35 (London: Her Majesty's Stationery Office).

Chappell, D. (1965), 'Regional crime squads', *Criminal Law Review*, 5–11.

Christoph, J. B. (1962), *Capital Punishment and British Politics: The British Movement to Abolish the Death Penalty, 1945–1957* (London: George Allen & Unwin).

Clarke, J. (1980), 'Social democratic delinquents and Fabian families', in National Deviancy Conference (ed.), *Permissiveness and Control: The Fate of the Sixties Legislation* (London: Macmillan).

Clarke, R. V. G. and Hough, J. M. (eds) (1980), *The Effectiveness of Policing* (Aldershot, Hants.: Gower).

Clarke, R. V. G. and Hough, J. M. (1984), *Crime and Police Effectiveness*, Home Office Research Studies no. 79 (London: Her Majesty's Stationery Office).

Cowperthwaite, D. J. (1988), *The Emergence of the Scottish Children's Hearings System* (Southampton: Institute of Criminal Justice, University of Southampton).

Cox, B., Shirley, J. and Short, M. (1977), *The Fall of Scotland Yard* (Harmondsworth, Middx: Penguin).

Critchley, T. A. (1978), *A History of Police in England and Wales*, rev. edn (London: Constable).

Downes, D. (1988), *Contrasts in Tolerance: Post-War Penal Policy in the Netherlands and England and Wales* (Oxford: Clarendon Press).

Field, S. (1990), *Trends in Crime and Their Interpretation: A Study of Recorded Crime in Post-war England and Wales*, Home Office Research Study no. 119 (London: Her Majesty's Stationery Office).

Garland, D. (1985), *Punishment and Welfare: A History of Penal Strategies* (Aldershot: Gower).

Gibson, E. (1960), *Time Spent Awaiting Trial*, Studies in the Causes of Delinquency and the Treatment of Offenders no. 2 (London: Her Majesty's Stationery Office).

Giddens, A. (1984), *The Constitution of Society* (Cambridge: Polity Press).

Grigg, M. (1965), *The Challenor Case* (Harmondsworth, Middx: Penguin).

Hall, S., Critcher, C., Jefferson, T., Clarke, J. and Roberts, B. (1978), *Policing the Crisis: Mugging, the State, and Law and Order* (London: Macmillan).

Halsey, A. H. (1988), *British Social Trends since 1900*, 2nd edn (London: Macmillan).

Hammond, W. H. and Chayen, E. (1963), *Persistent Criminals*, Studies in the Causes of Delinquency and the Treatment of Offenders no. 5 (London: Her Majesty's Stationery Office).

Harwin, J. (1982), 'The battle for the delinquent', in C. Jones and J. Stevenson (eds), *The Year Book of Social Policy in Britain, 1980–1981* (London: Routledge & Kegan Paul).

Home Office (1919), *Committee on the Police Service: Report* (London: His Majesty's Stationery Office) Cmd 253.

Home Office (1949a), *Second Report of the Police Post-War Committee* (London: His Majesty's Stationery Office).

Home Office (1949b), *Police Conditions of Service*, (London: His Majesty's Stationery Office) Part I: Cmd. 7674, Part II, Cmd. 7831.

Home Office (1959), *Penal Practice in a Changing Society* (London: Her Majesty's Stationery Office) Cmnd. 645.

Home Office (1960), *Report of the Committee on Children and Young Persons* (London: Her Majesty's Stationery Office). Cmnd. 1191.

Home Office (1963), *Sheffield Police Appeal Inquiry* (London: Her Majesty's Stationery Office) Cmnd. 2176.

Home Office (1964), *Report of Inquiry by Mr W. L. Mars-Jones, QC* (London: Her Majesty's Stationery Office) Cmnd. 2526.

Home Office (1965), *The Child, the Family and the Young Offender* (London: Her Majesty's Stationery Office) Cmnd. 2742.

Home Office (1966), *Report of the Inquiry into Prison Escapes and Security* (London: Her Majesty's Stationery Office) Cmd. 3175.

Home Office (1967), *Police Manpower, Equipment and Efficiency: Reports of Three Working Parties* (London: Her Majesty's Stationery Office).

Home Office (1968), *Children in Trouble* (London: Her Majesty's Stationery Office) Cmd. 3601.

Home Office (1969), *People in Prison* (London: Her Majesty's Stationery Office) Cmnd. 4214.

Home Office (1978), *Committee of Inquiry on the Police: Reports on Negotiating Machinery and Pay* (London: Her Majesty's Stationery Office) Cmnd. 7283.

Home Office, Department of Education, Department of Housing and Local Government, and Department of Health (1968), *Report of the Committee on Local Authority and Allied Personal Social Services* (London: Her Majesty's Stationery Office) Cmnd. 3703.

Home Office and Lord Chancellor's Office (1961), *Report of the Interdepartmental Committee on the Business of the Criminal Courts* (London: Her Majesty's Stationery Office) Cmnd. 1289.

Jackson, R. M. (1964), *The Machinery of Justice in England*, 4th edn (Cambridge: Cambridge University Press).

King, J. F. S. (ed.) (1958), *The Probation Service* (London: Butterworths).

King, R. D. and McDermott, K. (1989), 'British prisons, 1970–1987: the ever-deepening crisis', *British Journal of Criminology*, **29**, 107–28.

Klare, H. J. (1962), *Anatomy of Prison*, rev. edn (Harmondsworth, Middx: Penguin).

Lipton, D., Martinson, R. and Wilks, J. (1975), *The Effectiveness of Correctional Treatment: A Summary of Treatment Evaluation Studies* (New York: Praeger).

Lloyd, T. O. (1979), *Empire to Welfare State: English History, 1906–1976*, 2nd edn (Oxford: Oxford University Press).

Lodge, T. S. (1974), 'The founding of the Home Office Research Unit', in R. Hood (ed.), *Crime, Criminology and Public Policy* (London: Heinemann Educational Books).

McClintock, F. H. and Avison, N. H. (1968), *Crime in England and Wales* (London: Heinemann Educational Books).

Mannheim, H. and Wilkins, L. T. (1955), *Prediction Methods in Relation to Borstal Training*, Studies in the Causes of Delinquency and the Treatment of Offenders no. 1 (London: Her Majesty's Stationery Office).

Martin, J. P. and Wilson, G. (1969), *The Police: A Study in Manpower* (London: Heinemann Educational Books).

Marwick, A. (1982), *British Society since 1945* (Harmondsworth, Middx: Penguin).

Morris, A. and Giller, H. (1987), *Understanding Juvenile Justice* (London: Croom Helm).

Morris, T. (1989), *Crime and Criminal Justice since 1945* (Oxford: Basil Blackwell).

Neale, K. (1983), *Sir Lionel Fox, CB, MC* (Wakefield: Prison Service College).

Parker, T. (1963), *The Unknown Citizen* (Harmondsworth, Middx: Penguin).

Peters, A. (1986), 'Main currents in criminal law theory', in J. van Dijk, C. Haffmans, F. Ruter, J. Schutte and S. Stolwijk (eds), *Criminal Law in Action: An Overview of Current Issues in Western Societies* (Arnhem: Gouda Quint).

Radzinowicz, L. (1988), *The Cambridge Institute of Criminology: Its Background and Scope* (London: Her Majesty's Stationery Office).

Reiner, R. (1985), *The Politics of the Police* (Brighton, Sussex: Wheatsheaf Books).

Roach Family Support Committee (1989), *Policing in Hackney, 1945–1984* (London: Karia Press).

Royal Commission on Assizes and Quarter Sessions (1969), *Report* (London: Her Majesty's Stationery Office) Cmnd. 4153.

Royal Commission on Capital Punishment (1953), *Report* (London: Her Majesty's Stationery Office) Cmd. 8932.

Royal Commission on Criminal Procedure (1981), *Report* (London: Her Majesty's Stationery Office) Cmnd. 8092.

Royal Commission on the Police (1960), *Interim Report* (London: Her Majesty's Stationery Office) Cmnd. 1222.

Royal Commission on the Police (1962), *Final Report* (London: Her Majesty's Stationery Office) Cmnd. 1728.

Sparks, R. F. (1971), 'The use of suspended sentences', *Criminal Law Review*, 384–401.

Stevenson, S. (1989), 'Some social and political tides affecting the development of juvenile justice, 1938–64', in T. Gorst, L. Johnman and W. S. Lucas (eds), *Post-War Britain: Themes and Perspectives, 1945–1964* (London: Pinter Press and the Institute of Contemporary British History).

Stevenson, S. and Bottoms, A. E. (1990), 'The politics of the police, 1955–1964: a Royal Commission in a decade of transition', in R. Morgan (ed.), *Policing,*

Organised Crime and Crime Prevention, British Criminology Conference 1989, vol. 4 (Bristol: Bristol and Bath Centre for Criminal Justice).

Thomas, J. E. (1972), *The English Prison Officer since 1850* (London: Routledge & Kegan Paul).

von Hirsch, A. (1986), *Past or Future Crimes* (Manchester: Manchester University Press).

West, D. J. (1963), *The Habitual Prisoner* (London: Macmillan).

2 Crime, Community and Conflict: The Multi-Agency Approach

GEOFFREY PEARSON, HARRY BLAGG, DAVID SMITH, ALICE SAMPSON and PAUL STUBBS

There has been a large amount of discussion of 'inter-agency' or 'multi-agency' approaches to crime-related problems in recent years, often linked to a perceived need for these approaches to be locally based. It has figured prominently in Home Office thinking during the 1980s, summarised in the inter-departmental circular of 1984 on *Crime Prevention* which did much to stimulate interest in the multi-agency idea under the bold motto 'Preventing crime is a task for the whole community' (Home Office, 1984, p. 1). It is also central to the Labour Party's (1990) policy recommendations for a 'partnership' between local government and the police to ensure a 'comprehensive crime prevention' strategy and 'a safer Britain'. But what is the 'multi-agency' approach?

One of its difficulties, which might also have sometimes enhanced its attractiveness, is that it is a concept which can mean so many different things to different people. This is hardly surprising, given that the multi-agency philosophy has been invoked in such a wide variety of settings and contexts – neighbourhood-based crime-prevention schemes, child sexual abuse enquiries, juvenile liaison, environmental improvements such as street-lighting, and much more. Even so, there is also an abundance of conceptual confusion. Clearly, one overriding principle involves improved co-ordination between public services, although this can also lend itself to different interpretations: the elimination of wasteful overlap between services, for example, as against the identification of gaps in service provision, or the improvement of inter-professional communication which has loomed so large in many child-abuse scandals. A further level of potential confusion derives from ideological and political controversy. For some, the multi-agency concept involves a recognition of the important role which agencies other than the police can play in crime prevention, while for others it represents a sinister attempt to subordinate the work of these other agencies to the police. It can be seen both as a means by which to make the police more sensitive and accountable to the needs of the public, and as a mechanism to exhort public support for the police. It is thus both an emblem of the increasingly common assertion that 'the police alone cannot combat crime' and the fear of a threat to civil liberties through the extension of systems of control and surveillance.

The fundamental aim of our research project was to offer a preliminary assessment of how these policy discussions relate to actual working practices between agencies. Our overall objective was not only to study patterns of agency co-operation, but also to identify important areas of policy tension and potential conflict between agencies. The key agencies chosen for our research were the police, social services and the probation service. The assumption behind this choice was that the routine work of these agencies was most likely to bring them into face-to-face contact with both offenders and victims of a variety of different forms of crime, together with the fact that at the interface of these agencies there is a range of important decision-making processes. However, as the research evolved it also had to embrace certain aspects of the work of housing departments, education departments, health service personnel, voluntary bodies, community groups, residents' associations and tenants' associations.

Within this overall framework the research focused on a cluster of crime-related issues where inter-agency work seemed to have the most relevance: community-based crime-prevention initiatives; child-abuse and child sexual abuse enquiries; juvenile crime and juvenile liaison schemes; domestic violence; drug misuse and drug liaison initiatives; and inter-agency panels focusing on racial attacks. These are problems which obviously make very different impacts upon the routine work of the various agencies, and one aim of the research was to assist in understanding how these different perceptions influence the limits and possibilities of inter-agency strategies.

Elsewhere, we have already published accounts of different aspects of this work. These include a review of the multi-agency philosophy and its application to community-based crime-prevention (Blagg *et al.*, 1988) together with a more detailed analysis of conflicts in multi-agency work and how these can influence the lives and interests of groups of local residents (Sampson *et al.*, 1988). In addition, we have examined some aspects of the thorny issue of the public response to racial attacks and racial incidents (Pearson *et al.*, 1989) and given an account of how gender relations express themselves within the existing inter-agency relations between predominantly male organisations, such as the police, and social services departments, where the workforce contains more women (Sampson *et al.*, 1991). Here, we aim to set out the main policy implications of our research, focusing on potential obstacles to effective inter-agency co-operation and how these might be overcome.

THE RESEARCH LOCATIONS: MILLTOWN AND METROPOLIS

Our research work was located in two contrasting areas: inner London and a Lancashire town, 'Milltown'. This offered a basis for comparison within the research, both in terms of local needs and problems as well as variations in local working practices. In each of these areas a small number of localities were identified where there was some form of 'inter-agency' initiative and which also had the reputation of being 'problem estates' or 'problem neighbourhoods'. Interviews were conducted with the staff of different agencies which served these neighbourhoods, in order to enrich our understanding of how multi-agency policies were worked out and negotiated on the ground.

The neighbourhoods in which we worked were themselves quite different in many respects. In Milltown, fieldwork was undertaken on the Saxon Lane estate which lies on the outskirts of the town and consists of modern, conventionally built housing. The estate, built in the 1970s, had quickly established a local reputation as a 'dumping ground' for single-parent households and 'problem families', together with a high level of petty crime such as vandalism and gas-meter thefts. Subsequently, a multi-agency centre had been established by the police, the housing department and social services. The population of Saxon Lane was almost entirely white. By contrast, the Oldtown area of Milltown, which was our second fieldwork location, was the site of a substantial Asian settlement. Oldtown is an area of terraced housing dating from the turn of the century, close to the town centre. Here racial attacks and racial incidents were a major source of concern to local residents, although there were substantial areas of disagreement between the perceptions of residents and those of the Milltown police (Pearson *et al.*, 1989).

In inner London, three localities of a contrasting nature were chosen for our fieldwork. The Queen's Reach estate, again built in the 1970s, might almost have served as a stereotype of the popular image of the high-rise, inner-city 'problem estate'. Amidst a series of towering blocks of flats there was a bewildering maze of interconnecting walkways, ramps and balconies. From one point of view it was a spectacular architectural achievement, while from another it was a dismal 'concrete jungle'. Queen's Reach was also characterised by a vast mosaic of cultures, ethnicities and languages, with some disturbing rumours about 'criminal families' and major drug-dealing – although this was a view not shared by the local drug squad. An ambitious crime-prevention scheme had been established on the estate, involving a system of doors operated by electronic card-keys which sealed off the walkways, and an inter-agency forum which had been in existence for five years still met on a regular basis.

In contrast to Queen's Reach, the Empire Gardens estate was an inter-war development of three-storey walk-up flats, set out in a rigid grid-iron pattern. In its own time, Empire Gardens had also been regarded as an architectural triumph and stood as a landmark of municipal planning of the 1930s. Now a racially mixed neighbourhood with a substantial African-Caribbean population, it had for many year been regarded as a notorious den of crime and poverty. Even so, although feared by the local police as a potential site for social disorder, it was also seen by them as a 'low-crime' estate. This was, however, a view which could provoke a mixture of hilarity and hostility among local people, who took the view that there was an untapped reservoir of unreported crime – both in the form of petty burg-laries and domestic violence. Local people seemed to have given up on the police in Empire Gardens where numerous attempts to establish local crime-prevention initiatives and inter-agency schemes had always failed. A recent survey conducted by the local authority housing department con-firmed our own impression that there were deep divisions of opinion among residents as to the quality of life in Empire Gardens: some taking the view that it was a friendly place to live while others felt themselves to be trapped, and wished only to move elsewhere.

Finally, our research also embraced Gabriel's Walk in the St Michael's area of inner London, a neighbourhood which had been passing through a period of massive gentrification. At one time it was the home of a substan-tial Irish community, and since the 1950s there had been an extensive settlement of people from the Caribbean. Formerly, a large part of the housing stock had been in the private-rented sector, involving a pattern of multiple occupation. Increasingly, as flats and houses had been refurbished and sold to owner-occupiers, there had been a series of intense local political conflicts. Inter-agency efforts in this locality had come to act as a focus for the conflicting interests of the older residents, including many black people, and the new 'yuppie' influx. Problems associated with drug misuse and drug-dealing were highlighted by the new white residents, while the black community complained about racial attacks and police tactics of stop-and-search (Sampson *et al.*, 1988; Pearson *et al.*, 1989). Inter-agency co-operation had certainly not caused these conflicts in Gabriel's Walk, although it did sometimes seem that it had become a major vehicle for the expression of these tensions, helping to divide further an already divided community.

DOING RESEARCH: NEGOTIATING ACCESS AND FEEDBACK

At the outset, the research team had negotiated access for the research with all the principal agencies: borough social services departments, the Inner London Probation Service, the Lancashire Probation Service, the Lancashire Constabulary and the Community Relations Branch of the Metropolitan Police at New Scotland Yard. An important aspect of these negotiations was that we undertook to arrange, wherever possible, feedback sessions with interested and relevant parties.

The research strategy involved a dual approach: interviews with agency personnel who worked in the identified neighbourhoods, either individually or as groups, together with observational work of a number of key decision-making bodies which have a wider remit. These included a variety of committees and case conferences concerned with child abuse and child protection; juvenile liaison panels; drug liaison initiatives; inter-agency projects responding to racial attacks; and other less-formally constituted inter-agency meetings and forums. In London we attended police community liaison groups (which had recently been established under section 106 of the Police and Criminal Evidence Act) on a regular basis. These offered a vivid impression of police–public encounters in a formal setting. In these ways we hoped to show how policy discussions are worked through in a variety of different settings, whether these relate to decisions on specific cases or to attempts to bring together interested parties who might be assumed to share a common objective.

This dual strategy of interviews and observational methods sometimes revealed significant levels of disjunction between the attitudes and opinions of agency personnel towards multi-agency working, as against actual working practices. Someone well-versed in the multi-agency philosophy, for example, might be able to offer a 'word perfect' account of its necessity in effective crime prevention, while at the same time being observed to ignore the implications of this philosophy in practice. Or someone who had confessed to feelings of considerable hostility towards the aims and working practices of another agency would be seen to attempt to contain and conceal these feelings in inter-agency meetings, although not always with entire success.

This dual strategy also enabled us to explore with agency personnel what they felt subsequently about the procedures adopted in inter-agency forums, or issues which had risen in particular situations. It was a common complaint, for example, that inter-agency panels were no more than 'talking shops': as one senior police officer put it in the very first week of our research, 'When you take a close look at this inter-agency thing, you'll find it's a lot of "yap-yapping" . . . if you look in enough detail.' Or as another said: 'They're only talking shops because we want them to be. Because we don't want them to wield any authority.'

Tensions such as these indicate, as much as anything else, the scale of ambition involved in much thinking about multi-agency working: in that across the customary working practices and ingrained habits of different organisations it attempts to superimpose what are sometimes quite alien philosophies. Effective inter-agency work requires an openness towards the outside world, including an openness to criticism and self-criticism. This is not always easy to accomplish for any professional group, and does not always correspond to existing traditions of management and decision-making. In one interview with a divisional chief superintendent of the Metropolitan Police, for example, we had been given an articulate exposition of the virtues of multi-agency work and the need for policing to be sensitive to the needs of the local community. Later, as we chatted over a cup of tea, he was asked what the 'learning curve' was for a divisional police commander, and how long it might take someone to feel their way into the job. His response was immediate: 'There's no time to mess around. As soon as I sat behind that desk, I was in charge. From day one . . . .' He seemed to experience little sense of inconsistency between his stated views on the need for the police service to ground its practice in a sensitive response to community needs, as against the quasi-military assumptions of line-command in the police. Nevertheless, the lack of consistency was clearly in evidence. His superior officer, Deputy Assistant Commissioner at area level, had earlier explained to us his own doubts and misgivings about the multi-agency approach and community-oriented policing:

It's not that I'm against it. In fact, I'm all for it. The police should be accountable to the community, in some form or another, because we're public servants. But you try telling that to the lad on the beat. He's had it drummed into him since he was in training school, that when he puts on that police uniform he represents the Queen's peace. He represents authority. And then you tell him to listen to what other agencies are telling him to do? You tell him to listen to what the community says? You have to understand, we train them to play God . . . and we still do. You teach him to play God, and there's no reason he should defer to anyone else.

Although the project has benefited from the support and encouragement of all the relevant agencies, and although research access had been negotiated with top-level management before the research got underway, we nevertheless found that access to agency personnel had to be renegotiated at every level as the research progressed. As we have come to understand it, our negotiations at different levels in each organisation reflected the ways in which policy decisions formulated at management level were renegotiated as they came to be implemented (or not) on the ground.

The question of access is often discussed by social researchers as if it were merely an obstacle placing external limits on what can be achieved through research. In our view, and for our kind of research, this is an inadequate formulation of the problem of access. As already stated, principled access had been readily agreed by agency managers who gave us their full co-operation. Negotiations at a lower level, one might think, should therefore not have been necessary. However, they offered us an unrivalled opportunity to involve ourselves in the process of how different agencies engage with the 'outside world'. In other words, given that we were researching inter-organisational relations, the negotiations of access evolved as an important aspect of the research process itself.

Sometimes local agency personnel were suspicious of our motives: social workers in Empire Gardens, for example, initially formed the impression that it was our aim to further intensify the notorious reputation of the estate. This was a matter of considerable interest to us because we had already been informed by the police that Empire Gardens was, in terms of police statistics, a 'low-crime' estate; they took the view that it was nevertheless a serious problem for social workers because it housed so many 'problem people' and 'problem families'. The social work view, however, was that it was not an unusually difficult estate. It was true that there were many poor families living on Empire Gardens. It was also true that there was a high child-density, so that as a matter of course it generated a high childcare caseload. As for crime, social workers took the view that most crime on Empire Gardens went unreported. 'A low crime estate?' exclaimed the home help organiser, 'Low *recorded* crime, you mean!'

On other occasions, we were greeted with open arms by local agencies – either because it was hoped that our research might further their local interest, or because a key individual wished to show off some pet scheme in the locality. However, the most common problem in negotiating access was how to get busy professionals to fit us into their hectic schedules. Even so, there were some surprises which told us a great deal about the work-pressures in different agencies. To secure a one-hour interview with a social worker, for example, would invariably mean planning several weeks in advance, always with the possibility that this arrangement might be cancelled at short notice owing to other demands, such as the requirement to be present at a case conference or court hearing. The police, on the other hand, were often able to offer an interview at a few days' notice. Moreover, it was not uncommon for interviews with the police to involve a whole morning and to run through the lunch hour, whereas interviews with social workers and probation officers needed to observe strict timescales. In part, this is no doubt a reflection of the higher priority given to 'multi-agency' approaches by the police, although we found the same disparities in Lancashire where the multi-agency concept was much less well-developed as a policing philosophy than in London. Even so, it speaks volumes for the resource availability of different state agencies. This itself reflects upon the ability of those agencies to engage in multi-agency forums that can easily be seen as a distraction from their more immediate and pressing responsibilities.

High rates of staff turnover were another issue which impacted on our research strategies, and which must also bear heavily upon the capacity of state agencies to sustain continuity in their dealings with each other and with the wider community. In the case of the police, it is a matter of policy that officers often stay only for two years in any given posting. In the case of social services and probation, there was a marked discrepancy between London and Lancashire. In Milltown, many of the social workers and probation officers had worked in the same town for many years – offering a still, if sometimes stagnant, pool of accumulated experience. In London, amidst a general difficulty experienced by social services departments in recruiting and retaining social work staff – a difficulty no different from the much-publicised London staffing crisis with schoolteachers and nurses, although less often remarked upon – it was a whirlpool of constant staff arrivals and departures. It would be easy to regard these staffing changes simply as a nuisance which got in the way of our research: as when agency contacts which had been carefully nurtured over some months fell apart when key members of staff moved to fresh jobs. But it also offered a powerful indication of the difficulties of maintaining continuity in inter-agency relations under circumstances such as these.

If access negotiations proved to be a vital, although unanticipated, aspect of the research process, the same is true of the feedback meetings which we had planned to undertake towards the end of the research. These were arranged with teams of social workers, probation officers and police officers in order to report on our findings. A small number of multi-agency meetings were also convened for this purpose, sometimes involving representatives of local community groups and residents' associations.

Our usual practice was to prepare a short paper which was either circulated prior to the meeting or formed the basis of an introductory talk followed by discussion. We found that agency personnel gave an enormous welcome to these feedback sessions, frequently commenting that this was a more agreeable approach than that which they had previously experienced from social researchers – disparagingly known as 'hit-and-run' research. At this level, as a matter of common courtesy and public relations, we would therefore recommend this procedure as an effective research strategy.

We also found, however, that feedback meetings were an extremely valuable investment of our own time, in that they proved to offer an enrichment of the research process itself. Not only were agency personnel able to reflect upon our findings and sometimes to correct misperceptions of their work and inaccuracies, they were also able to point us in new directions and, through the process of discussion itself, to offer new insights into how work-teams operated.

In the case of the probation team located near the Queen's Reach estate, for example, through the feedback meeting we had suggested that a major finding of our research was that the probation service was proving to be marginal to most inter-agency initiatives. The team had already indicated its own reservations about the meaning of 'multi-agency' work and its relevance to the probation service, but some team members fought back with an impressive list of agencies with whom they were in regular contact: housing departments, social security offices, psychiatric services and drug services, victim support schemes, prisons, and a whole host of temporary accommodation schemes and hostels run by the Salvation Army, the Church Army and other voluntary groups. However, these contacts were maintained on a case-by-case basis, and were not seen as part of a formal scheme of inter-agency co-operation, so that they were largely invisible within the emerging framework of the 'multi-agency' philosophy. Police officers, in another feedback session, were also able to identify what they saw as gaps in inter-agency provision which might otherwise have been overlooked: principally, from their point of view, the lack of a locally available detoxification centre for problem drinkers. This resulted in a significant amount of police time being spent watching over snoring drunks in the cells of the local 'nick'.

Feedback sessions arranged for multi-agency gatherings were particularly illuminating. It was not only that we sometimes found it necessary to introduce various key personnel to each other, in spite of prior assurances from all concerned that they enjoyed 'good working relationships' with their counterparts. On occasion the participants in such meetings began to exemplify, in living detail, what the research had begun to indicate: namely, that it can be extremely difficult to find common ground within multi-agency forums. This allowed us to explore in some depth with participants what these difficulties amounted to. It is as well to say, however, that it was not always easy going. In the sanctuary of the academic seminar we can explore at our leisure the intellectual complexities of negotiating between the 'multiple realities' experienced by different audiences when faced with what is apparently the same, common universe of difficulties. Out there in what we call the 'real world', the same multiple realities could come crashing through with unexpected force.

One sunny afternoon in mid-summer the research team gathered at the community centre on the Empire Gardens estate with a group of representatives from the police, probation, social services, housing department, youth workers and community workers. We had also invited local residents, including representatives of the old people's club, the women's self-help health group and the tenants' association. By way of an introduction a member of the research team talked briefly about the different ways in which different interest groups understood the problems of Empire Gardens. Four competing arguments were outlined. The first was that social deprivation led to stress which manifested itself in mental breakdown, alcohol abuse and domestic violence. The second located the estate's difficulties in a housing policy which had used Empire Gardens in the past as a 'sink' estate, with the result that there were too many of the 'wrong kind of people' living there. The third argument was that the estate's problems were those of poor people (the 'have-nots') who were trapped within a downward spiral from which they could not escape. The fourth and final view was that the estate suffered from a bad reputation which was in fact unjustified, but which nevertheless refused to lie down, and affected the lives of all people who lived there.

After this introduction to the 'multiple realities' of Empire Gardens, the discussion was opened.

> CHAIR: Well, you've heard those different views. Perhaps they have something to do with why it's always been so difficult to get effective inter-agency cooperation on Empire Gardens. Perhaps we can return to that later. First, perhaps you would like to give us your initial reactions to what Alice has just said?
>
> RESIDENT 1: Bullshit!
>
> RESIDENT 2: Absolute rubbish . . .

The meeting had got off to a good start.

CONFLICT AND CO-OPERATION IN PRACTICE: THE CENTRAL ISSUES

It will already have become apparent that in trying to reach an understanding of multi-agency co-operation, we have come to place an emphasis on a prior and necessary understanding of how and why different state agencies often come into conflict. The desire to devise well-co-ordinated multi-agency responses is understandable. However, any number of difficulties lie in the path of effective inter-agency co-operation.

In one recent contribution to the debate on multi-agency working, specifically concerned with the relations between the police and social workers, stress was placed on the 'shared uncertainties' faced by these two professional groups, leading to the suggestion that they have a great deal in common (Holdaway, 1986). Our understanding departs radically from such a view. It is not only that social workers and police officers have very different jobs to do, with different tasks and responsibilities. The way in which the 'same' problem makes a very different impact upon the routine workloads of the various agencies means that agency personnel will often have widely divergent perceptions of various problems and neighbourhoods. Another vital difference is that the police force is an unambiguously male organisation, while the majority of social workers are women, and gender relations can have a powerful impact on the relations between these two agencies (Sampson *et al.*, 1991). Power-differentials between agencies also mean that some agencies (notably the police and the housing departments) tend to dominate the agenda of multi-agency forums, and at the same time have more leverage to act upon any given problem – and indeed to define what the 'problem' is, and what forms of action might be considered legitimate.

The workforce of the police service is, of course, much bigger than that of any of the other state agencies relevant to our research, so the police service is in a powerful position by this criterion alone. Overall, however, it is perhaps more important to recognise that there are deeply rooted structural oppositions between stage agencies working in the sphere of criminal justice, with the dominant tendency for organisations such as social services to be structurally subordinate to police-led agendas. In practical terms what this means is that if they are to be effective, multi-agency initiatives would do better to start from an understanding of actual and potential sites of conflict rather than from a naïve view that co-operation is a 'good thing'.

At the outset of this research, this had not been our position. Our initial intention had been to explore the ways in which varied local traditions and customary working practices might influence relations between state agencies. This was the primary reason for building in an element of comparison between Milltown and Metropolis, and selecting a small number of contrasting neighbourhoods for detailed research. However, these differences have not proved to be as significant in many respects as might be imagined.

Beneath a pattern of immense variation – in terms of local demography, local problems and specific schemes of inter-agency working – we have found that problems of co-operation and conflict between state agencies assume directly similar forms, reflecting the structural relations between these agencies.

The general form of these conflicts and dilemmas which are thrown up within multi-agency initiatives can be easily summarised. In most if not all areas of concern, where the multi-agency approach is advocated there are problems of confidentiality and how to devise accountable systems of information exchange. The aims, objectives and priorities of agencies can (and do) conflict. Different agencies have different sources of authority and legitimacy. There is sometimes competition over scarce resources, with agencies being encouraged to attempt to define problems in ways which justify (or increase) the agency's own resource level. Differences in management structures and management styles can add a further obstacle, and it can also be difficult to establish at what level in an organisation's hierarchy it is most appropriate and effective to attempt to establish inter-agency liaison. These sites of tension and conflict overlap to a considerable degree. Nevertheless, for the sake of clarity and conceptual analysis the key issues can be addressed under a series of separate headings, together with some illustrations of how these issues express themselves within practical undertakings.

Defining a Localised Focus

The most fundamental difficulty to inter-agency co-operation is how to agree on a definition of the locality and its problems. The inter-departmental memorandum *Crime Prevention*, which is usually known as HO 8/84 and which did much to stimulate thought and action on the multi-agency approach, can serve as a starting point, in that it provided a policy formulation which offered a pivot for our original research proposal to the ESRC (Home Office, 1984).

In one sense, our research has confirmed a central thrust of HO 8/84, in that it seems clear that multi-agency initiatives stand more chance of being effective where they are closely focused on specific issues and attuned to local needs and circumstances, including local resources. Against that, what must also be said is that the evidence accumulated by the research led us to depart significantly from the original proposal in terms of how we came to attempt an analysis of multi-agency initiatives. Originally, the research project had been conceived as one which would place an emphasis on local traditions and variations in local working practices. However, our analysis has had to move in the direction of stressing the structure of power relations which inform the relationships between state agencies, irrespective of other important local variations.

Nevertheless, at a practical level it remains true that multi-agency initiatives will have more coherence where they are directed towards specific issues and locally defined problems. Even so, our research has repeatedly shown that there are significant areas of difficulty in an approach such as that advocated in HO 8/84, in terms of who defines the boundaries of a locality, its problems and its needs.

We can offer one or two illustrations of this apparently elementary difficulty. The first comes from the Saxon lane estate in Milltown, where already abundant conflicts about the scope and intent of the local multi-agency initiative (cf. Blagg *et al.*, 1988) were compounded by a somewhat perplexing inability on the part of the agencies concerned to arrive at a firm agreement on the precise geographical boundaries of the inter-agency initiative. The perplexity was deepened by differences in usage about the name of the locality in question. So that, although the estate was generally known as Saxon Lane, for reasons which were never entirely clear – but which probably had to do with historical considerations of divisional police responsibilities – the police invariably referred to the area as 'Cowmarsh'.

If the agencies could not agree on the exact name and territorial definitions of Saxon Lane (or Cowmarsh) then what was the problem? Was it crime, for example, or family poverty? Was the self-evident decay of the estate the result of vandalism or inadequate maintenance? Was the environment the problem or was it the people who lived there? These different formulations of Saxon Lane's difficulties were championed by the various agencies. The multi-agency initiative had to find its feet amidst this conflicting set of perceptions and priorities.

If a given locality could generate a divergence in agency definitions of the nature of the problem in hand, then it is also true that any given problem could generate similar discrepancies. In inner London, for example, problems associated with the motor car were the focus for a great deal of discussion at the meetings of police consultative groups. But what exactly was the 'problem'? For the police, reflecting a London-wide crime-prevention campaign, the question of thefts of and from vehicles was the central issue. For those representing the interests of local residents, it was a question of the lack of police attention to untidy parking, which blocked emergency access routes or made it exceedingly difficult to get about with a wheel-chair or push-chair. For those representing local commercial interests, on the other hand, there was a frequent complaint that the excessive zeal of the police in pursuing parking offences was driving high-street shopkeepers out of business. So even such an apparently straightforward issue as the motor car could generate multiple versions of the nature of the problem. Drug issues could also generate conflict and misunderstanding. In all three of our inner-London neighbourhoods – Queen's Reach, Empire Gardens and Gabriel's Walk – there was scope for sharp disagreements between different groups of residents as to whether drugs were a problem in the area. Moreover, even when it was agreed that there was a local problem, what was its precise nature and what was its solution? Was it a question of law enforcement? Or health education? Or the provision of treatment and rehabilitation services? These can be readily agreed as the three constituent elements of any effective drug-prevention strategy – health education, law enforcement and treatment and rehabilitation – and yet they do not add up to a single, unified course of action (Pearson, Gilman and McIver, 1986). Where drug-liaison initiatives had been established, even the question of the substance of abuse could be a matter of conflict in terms of priority and action. Where there has been a recent increase in heroin misuse during the course of the 1980s' heroin epidemic, self-help groups and parents' groups would attempt to focus attention on their understandable difficulties. Drug agencies in the voluntary sector, on the other hand, not uncommonly reported that their major source of self-referrals was people experiencing difficulties with medically prescribed tranquillisers. At the same time, there would invariably be an articulate and insistent voice on drug liaison committees that alcohol and tobacco were the major source of ill-health, rather than minority pursuit drugs such as heroin and cocaine. Whereupon police representatives would visibly yawn – why should they waste valuable time pondering the health consequences of licit drugs when there were already enough crimes and criminals to be detected, arrested and convicted within the illicit drug economy?

As a final instance of conflicting definitions of local problems, we can return to the Empire Gardens estate. We have already hinted at the different ways in which various interest groups viewed Empire Gardens and its problems. For the police, although it had priority status because of the perceived risks of social disorder, Empire Gardens was a 'low-crime' area which was nevertheless assumed to pose a major problem for social workers. For social workers, on the other hand, the estate's problems were generally seen as those associated with poverty, with the additional difficulty that residents suffered from a large amount of petty crime which went unreported. The housing department's view was different again. Empire Gardens loomed large in the housing department's concerns if only because it represented approximately one-tenth of the local authority's entire housing stock, and its problems were seen as resulting from design faults together with chronic under-funding which had led to dilapidation – a view which, quite apart from its obvious merits, helped to justify the housing department's claims for a substantial increase in its budget.

This was certainly not the only instance that we came across where an agency would 'talk up' particular aspects of a neighbourhood's difficulties in order to enhance that agency's claims on resources. In this case, the housing department and the police were able to find a certain amount of common ground: the police were well-versed in arguments which suggest that crime problems can be exacerbated by architectural design-faults (cf. Newman, 1973; Coleman, 1985). It seems likely, however, that this powerful coalition of interests represented by the police service and the housing department enabled other issues on the estate to be marginalised: particularly the question of domestic violence, to which, women's groups on Empire Gardens insisted, the response of police and social services was woefully inadequate.

Power and Representation

Two more specific questions emerge when the problematic aspects of such definitional processes are scrutinised. The first is the problem of representation – both in terms of how agencies themselves are represented within multi-agency forums, and how the needs of a locality are represented. Agency representatives invariably reflect the preoccupations of a particular individual's position within the organisational hierarchy, often to the neglect of other relevant sets of preoccupations. Systems of local representation, on the other hand, invariably reflect complex and competing 'sectional interests' within any given locality (Pearson, 1986). These sectional interests include such considerations as age, gender, race and ethnicity, and whether or not a household contains dependent children. Communities are never homogeneous entities, and those who claim to represent the 'community' draw their sources of authority from specific sectional interests and tend to act, however unwittingly, on their behalf. In the case of Empire Gardens, for example, although somewhere between one-quarter and one-third of residents were of African-Caribbean descent, local systems of representation – such as the tenants' association and the old people's club – were almost exclusively white. Equally, although almost one-half of heads of households were aged under 35 years, the substantial majority of representatives were middle-aged or elderly. Distortions were therefore necessarily entered into local systems of representation. So that, while the view taken in HO 8/84 that multi-agency initiatives should be closely tailored to local needs has an easy ring to it, it nevertheless conceals a host of complexities, given what are necessarily imperfect systems of representation.

A second consideration is that an uneven traffic of power runs both between the different state agencies and also between them and the communities which they serve. A major consequence of these power differentials is that it is invariably the more powerful agencies (principally the police service and housing departments) whose interests prevail in the definition of local needs and local problems. A further consequence is that significant groups and interests are often marginalised or even ignored (Sampson *et al*., 1988).

In the Gabriel's Walk neighbourhood of inner London, the local inter-agency forum was often dominated by discussions of drugs and drug-dealing. These complaints came largely from recently arrived white middle-class residents who had benefited from the gentrification of the area, and who on this issue entered into a powerful alliance with the police. Local opinion within the black community, however, was often found to be divided on the question of drugs, one source of conflict being the amount of attention given by the police to cannabis possession. Stop-and-search tactics had, on this view, compounded an already existing problem of racial discrimination. Other complaints from within the black community centred on racial attacks. Time and time again, however, the discussion drifted back towards drugs and drug-dealing. The African-Caribbean community had over many years established its own power-base in Gabriel's Walk, and was often able to provide an articulate defence of its interests. Meanwhile, more recently arrived immigrants, such as the tiny Moroccan and Vietnamese communities – who were themselves the focus of sometimes quite vicious racial attacks – experienced considerable difficulty in fighting for the space to voice their own concerns, which centred both on racial harassment and the inadequacy of language translation facilities provided by public services. A complex interweaving of power differentials in the Gabriel's Walk neighbourhood thus served to marginalise some of the most vulnerable sections of the community.

Policy Formulation and Implementation: Unintended Consequences

The research has also confirmed that there is room for considerable disjunction between central and local government policy statements on multi-agency working, as against what it actually means on the ground. Policy agreements conceived at chief-officer level between agencies can therefore sometimes be difficult for 'front-line' personnel to negotiate and implement with their colleagues. Here a number of illustrations from fieldwork might clarify what is at issue.

The joint-agency initiative between the police and a local authority housing department on the Saxon Lane estate had been intended to foster more-co-operative working relations. However, in its practical effects it actually generated tensions and hostilities between front-line workers because of the way in which local housing officers felt that it was being used by the local police to off-load nuisance-value illegalities (defined by the police as not 'real' crime) on to neighbourhood workers. Although this provided a partial solution to the local police's perception of their difficulties, neighbourhood workers interpreted this action as a subversion of their own role, which they defined as working with local residents in order to improve the environment and the quality of life and not as ancillary police officers.

Conversely, in an area of inner London, police officers were dismayed by the requirement of a juvenile liaison scheme that they should consult with the social services department when taking decisions on young offenders, adopting the view that this interfered with their ability 'to do the job properly', while also turning them into 'bloody social workers'. In part, these officers were responding to tensions within their own organisation. In this and other parts of London, police officers working in juvenile liaison schemes were known disparagingly by their colleagues in the uniformed and CID branches as 'Care Bear', the 'Toy Squad' and the 'Teeny Sweeney'. We shall return in a later section to the ways in which intra-organisational tensions can express themselves as inter-organisational conflicts.

There were also unintended consequences which resulted from the high-technology crime-prevention scheme which had been introduced on the Queen's Reach high-rise estate. Devised and agreed through multi-agency co-operation at chief-officer level, it produced a host of difficulties in implementation. Elderly residents found themselves barricaded inside a fortress-like construction of metal doors which they found difficult to open, operated by electronic-card devices which they found equally difficult to understand or utilise. Neighbours were similarly unable to keep a friendly eye on elderly residents because of these obstructions, and this problem was compounded by operating difficulties in the system. At the same time a running battle ensued between agency personnel around who should (and who should not) have access to a master-key. Initially, it had been agreed that the CID and the milkman should possess cards, whereas the homebeat officer and social workers were excluded. During some months of struggle and negotiation, the crime-prevention scheme became an all-consuming preoccupation for the estate's multi-agency forum. In other words, instead of being the 'solution' it became the 'problem'.

One of the original issues which had inspired the Queen's Reach security system was that young people with skate-boards had been using the walkways and corridors, to the annoyance of residents. It was our impression that skate-boarding had been 'talked up' so that it had come to assume the proportions of a major problem which could justify a major high-technology intervention – in the same way as, during the summer of social disorder in 1981, a fight outside a chip shop on the Saxon Lane estate had come to be defined as a 'riot' which had helped to justify Saxon Lane's multi-agency initiative. It became something of a joke among our research team that on the Queen's Reach estate one might find old people, clutching their electronic card-keys but confronted with heavy metal doors which they were unable to open, hoping and praying that a skate-boarder might chance by with the physical strength and high-tech literacy to do the job for them.

Similar disjunctures between policy formulation and implementation have been noted in other research into crime prevention schemes (Hope, 1985; Allatt, 1984a & 1984b) and these kinds of difficulties were repeatedly encountered in our own research. Whether more thoughtful forward planning could obviate these types of implementation problems is an obvious consideration.

The Question of Hierarchy: Formality and Informality

A related question, which recurred throughout our research, is at what level in the hierarchy of each organisation should joint-agency strategies be addressed. It was a frequent complaint by agency personnel that multi-agency panels were too often located at management level, and hence remote from the actualities of day-to-day work. Quite commonly, there were also disparities within multi-agency forums in terms of the seniority of participants within their own organisations. Different conceptions and structures of line management and decision-making, together with different interpretations of confidentiality and accountability, could also jar against each other when agency personnel were brought together. Perhaps the issue underlying these varied difficulties is whether multi-agency initiatives should strive for formal systems of representation and liaison, or whether they work more effectively on an informal basis.

The multi-agency forum on the Queen's Reach estate offered a good example of the strengths and weaknesses of informal working practices. On the one hand, members of the forum drew considerable personal satisfaction from its workings. They would repeatedly say that as a result of the forum's regular meetings their relationships with their counterparts in other agencies were on a much better footing. Policemen valued the fact that they could be acknowledged as human beings, with a capacity for sensitivity and tact, rather than simply as stereotypical representatives of the 'Met', the 'Bill' or the 'Filth'. Social workers, similarly, enjoyed their recognition as skilled professionals rather than as 'namby-pamby, pussy-footing do-gooders'. Generally, there was a feeling that forum members gathered together as rounded human beings: 'We're on personal-name terms now, it's not just a voice on the end of the telephone.'

Against this, the lack of any formal representative status within the Queen's Reach forum meant that a number of significant issues could not be resolved. At one point the territorial responsibilities of the local home-beat officer were changed, resulting in complaints from other forum members that the level of service delivery to the estate was threatened with deterioration. The response of the police representative to these complaints was neither to defend the police decision and the reasoning behind it, nor to take the complaint back and argue the case with his senior officers. Rather, he simply echoed the grumbles of other members and turned to the group for support and sympathy: 'It's typical of the management,' he said. 'They're always chopping and changing.' The housing representative shrugged off frequent complaints about the level of rents on the estate in a similar way: 'You know what they're like, bureaucrats, they've no idea what it's like on the ground.' So that although the Queen's Reach forum met the needs of its members in terms of mutual support and encouragement, it remained highly questionable whether it was meeting the needs of the estate itself and its residents.

Our research uncovered sufficient evidence of weaknesses and lapses in systems of representation to suggest that a degree of formality, with agreed areas of delegated authority for participants in multi-agency forums, would be appropriate. More formal systems of representation would also clarify boundaries between different agencies, prevent the blurring of roles and identities which is not conducive to effective inter-agency work, and enable agency members to articulate their own specific identities, tasks and re-sponsibilities. Nevertheless, informants from all agencies repeatedly stressed that, in their experience, multi-agency work only became meaningful when it operated at a low level and on an informal basis. Having said that, our research also showed that within informal multi-agency forums it is not uncommon to encounter excessive breaches of confidentiality in informa-tion exchanges, together with other unacceptable working practices which, because of their informality, are also unaccountable.

Our response to this issue may seem unnecessarily hesitant, or even confused. It must be frankly acknowledged, however, that there is a signifi-cant contradiction within our research evidence. On the one hand, informal systems of inter-agency working and information exchange are risky encounters which can endanger important confidentialities and might even sometimes constitute a threat to civil liberties. On the other hand, more informal and fluid systems of inter-agency relations seem to offer a more workable basis for communication and negotiation. This contradiction remains an unresolved tension within our research, and more importantly in the theory and practice of the multi-agency approach to crime prevention and crime reduction.

Inter-Organisational and Intra-Organisational Conflicts

One further theme that ran through our research, and that had not been fully anticipated, is that what often appear as *inter*-organisational conflicts are sometimes more appropriately understood as *intra*-organisational conflicts. We have already alluded to this, through the way in which policy formulation at management level can have unintended consequences in policy implementation on the ground; for example, when local police officers used the Saxon Lane joint-agency initiative as a means to off-load 'nuisances' on to neighbourhood workers employed by the local authority housing department. In this way, the housing department's initiative to bring agencies together in a common effort partially backfired because of conflicts between different levels of the hierarchy of the police service as to how the 'real' problem on the estate should be defined.

The highly complex division of labour within the police service – homebeat officers, the shift-system 'relief', the CID, specialist 'squads', rapid deployment units such as the Territorial Support Groups in London, community liaison functions, youth and community sections, and so on – means that it is the police who most commonly become the focal point of inter-organisational conflicts which more accurately reflect intra-organisational tensions. It is commonplace to observe that a homebeat officer's patient work of nurturing good community relations over a period of years can be damaged, even destroyed, through a hasty intervention by the TSG or the 'relief'; and we have ample evidence to support these kinds of claims. Indeed, they were acknowledged as a significant managerial issue in interviews with senior and intermediate command ranks of the police service itself.

A similar issue is the role-confusion seemingly experienced by specialist officers when they are deployed to give drugs education talks in schools and youths clubs: is their function 'community liaison' or 'intelligence gathering' (cf. Grimshaw and Jefferson, 1987)? Even where police officers feel confident that they are able to distinguish their different roles, and to keep them separate, this will not always be apparent to schoolteachers and youth workers, who thereby come to mistrust the motives of the police. Indeed, for these and other reasons, the police have discontinued the practice of offering drugs talks to schools in some areas, believing that police involvement risks a glamourous overemphasis of drug misuse and that drugs education should be more firmly located within a basic school curriculum of health education (cf. Pearson, Gilman and McIver, 1986; ACMD, 1984).

Confusions also arise in the minds of ordinary citizens when confronted with representatives of state agencies that embrace a complex division of labour. An informal visit to the local residents' association by the homebeat officer is interpreted as 'snooping' and surveillance. A social worker's enquiry about a mother's domestic arrangements or the well-being of her children is read, not as a concerned interest in child welfare, but as an anxious concern with child protection. A housing officer's approach to the question of racial incidents is seen as an investigation of possible grounds for the eviction of a neighbour. As a consequence, people close off against lines of communication which are being offered to them. Suspicions about 'hidden agendas' abound. Sometimes, of course, these suspicions are entirely appropriate, although essentially what one is dealing with is not so much a conflict between different agencies and interest groups as a failure of that agency to define clearly to itself and to its public what are its principle aims and objectives in any given situation.

The complexities of the division of labour within state agencies, however, which are often enshrined in statutory responsibilities, mean that these problems are sometimes beyond the reach of more efficient managerial solutions. Structural conflicts of power and direction exist not only between agencies, resulting in inter-agency rivalries and conflicts, but also within them – so that intra-organisational conflicts can assume as much significance in this area as inter-organisational differentiations of responsibility and power.

Gender Relations

One vital area of difficulty within multi-agency approaches to crime and crime prevention, to which we had not given sufficient recognition in our original formulation of the research, proved to be that of gender relations. In the light of our fieldwork, however, it becomes necessary to afford a central significance to the question of gender: both as a means by which power is exercised between agencies and also as a fundamental issue which informs a number of aspects of multi-agency co-operation and conflict (Sampson *et al.*, 1991).

Gender issues asserted themselves almost immediately within our field-work, when it became apparent that the two full-time research workers (one of whom was a woman) were encountering sharply differing experiences in negotiating access, particularly with the police service. These experiences are amply supported by the findings of the Policy Studies Institute survey of the Metropolitan Police, which detailed discriminatory attitudes and practices towards women by policemen (cf. Smith and Gray, 1983). 'The police world', as Reiner (1985, p. 216) has described it, 'remains aggressively a man's world.'

Nevertheless, although research on the occupational culture of the police has sometimes drawn attention to the 'cult of masculinity' in police work, gender relations have been given scant recognition in recent approaches to an understanding of the tensions inherent in the relations between the police and social workers (cf. Holdaway, 1986; Thomas, 1986). This is all the more surprising, given that while the police service is predominantly male, the workforce of social services departments is predominantly female, as is its welfare clientele. Moreover, the possibilities of fostering links with the community are also structured by gender, reflecting the predominant tendency for informal care networks and 'neighbouring' to be heavily dependent on the work and activity of women (cf. Bulmer, 1986; Finch and Groves, 1980). So that whenever the police become involved in multi-agency negotiations with welfare professionals, or with community groups through such initiatives as neighbourhood-based crime-prevention schemes, gender divisions are invariably in play.

Our research evidence suggests that it is only where joint investigative procedures have been developed in recent years in response to cases of alleged child sexual abuse that gender issues have been addressed in multi-agency work, and even then in a most uneven manner and in many different and opposed ways. Domestic violence is another area of concern where, at least within the Metropolitan Police, policy-level discussions were ongoing at the time of our research with the aim of improving the police response to violence against women in the home. However, domestic violence remained a marginal issue for the front-line personnel of all agencies. Indeed, there is an urgent need for gender issues to be prioritised in a variety of spheres of multi-agency involvement.

As a general principle, gender issues could be a significant obstacle in inter-agency relations. Women front-line workers from social services, the probation and health-care services were often reluctant to liaise with the male-dominated police service, minimising their contacts because they felt that they were not seriously valued as professional workers. Some women would take avoidance action, such as not eating their meals in the court canteens because of their dislike of the verbal and even sexual harassment that they sometimes experienced.

Common to the gender divisions within many work-settings, resentment was also expressed by women workers about the tendency for the management hierarchy to be dominated by men. This was accentuated among women police officers – who are a vastly under-researched occupational group – where we found high levels of antagonism and resentment against sexual discrimination and degradation by male officers (cf. Jones, 1986; Heidensohn, 1989). Even so, it is from these day-to-day experiences of women with their separate organisations that inter-agency work can actually precipitate new patterns of working relationships, specifically among women, between agencies which have otherwise historically, ideologically and professionally been in conflict with each other (Sampson *et al.*, 1991). The reaction of women workers is sometimes to attempt to support each other across these barriers to agency co-operation, as a response to the discrimination which they encounter within their own agency. We have found this particularly in the case of child sexual abuse, although it can sometimes explain some of the other informal networks between workers which grow up alongside formal inter-agency mechanisms. Gender relations are, therefore, clearly a complex and unreckoned force within multi-agency initiatives.

SUMMARY AND CONCLUSION: THE SCOPE OF MULTI-AGENCY WORK

By way of summary and conclusion, it should be stressed that we found much more evidence of multi-agency work than had been anticipated in our original research proposal, although it has to be said that much of it had been only very recently initiated. One consequence of conducting research in such a novel area of policy development was the poverty and inadequacy of the background literature on the multi-agency approach to crime prevention. The research also had to be carried out within a rapidly shifting terrain, with a number of new developments and initiatives emerging only when the research was already well-advanced. In view of this, our work should be regarded only as a first step in attempting to understand working difficulties in the implementation of multi-agency initiatives, leaving a number of blind-spots and areas of remaining uncertainty.

There is still considerable scope for research in this area. The multi-agency idea is not only central to recent Home Office departures, such as the Safer Cities initiative and the newly created Drug Prevention Units. It is inscribed across the entire government strategy for reforming the criminal justice system and the work of the Probation Service in supervising offenders in the community (Home Office, 1990a and 1990b). One direction for future research could be tightly focused evaluations of the outcomes of specific multi-agency initiatives. Such research would encounter formidable difficulties in establishing effective performance indicators. More attention also needs to be paid to the informal workings of locality-based crime-prevention schemes, in terms of how these are experienced and understood not only by front-line agency personnel but also by local residents. Our research has been able to map out the general terrain of a number of these issues, indicating some of the areas of difficulty and complexity which must temper enthusiasm for multi-agency approaches within the criminal justice system. Although the emphasis on state agencies co-operating more effectively in crime prevention has been repeatedly stressed in recent years, the difficulties which are encountered in attempts to establish meaningful and relevant forms of inter-agency working have been invariably underestimated.

Too often multi-agency initiatives begin from a somewhat naïve, albeit well-intentioned, impulse to foster improved systems of co-operation, without giving sufficient consideration to actual and potential conflicts between agencies. A number of these conflicts derive from the fact that different state agencies have different aims and objectives, while their staff also adhere to different professional ideologies. Matters of considerable importance in terms of principle are thereby put on the line – confidentiality, civil liberties, accountability. Even so, conflicts also arise from the quite humdrum fact that any given issue, or any given locality, will tend to make a widely varying impact upon the routine workloads of different agencies. Indeed, although the first site of potential conflict has often been acknowledged in discussions of the inter-agency approach – for example, in debates on conflicts between 'justice' and 'welfare' principles in response to juvenile crime, or the need to provide for the welfare of children as against the punishment of offenders in the sphere of child abuse – it might be that the second set of conflicts is more of an obstacle in attempts to devise multi-agency initiatives. Where any given problem or locality makes only an insignificant impact on an agency's routine workload, whereas for another agency it is an all-consuming preoccupation, then it is clearly difficult to find common ground, even where aims and objectives might be shared.

Where conflicts such as these are in play, then even where there is a consensus on the need to co-operate there is always a possibility that multi-agency initiatives will fritter away their energies. At a practical level, it would seem better for agencies first to identify possible and actual sites of conflict. To recognise, in fact, that conflicts between agencies are often an entirely healthy expression of their different roles and responsibilities. Where conflict can be maturely addressed in these terms, acknowledged and understood, then a platform of mutual consideration can be established. Identified areas of conflict might, of course, place limits upon inter-agency working, so that what might emerge is a narrower platform of agreement than had been originally envisaged, although it will in all probability be more secure. What is implied in these observations, quite obviously, is a more socially nuanced understanding of the multi-agency approach than currently prevails. It is such a stance that we have aimed for in this research, a requirement that has been forced upon us by the complexities which have emerged in our fieldwork.

In spite of these abundant complexities, it is possible to summarise the practical outcomes of our research in the form of eight central policy issues which should be taken into consideration when planning and attempting to implement multi-agency strategies within the sphere of criminal justice:

1. There is a clear need for a local focus in multi-agency initiatives, both in terms of identified needs and problems, and also local resource availability.
2. Even so, different problems and different localities make widely varying impacts upon the routine workloads of different state agencies, so that it can be extremely difficult for these agencies to find common ground for an inter-agency strategy.
3. Some agencies are more powerful than others (the most powerful state agencies are the police and the housing departments) and there is a tendency for the preoccupations of these agencies to dominate inter-agency agendas, with a corresponding likelihood that other important interests become marginalised or ignored. Gender relations provide one vital means by which power is expressed and should be addressed in all inter-agency initiatives.
4. Difficulties are often encountered when negotiating between agencies, in terms of the seniority of representatives from each agency within their own organisational hierarchy. Questions of representative status are more generally problematic, whether one is thinking of inter-agency forums or the representation of local needs and opinion within community-based crime-prevention schemes.
5. A largely unanswered question concerns whether multi-agency forums are more effective when they work on a formal or an informal basis.
6. There are large differences between policy formulation and its implementation by front-line personnel.

7. Difficulties and conflicts which can often appear at a surface level to be inter-organisational on closer scrutiny can sometimes be seen to involve intra-organisational tensions. For example, they reflect conflicts between different levels of an organisation's hierarchy, tensions within an organisation's complex division of labour, or the opposing directions of the organisation's various statutory responsibilities.

8. Finally, when attempting to devise systems of closer co-operation in relation to criminal justice or crime prevention, it would be more advisable to address first the actual and potential sites of conflict between different interests, rather than to embark upon multi-agency initiatives with a naïve view of consensus.

REFERENCES

Advisory Council on the Misuse of Drugs (1984), *Prevention* (London: Her Majesty's Stationery Office).

Allatt, P. (1984a), 'Residential security: containment and displacement of burglary', *Howard Journal of Criminal Justice*, **23**, 99–116.

Allatt, P. (1984b), 'Fear of crime: the effect of improved residential security on a difficult to let estate', *Howard Journal of Criminal Justice*, **23**, 170–82.

Blagg, H., Pearson, G., Sampson, A., Smith, D. and Stubbs, P. (1988), 'Inter-agency co-operation: rhetoric and reality', in T. Hope and M. Shaw (eds), *Communities and Crime Reduction* (London: Her Majesty's Stationery Office).

Bulmer, M. (1986), *Neighbours: The Work of Philip Abrams* (Cambridge: Cambridge University Press).

Coleman, A. (1985), *Utopia on Trial: Vision and Reality in Planned Housing* (London: Hilary Shipman).

Finch, J. and Groves, D. (1980), 'Community care and the family: a case for equal opportunities?', *Journal of Social Policy*, **9**, 486–511.

Grimshaw, R. and Jefferson, T. (1987), *Interpreting Policework: Policy and Practice in Forms of Beat Policing* (London: Allen & Unwin).

Heidensohn, F. (1989), *Women in Policing in the USA* (London: Police Foundation).

Holdaway, S. (1986), 'Police and social work relations: problems and possibilities', *British Journal of Social Work*, **16**, 137–60.

Home Office (1984), *Crime Prevention*, Circular HO 8/84 issued by the Home Office, Department of Education and Science, Department of the Environment, Department of Health and Social Security and Welsh Office (London: Home Office).

Home Office (1990a), *Crime, Justice and Protecting the Public: The Government's Proposals for Legislation*, Cm. 965 (London: Her Majesty's Stationery Office).

Home Office (1990b), *Supervision and Punishment in the Community: A Framework for Action*, Cm. 966 (London: Her Majesty's Stationery Office).

Hope, T. (1985), *Implementing Crime Prevention Measures*, Home Office Research Study no. 86 (London: Her Majesty's Stationery Office).

Jones, S. (1986), *Policewomen and Equality* (London: Macmillan).

Labour Party (1990), *A Safer Britain: Labour's White Paper on Criminal Justice* (London: Labour Party).

Newman, O. (1973), *Defensible Space* (London: Architectural Press).

Pearson, G. (1986), 'Developing a local research strategy', in P. Wedge (ed.), *Social Work: Research into Practice* (Birmingham: British Association of Social Workers).

Pearson, G., Gilman, M. and McIver, S. (1986), *Young People and Heroin: An Examination of Heroin Use in the North of England*, Health Education Council Research Report no. 8 (London: Health Education Council; Aldershot: Gower).

Pearson, G., Sampson, A., Blagg, H., Stubbs, P. and Smith, D. (1989), 'Policing racism', in R. Morgan and D. J. Smith (eds), *Coming to Terms with Policing* (London: Routledge).

Reiner, R. (1985), *The Politics of the Police* (Brighton, Sussex: Harvester).

Sampson, A., Stubbs, P., Smith, D., Pearson, G. and Blagg, H. (1988), 'Crime, localities and the multi-agency approach', *British Journal of Criminology*, **28**(4), 478–93.

Sampson, A., Smith, D., Pearson, G., Blagg, H. and Stubbs, P. (1991), 'Gender issues in inter-agency relations: police, probation and social services', in P. Abbott and C. Wallace (eds), *Gender, Sexuality and Power* (London: Macmillan).

Smith, D. J. and Gray, J. (1983), *Police and People in London* (London: Policy Studies Institute).

Thomas, T. (1986), *The Police and Social Workers* (Aldershot: Gower).

3 Discourse and Decision-Making in Scottish Prisons

MICHAEL ADLER and BRIAN LONGHURST

INTRODUCTION

For the last few years we have been attempting to study day-to-day administrative decision-making within the Scottish prison system. We have focused on adult, male, long-term prisoners, who constitute the largest and most problematic of the various groups which make up the prison population, and have analysed in detail several major areas of decision-making including: the initial allocation of prisoners to establishments by the National Classification Board; transfers between establishments; security categorisations; the allocation of work and education; the distribution of privileges; recommendations for parole; the handling of requests and grievances through petitions to the Secretary of State; appeals to the domestic courts, the Parliamentary Commissioner for Administration and the European Commission on Human Rights; and the activities of the Prisons Inspectorate. In each case we have sought to establish what decisions are accomplished; why the system operates in the way it does; what problems are created by existing practices, for whom they are problematic and to what extent they have given rise to pressure for change; what are the obstacles to change; how effective are the different forms of accountability; what alternatives to the existing system are being canvassed and what their implications for day-to-day administrative decision-making would be.

During the course of our fieldwork, we used three main research techniques: documentary analysis, observation and interviews. Documentary analysis involved the study of files and other official records; observation entailed attending meetings of, for example, the National Classification Board and local induction boards, and sitting in with various staff groups at headquarters; while interviews were conducted with a wide range of individuals from inside and outside the prison service. We conducted a total of 60 interviews, 31 with governor-grade staff, seven with industrial managers, three with education officers, five with social workers, eight with civil servants (including the Director and three Deputy Directors), two with the Inspectorate and four with well-informed outsiders.

73

We were initially drawn to the study of day-to-day administrative decision-making by two interrelated sets of concerns. Notwithstanding the lack of any consensus about the aims of imprisonment or any agreement about the future direction of penal policy in Scotland, we were struck by the ability of those who ran the prisons to produce a semblance of social order, at least for much of the time. Although the spate of violent incidents which took place in Scottish (and likewise English) prisons drew attention to the fragility of this situation, and was quite rightly the subject of a good deal of attention, we felt that it was important not to lose sight of the fact that these incidents constituted the exception rather than the rule. Equally, we were struck by the secrecy which characterised the activities of the Scottish Prison Service (SPS) and the fact that so little information relating to day-to-day administrative decision-making was available to the public. As Cohen and Taylor (1979) pointed out (in their critique of the Home Office), this secrecy 'insulates prisons and their administration from the type of reasonable criticism which is regularly incurred by other institutions in our society' (p. 94). This seemed to us to be particularly unhelpful at a time when the future direction of the Scottish Prison Service was becoming a matter of public concern.

It is clear that no programme of empirical research can be pursued adequately without first developing an appropriate analytic framework. In developing such a framework we have drawn on and sought to integrate the two academic traditions and approaches we brought to the research. One of us (BL) came to the research with a background in sociology and a special interest in the sociology of knowledge; the other (MA) came with a background in social policy and a special interest in socio-legal research, in particular the concept of administrative justice. It is unusual for these traditions and approaches to be brought together but their integration has been particularly fruitful: the analytic framework we have developed has not only helped us to understand the research agenda set out above but has also led to a new and distinctive approach to the study of imprisonment.

Our chapter is in three parts. We begin by outlining the nature of the Scottish prison system and the approach to the study of day-to-day administrative decision-making which we took in our research. We then use this framework to contextualise the study of two different substantive areas of investigation: the work of the National Classification Board and the recent development of penal policy in Scotland. In our conclusions we assess the usefulness of our analytic framework and offer some brief normative comments on the future of imprisonment.

AN ANALYTICAL FRAMEWORK FOR THE STUDY OF THE SCOTTISH PRISON SYSTEM

It is impossible to study contemporary imprisonment without paying attention to the ideas and beliefs (which we shall term discourses) which shape and contextualise it. In general, we maintain that groups of social actors in specific social settings produce discourses which reflect and construct their social interests in the course of competitive struggle (see further, Longhurst, 1989). In any case study, the analyst will be interested in the conflicts and accommodations between the most significant social actors in a particular domain, in this case the Scottish prison system. This can be seen to consist of a series of layers which are represented diagrammatically in Figure 3.1 as four concentric circles. We shall refer to these concentric circles as the inner core, the outer penumbra, the layer of political accountability and the layer of legal accountability.

There are five potentially significant groups of actors within the inner core of the Scottish prison system: civil servants who are located in the headquarters of the Scottish Prison Service in Edinburgh; prison governors, prison officers and several groups of prison professionals, most of whom work in establishments; and the prisoners themselves. The Director of the Prison Service is a senior civil servant with the rank of Under-Secretary

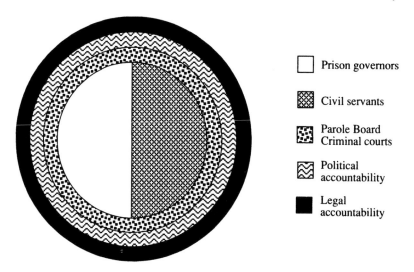

FIGURE 3.1 *Simplified model of the criminal justice system as it relates to prisons*

(Grade 3), and the 150 or so staff who work at headquarters are organised into divisions, each under the control of a Deputy Director. Although a unified grading system known as 'Fresh Start' was introduced in 1987, a distinction can still be made between the erstwhile governor grades (now often called managers) and the uniformed staff. Each of the 22 establishments is under the control of a governor and, depending on its size, may contain up to ten governor-grade staff. There are currently about 90 governor-grade staff, a small number of whom have jobs at headquarters (usually about six), with the Inspectorate (two) or at the Staff College (two). There are, of course, many more prison officers – currently about 2500 to deal with an average daily population of 5000 or so prisoners. And finally there are some 60 chaplains, 50 social workers, 30 full-time education officers, 25 medical officers and smaller numbers of psychologists and psychiatrists. In Scotland, unlike England and Wales, few of these professionals are actually employed by the prison service – on the whole, they are employed by external agencies and engaged to provide a service on a contractual basis.

Different groups of staff exercise power in different circumstances. In terms of day-to-day activity in the halls or in the workshops, the most important groups are prison officers and prisoners, and what does and does not go on is best understood in terms of a power struggle between these two groups. On the other hand, in terms of the specific services which they can provide and, in some cases, the particular decisions which they can influence, the power of some of the professional groups can be considerable. However, with respect to the large majority of administrative decisions which affect the prison careers and the quality of life of prisoners, prison governors and headquarters personnel, in particular those in the casework branches, are the most important groups of staff. In fact, the nature of the decisions that are taken not infrequently reflects the outcome of a power struggle between these two groups of actors.

To argue that prison governors and headquarters staff have the greatest influence on administrative decision-making is not to deny that other groups can also influence the outcome of decisions. Prison officers are clearly involved in administrative decision-making, in that they write reports and make recommendations on a wide range of issues, for example, a prisoner's suitability for a change of work party, an upgrading of security category, or a move to semi-open or open conditions. However, their recommendations and opinions are nearly always 'translated' by the more powerful governor grades. To a quite surprising extent, considering their status in the world outside, the position of many of the prison professionals is very similar to that of the prison officers. The position of the prisoner is not so different either. Although adult, male, long-term prisoners are now able to express a preference for one of three 'prisons of classification' (Glenochil, Perth and Shotts) at which to begin their sentence (see below) and may ask for a change of work-party, they have few legally enforceable rights and must always persuade someone in authority to support their request. Thus, prisoners do not feature prominently in our analysis which focuses on those who exercise the greatest influence over administrative decision-making.

Thus, in relation to administrative decision-making, the most important groups of actors in the inner core are civil servants, who are located in the headquarters of the Scottish Prison Service in Edinburgh, and prison governors, who are mainly to be found in the various penal establishments. The inner core is surrounded by an outer penumbra of institutions whose activities impinge directly on the Prison Service, the most important of which are the criminal courts that decide who is sent to prison and for how long, and the Parole Board that determines who should be let out before completing their sentence. In turn, this is surrounded by a layer of political accountability, in particular to the Scottish Office, other government departments and the Cabinet. Finally, there is a layer of legal accountability, primarily by means of judicial review in the domestic courts and applications to the European Commission of Human Rights.

So far, we have characterised the most salient administrative features of the Scottish prison system. It is in this context that we focus on the discourses of different actors and the struggles between competing discourses associated with different actors. We distinguish between discourses which are concerned with the ends of imprisonment, with what prisons are for – *ends discourses* – and discourses which deal with the means of imprisonment, that is, with how prisons should be run – *means discourses*. Within the Scottish prison system we have identified three significant ends discourses: those of rehabilitation, normalisation and control. We have also identified three significant means discourses: those of bureaucracy, professionalism and legality. We shall now characterise each of these in turn, beginning with ends discourses.

Whilst many commentators run reform and rehabilitation together, it is important, both analytically and historically, that they be separated (Hudson, 1987). The nineteenth-century prison was concerned with reform. The state constructed the orderly prison so that the individual could be provided with the space to reform on the basis of his or her free will. The prison as we know it was founded on these principles (see, for example, Foucault, 1977) and the famous penal reformers such as John Howard and Elizabeth Fry desired better penal conditions so that 'better' people would result after having reformed themselves. However, in the late nineteenth century the prison began to change (Garland, 1985). With the expansion of the state and the development of disciplines such as criminology, psychology and psychiatry, reform was superseded by rehabilitation. The state actively sought to change the criminal using these new forms of knowledge. The first wave of rehabilitation was followed after the Second World War by a second wave, which reached its crescendo in the late 1960s (Hudson, 1987).

The focus of rehabilitation discourse is on the 'deviant individual' who is deemed to be psychologically disturbed, socially maladjusted or otherwise out to step with the rest of society in some way. The nature and degree of the deviance are to be ascertained by the new disciplines. The aim of the prison as a state agency is to socialise the individual back into society. Ultimately, advocates of rehabilitation believe that this will lead to reduction in crime and hence to the 'protection' of society.

In the early 1970s rehabilitation came under attack from those who thought it unjust and from those who thought it insufficiently punitive. As summarised by Hudson (1987), adherents of the 'justice model' argue that punishment should be in proportion to the crime, rather than the individual's response to prison. Hence, sentences should be determinate, there should be 'an end of judicial and administrative discretion' and 'disparities in sentencing' should be eliminated. In addition, prisoners would be protected by 'due process'.

From the above account it can be seen that the justice model is primarily concerned with sentencing and says relatively little about the nature of the prison itself. In Britain, the most interesting application of justice-model-type thinking to the prison came in King and Morgan's (1980) unsuccessful attempt to persuade the May Committee (Home Office, 1979) to adopt the philosophy of 'humane containment'. They argued, first, for the 'minimum use of custody': prison sentences should be short and 'used only as a last resort'. Secondly, they maintained that prisons should function at the minimum security level needed, calling this the principle of the 'minimum use of security'. Hence, far more prisoners would serve their sentences in less-restrictive conditions than they currently do. High security is not only expensive but also deprives prisoners of contact with their families. Thirdly, King and Morgan argued for the 'normalisation' of the prison, which they explained as follows:

> By this rather inelegant phrase we mean that as far as resources allow, and consistent with the constraints of secure custody, the same general standards which govern the life of offenders in the community should be held to apply to offenders in prison.

Normalisation discourse seeks to obviate the negative effects of prison, merely aiming to ensure that the individual will not become 'worse' during the period of incarceration. This contrasts in an extreme way with rehabilitation discourse, which maintains that the individual can get 'better' in prison. The focus in normalisation discourse is on the normality of the incarcerated individual. He or she is seen as a normal individual who happens to have committed a crime, for which he or she has been punished (by being sent to prison) but for whom the experience of the prison itself should not be punitive. The contrast with the 'deviant' individual in rehabilitation discourse is clear. The familiar adage that prisoners are sent to prison *as* punishment rather than *for* punishment is central to normalisation discourse.

The final 'ends' discourse which we see as particularly important is that of control. The development, nature and ramifications of control discourses in society have been elegantly and illuminatingly discussed by Stanley Cohen (1985) who detects their increasing prevalence in the 1980s. In the penal context, this discourse focuses on the control and smooth operation of the prison and the prison system. 'Good order' and control are perceived to be threatened by the 'disruptive' individual who constitutes the focus of this discourse. Of course, control is an inherent problem in prisons and all prisoners are inevitably subject to various forms of control. However, in control discourse the 'difficult' prisoner has become increasingly prominent. Moreover, as we shall see below, the desire to implement a control strategy for the minority of difficult prisoners can have important effects on the nature of imprisonment for all other types of prisoners. In particular, it can have 'knock on' effects on the potential for normalisation.

An important source of support for this discourse stems from its attention to the protection of prison staff, in particular prison officers. The short-lived complete 'lock-down' of all prisoners in Scotland, following the spate of rooftop incidents in 1986–7, some of which involved the taking of hostages, can be seen as the implementation of a control strategy for a short period of time. Of course, it would be very difficult to maintain such a strategy for very long and, in our interviews with prison governors, many of them maintained that this was unreasonable and unnecessary anyway.

Control discourse tends to stress conformity. It does not worry about the rehabilitation or reform of the individual (with the demand that the offender should really change) or the normalisation of the prison (with the demand that prisoners should be treated as much like individuals in the community as possible). Rather, it maintains that the individual should conform to whatever measures are deemed to be necessary for the maintenance of order

and discipline in the prison. The characteristic features of the three competing forms of ends discourse are summarised in Table 3.1.

TABLE 3.1   *Characteristic features of three competing forms of 'ends' discourse*

Discourse:	Rehabilitation	Normalisation	Control
1. Source of legitimacy	Improving the individual	Prevention of negative effects of prison; treating prisoners like individuals in the community	Control of disruption; 'smooth functioning'
2. Focus	'Deviant' individual	'Normal' individual	'Disruptive' individual
3. Concerns	Socialising the individual back into society through the provision of training and treatment	Minimum security, contact between prisoner and family, improved living conditions	Conformity to social order; protection of prison staff

Having characterised rather briefly these ends discourses, we now move
to the consideration of means discourses. Our discussion here is influenced
by the work of Jerry Mashaw (1983) who, in analysing the specific nature
of the United States' Disability Insurance scheme, reorients the study of
administrative decision-making by integrating the normative concerns of
administrative law (which sets out standards for 'good' administrative
decisions) with the positive concerns of organisation theory (which deals
with how organisations actually work).

Mashaw develops three ideal types of administrative justice:
'bureaucratic rationality', 'professional treatment' and 'moral judgement'.
Different forms of discourse are associated with these ideal types. The
bureaucratic discourse of civil servants derives its legitimacy from its
claims to fairness and impartiality. In contrast, governors' discourse is
'professional' but despite the recent interest in managerial techniques, is
'grounded' in experience rather than in some esoteric body of knowledge.
As such it derives its legitimacy from the governors' knowledge of establishments and inmates. Whereas bureaucratic discourse focuses on the

prison system as a whole, professional discourse concentrates on the individual establishment. And while bureaucratic discourse has, as its primary concerns, the achievement of uniformity, consistency and fidelity to the rules, professional discourse emphasises leadership, experience and judgement as means of enhancing the institutional ethos. Likewise, bureaucratic discourse advocates the direct administrative accountability of establishments to headquarters and thus of governors to civil servants, while professional discourse envisages a greater degree of decentralisation and negotiated forms of accountability.

While the bureaucratic and professional discourses associated with civil servants and governors are the dominant forms of discourse, there is a third type. However, this has, so far, only been evident in relatively muted form in Scotland. We refer here to a legal or juridical discourse, since it is associated with the courts and the legal system. This form of discourse derives its legitimacy from the rule of law, it focuses on the individual prisoner and its primary concerns are with protecting prisoners' interests and strengthening the means available to individual inmates to assert their 'general' and 'special' rights (Richardson, 1984). This form of discourse stresses that prisons should be held accountable to the rule of law as interpreted by the courts. The characteristic features of the three competing forms of means discourse are summarised in Table 3.2.

TABLE 3.2 *Characteristic features of three competing forms of 'means' discourse*

Discourse:	Bureaucracy	Professionalism	Legality
1. Source of legitimacy	Fairness, impartiality	Intimate knowledge	Rule of Law
2. Focus	On the system	On establishments (and prisoners collectively)	On individual prisoners
3. Dominant concerns	Uniformity, consistency, fidelity to the rules	Leadership, experience, judgement, enhancing the 'organisational ethos'	Respect for prisoners' rights
4. Accountability for decisions	Internal – to Secretary of State directly	Negotiated – to Secretary of State indirectly	External – through courts

If ends discourses are combined with means discourses the result is the three by three, nine-cell matrix shown in Table 3.3.

TABLE 3.3   *Discourse matrix*

	Rehabilitation	Normalisation	Control
Bureaucracy	1	2	3
Professionalism	4	5	6
Legality	7	8	9

It is possible to locate, *inter alia*, significant actors; institutional and administrative practices; and policy statements on this matrix. Further, it is possible to chart changes in policy and practice by showing moves from one cell to another or from one area of the matrix to another. Our research suggests that the framework has great potential for the study of the Scottish prison system and, we suspect, many others besides. We illustrate its usefulness with two examples taken from our research on the Scottish prison system. First, the work and position of the National Classification Board; and secondly, the development of penal policy in Scotland over the period 1988–90.

THE NATIONAL CLASSIFICATION BOARD

The National Classification Board (NCB) decides the prison to which the newly sentenced adult, male, long-term (over 18 months) prisoner should be sent at the start of his sentence. The NCB meets alternately at Scotland's two main local prisons, Barlinnie in Glasgow and Saughton in Edinburgh, with occasional meetings taking place in some of the other local prisons, most notably Perth. It consists of a governor, the industrial manager from the prison where the Board is held and, in Edinburgh, a social worker who sometimes participates in the discussion of individual cases although he/she is technically not a member of the NCB. The NCB is administered by an induction officer who also takes part in discussions on occasions and offers advice when requested.

When we first visited the NCB in 1986 and early 1987 it used two main principles to classify offenders. First, it established whether or not the prisoner was a first offender. It is important to point out that a 'first offender' in Scottish prison terms is not necessarily what would be understood as a 'first offender' by the general public. The term 'first offender' is used to refer to someone who has not served a sentence in an adult prison in the last ten years and is therefore applied to prisoners who have served long sentences in the more distant past as well as those who have more recently completed a sentence in a Young Offenders Institution. First offenders would be sent to Edinburgh, but for recidivists the choice was between Perth and Peterhead/Aberdeen. Here, the second principle, of 'trainability', came into play. The NCB would decide whether a prisoner was trainable or not, by considering his likely response to the regime in a training prison. Trainable prisoners would be sent to Perth, those under 35 years of age who were not trainable would be allocated to Peterhead, those over 35 to Aberdeen. At this point, prisoners were also being classified to Shotts for two main reasons. First, continuing existing practice, a certain number were 'creamed off' by the NCB at Barlinnie to work in the laundry. Secondly, a larger number were so classified in anticipation of the opening of the main body of the new prison at Shotts (Phase II) in June 1987.

The NCB arrived at its decisions through the following processes. At Edinburgh prison the prisoners were kept outside the room in which classification took place. They were called in individually and interviewed by the Deputy Governor (or, if he was unavailable, the Training Governor) who acted as chairperson of the Board, the industrial manager (or one of his deputies) and a social worker. Simple tests of English and arithmetic had been taken by the inmates prior to the meeting of the Board. The Social Work Unit in the prison used the Board as a convenient place to interview long-term prisoners on admission, and the social worker played little or no part at all in the actual decision-making processes of the Board. A social worker explained this to us, saying: 'The main reason I use the Classification Board is that I can't find anywhere else in the prison to interview newly sentenced prisoners.'

The interviews were fairly brisk and normally quite short (5 minutes would be a very long interview), but, of course, the length of the interview varied depending on who was carrying it out as well as the character and response of the prisoner. Some interviewers, for example, would use the interview for a chat with the prisoner or to ask specific questions about his situation. The latter was more common with 'genuine' first offenders who would not know the system as well as those who had been in and out of it several times. When all the prisoners had been interviewed, the members of the Board (including the induction officer who supervised the mechanics of the Board and quite often answered specific queries) sat together and decided to which prison to allocate the inmate. Decisions were reached fairly briskly and, while there was sometimes a brief discussion and Board members often passed comment on the prisoners and their classification, systematic or fundamental disagreement was rare. At the conclusion of this meeting, the decisions of the Board were sent to Casework Branch in HQ for formal ratification. The decisions made by the Board were rarely challenged, though the chairperson of the Board was occasionally asked for clarification of a particular decision which appeared unusual. Such questions were normally dealt with quickly and again without deep disagreement.

The operation of the Board at Barlinnie differed in a number of small respects. The chairperson was the Deputy or Training Governor from Edinburgh prison, the industrial manager was from Barlinnie and no social worker was ever present. All the prisoners took simple induction tests immediately prior to the meeting of the Board in the room that was used for the interviews and sat around at the back of the room until called for interview.

The destinations of the newly sentenced prisoners at the five Boards we observed at this stage are summarised in Table 3.4.

TABLE 3.4 *National classifications observed, 1986–7*

Prison	Number	Percentage
Perth	19	38
Edinburgh	10	20
Peterhead	1	2
Peterhead (Protection Unit)	1	2
Shotts	15[1]	30
Perth/Shotts, Shotts/Perth	2	4
Others	2	4
Total	50	100

[1] 8 classified for Shotts at the last meeting we attended in anticipation of the opening of Phase II.

It is clear, therefore, that there was little scope for individualised decision-making here. Two basic features of the prisoner had to be established: first offender/recidivist and trainable/not trainable. It might be thought that there could be scope for debate over the meaning of the latter, but those classifying had a clear idea. As one classifier subsequently explained: 'It was fairly straightforward; I assessed from my knowledge of the prisoners and from my information if he was an arsehole or if was'nae an arsehole.'

The classifiers disagreed rarely (6 out of 28 cases analysed in detail). These disagreements often reflected some confusion or simple errors of interpretation (for example, a prisoner telling a classifier he was a first offender when in fact he was a recidivist) rather than principle, and were quickly (in seconds) resolved.

At this point, therefore, the activities of the NCB were primarily those characterised by cell 1 of our matrix in Table 3.3, although the Board also exhibited some features characteristic of cell 4. The Board used a simple set of rules to distinguish between first offenders and recidivists, and to some extent between prisoners who were trainable and those who were not. Both these distinctions reflect a residual commitment to rehabilitation. Prisoners who refused to take the tests were automatically deemed to be untrainable. However, there was some scope for professional judgement of the individual prisoner. Professional knowledge and expertise were also used in the passing of information to the prisoner in the interview. Thus, the activities of the Board represented a confluence of bureaucratic and, to a lesser extent, professional forms of discourse with those of a rather muted version of rehabilitation.

During 1987 the position of the NCB became increasingly tenuous. Two sets of forces combined to make the NCB almost irrelevant. First, there were practical and institutional pressures. Overcrowding, changes in the nature of the prison population, in particular the marked increase in the number of sex and drug offenders, and the spate of hostage-taking incidents threw classification into crisis. Prisoners were classified to a prison, in the full knowledge that it was unlikely that they would reach there for a long time, if at all. Likewise, prisoners were classified to the Peterhead Protection Unit when it was clear that, on the basis of the plans then current, it might take years before a space became available. Although the classification system was rational in its own terms and perhaps in relation to the relatively stable system that had existed hitherto, it moved increasingly out of line with operational considerations as other factors seriously curtailed the room for manoeuvre. One response of the Scottish Prison Service to these sorts of pressures was a transfer of spare capacity in Young Offenders Institutions to the overcrowded adult long-term system. Under 'Grand Design' as the reorganisation was known, two prisons, Dumfries and Greenock (which had only recently reopened as a prison for adult long-term prisoners (LTPs), became Young Offenders Institutions (YOIs) while Glenochil YOI became an adult, long-term prison, and Noranside Open YOI became Scotland's second open prison. This, and the opening of Shotts Phase II, altered the situation considerably and greatly relieved the overcrowding referred to above. Henceforth, all male long-term prisoners would normally begin their sentence at one of three new 'core' establishments: Shotts, Glenochil or Perth. The place of Edinburgh was left undefined although there was talk of it becoming a 'progression' prison, taking upgraded prisoners from one of the core establishments.

During 1987, in tandem with Grand Design, the Scottish Prison Service came increasingly under the sway of a normalising strategy. The language of 'training' and 'progression' was challenged by that of normalisation and 'parity of regimes'. The initial thinking through of this strategy is contained in *Custody and Care* (Scottish Prison Service, 1988a) which we discuss more fully below.

Classifiers were also thinking along these lines. As a chairman of the NCB told us:

> Trainable or non-trainable are out of date concepts because in actual fact, if you analyse what we have called training in the past, I think training is a misnomer. We have provided work opportunities and the opportunity for people to learn one or two skills. There has been little attempt at training in social skills or even in training people for release. We have done it on some occasions and in some prisons, but not for the mass. So training in that respect really was a misnomer. What I think we ought to be providing is a system where we make opportunities available because it is then up to the individual to avail himself of these opportunities.

These developments threw the NCB into crisis. While the format of the Board remained essentially the same, by late 1987 its rationale had ceased to exist.

In theory, the classification system was now based on prisoner choice, geographical location and security considerations. However, one governor we interviewed explained that 'We are changing the classification system to meet the needs of the moment as we go along' and that furthermore, 'because of the Peterhead incidents . . . the classification system virtually broke down'. Indeed, one respondent explained: 'Classification is virtually a waste of time. Shotts or Glenochil – there are no clear guidelines.'

The destinations of the newly sentenced prisoners at the four Boards we observed at this stage are summarised in Table 3.5.

Disagreement between the classifiers was even rarer than before, as there was now even less to disagree about. Discussion at the full Board was even more perfunctory than before. Furthermore, prisoners were quite often upset at interview. They were being asked to make a choice between establishments on the basis of little background information. Some said that they would like to go to open conditions and were irritated when it was explained that this would only be possible for a tiny number.

TABLE 3.5   *National classifications observed, early 1988*

Prison	Number	Percentage
Glenochil	23	47.9
Shotts	13	27.1
Perth	8	16.7
Edinburgh	3	6.3
Others	1	2.1
Total	48	100.1

The increasing dominance of normalisation discourse and the attempt to move the prison system in this direction shattered the rationale and practice of the NCB. A prison system moving in the direction of normalisation had no use for a system of classification based on distinctions between first offenders and recidivists and between prisoners who were deemed to be trainable and those who were not. Not only was the muted form of rehabilitation undercut by normalisation, the combination of bureaucratic and professional discourses was undercut by a weak form of legality in that, subject to the availability of places, adult, male, long-term prisoners could choose in which of three prisons they wished to start their sentence. At this later stage, the activities of the Board could be characterised primarily by cell 2 of our matrix although the Board also exhibited some features characteristic of cell 8.

PENAL POLICY IN SCOTLAND

So far, we have considered the impact of discursive strategies and practices on classification practice in the Scottish prison system, showing the heuristic value of our overall framework. We also believe that this framework aids the understanding of the movement of penal policy in Scotland since 1988 and will now consider this. We shall be concerned with three documents: *Custody and Care* (Scottish Prison Service, 1988a), *Assessment and Control* (Scottish Prison Service, 1988b) and *Opportunity and Responsibility* (Scottish Prison Service, 1990).

Custody and Care (C & C) addresses four main topics: 'Task and responsibilities of the Scottish Prison Service (SPS)'; 'Policy and priorities for inmates'; 'Planning for individual establishments'; and 'The training and development of staff'. The 'task' of the SPS is:

(i)   to keep in custody untried or unsentenced prisoners, and to ensure that they are available to be presented to court for trial or sentence;

(ii) to keep in custody, with such a degree of security as is appropriate, having regard to the nature of the individual prisoner and his offence, sentenced prisoners for the duration of their sentence or for such shorter time as the Secretary of State may determine in cases where he has discretion;

(iii) to provide for prisoners as full a life as is consistent with the facts of custody, in particular making available the physical necessities of life; care for physical and mental health; advice and help with personal problems; work, education, skill training, physical exercise and recreation; and opportunity to practice their religion;

(iv) to promote and preserve the self-respect of prisoners;

(v)   to enable prisoners to retain links with family and community; and

(vi) to encourage them to respond and contribute positively to society on discharge.

C & C also makes clear that:

> The appropriate balance of elements of the task is a matter of judgement based on experience, specialised advice, perception of the risk or positive potential of inmates, and availability of facilities or resources.

Although priority is given first to security and then to control, the balance between the various tasks and thus the aims and objectives of the SPS are still left open. C & C outlines the legal framework of imprisonment in Scotland and sets out proposals to produce a consolidation of the Prisons (Scotland) Act 1952 and subsequent amendments and to amend and update the Prison (Scotland) Rules, which likewise date from 1952, and the Standing Orders derived from them.

Under the second head, C & C considers the initial classification of long-term prisoners to establishments and examines the role of the National Classification Board. It proposes that 'regime prospectuses' be drawn up for every prison and made available to prisoners. It argues for the introduction of 'sentence planning' for all long-term inmates, saying that 'the aim is to get the individual to come to terms with his sentence and to complete it as peaceably and constructively as possible' and that 'sentence planning' in the sense of continuous assessment and dialogue with the inmates should begin 'immediately the sentence is known'. These proposals have important implications for *Assessment and Control* (A & C), as we shall demonstrate.

To facilitate 'sentence planning' C & C proposes that each establishment will produce a regime plan. In general, establishments will be kept in line with each other so as to ensure 'parity of regimes', that is, as equal treatment as possible of like prisoners. Finally, more and better staff training is proposed and the roles of governors and staff are set out.

The later document *Assessment and Control* consists of three main parts: first, an analysis of explanations and reasons given for the recent spate of rooftop incidents in Scottish prisons, which puts forward the case for developing 'control risk profiles' as a means of identifying potentially disruptive and violent individuals; secondly, an elaboration of plans for the future pattern of specialised units in which such individuals would be held; and thirdly, a very brief update on C & C.

A & C begins with a consideration of the reasons that have been given by inmates for the recent spate of disturbances in Scottish prisons. The reasons examined are: ill-treatment by staff; overcrowding and conditions of accommodation; changes in parole policy; quality of regimes and availability of privileges; the remoteness of Peterhead and the difficulties this creates for visits. Except for the remoteness of Peterhead, which is left open, all these reasons are rejected. However, the reasoning involved is remarkably loose and unconvincing. The analysis infers from the possible (or known) consequences of an act that it was not rational for the actor to engage in it.

Further, A & C transforms 'reasons' – a non-judgemental characterisation – into 'justifications': 'In themselves, the various reasons which have been given by inmates as *justification* for the incidents do not, on investigation, give any *justification* at all for the actions taken' [our emphasis].

It would, of course, be quite proper to cite all the reasons given as possible explanations for a pattern of events without arguing that they justified the events. Explanations and justifications are not necessarily related.

The rejection of these 'reasons' allows A & C to conclude that the explanation for disruption lies with the individual:

> rather than looking to changes in the way in which the Prison Service as a whole goes about its task (although clearly this is an area which must be kept under review) a more productive approach may be to concentrate attention on the individual personality and 'repertoire' of particularly disruptive and violent inmates.

A & C attempts to provide a profile of this type of inmate, maintaining that 'violent and disruptive prisoners tend to display a combination of the following features'. The list of features comprises: a hostile attitude towards authority; an inability to come to terms with their sentence or its length; the experience of being separated from their families; peer group pressure from the criminal community; an inability to live to order; the intensifying effect of the prison environment; drugs; and personality disorder. This catalogue is quite incoherent in its own terms, in that it covers personality attributes, experiences, attitudes and behaviour. Thus, it is hard to envisage it forming the basis of any set of diagnostic tests.

By adopting this strategy, the 'problem' for the SPS becomes that of identifying those prisoners who are *potentially* disruptive in order to remove them from the mainstream of prison life. In order to do this, prisoners need to be continuously assessed. The link back to the proposals made in C & C is clear. The use which is envisaged for continuous assessment in A & C undercuts the normalising aspects of this strategy outlined in C & C. In addition, the SPS planned a substantial expansion of 'alternative units' to accommodate these 'violent and disruptive' prisoners.

These documents can be analysed in terms of the framework outlined above. In certain respects, with the publication of C & C, the SPS could be seen to be moving in the direction of normalisation. Examples of this are the commitment, as part of the task of the SPS, 'to provide for prisoners as full a life as is consistent with the fact of custody', 'to enable prisoners to retain links with family and community' and give a measure of choice to LTPs about initial allocation. Further, there is the desire to plan sentences in dialogue with the prisoner, and the attempt to ensure some kind of parity of regimes, so that, as far as possible, prisoners serving similar sentences and prisoners at similar stages of their sentences are treated more or less equally. Control discourse is still discernible but rehabilitation is more or less absent. However, the main move towards normalisation was undercut by the discourses of A & C. Take the following for example:

> The priority is prevention and this means that judgements have to be taken which anticipate possible or intended trouble. The test of preventive measures cannot be 'proof beyond a reasonable doubt' because the only such proof would be the actual occurrence of the events which it is hoped to prevent. Necessary intervention in advance of anticipated trouble, therefore, will always be open to objections that it is unfair or unreasonable.

The abandonment of criteria of proof proposed here infringes the very basis of claims to normalisation in practice.

The priority which A & C gave to the need for greater control in the Scottish Prison System effectively undercut the normalising strategy of

C & C. The confluence of bureaucratic and normalisation discourses in C & C was subverted by the accommodation of bureaucratic and control ones in A & C.

A & C provoked a large measure of concern amongst commentators on penal affairs, and indeed was not welcomed by more 'progressive' elements inside the prison service itself. This led to a new policy document, *Opportunity and Responsibility* (O & R) published in May 1990. O & R outlines a new philosophy of imprisonment based on the twin assumptions that prisoners should be treated as responsible persons and that the prison system should aim to offer prisoners a full range of opportunities for personal development and the resolution of personal problems. It acknowledges that mistakes were made in the shifts of administrative practice during 1987, and it dismisses almost completely the specific and general approach of A & C. It maintains that

> we should regard the offenders as a person who is responsible, despite the fact that he or she may have acted irresponsibly many times over in the past, and that we should try to relate to the prisoner in ways which would encourage him or her to accept responsibility for their actions by providing him or her with opportunities for responsible choice, personal development and self-improvement.

Central to this approach are proposals which will allow the prisoner to participate at each stage in planning his or her sentence and that recognise the need to structure opportunities in a sensible and appropriate manner. This entails the retention of a system of progression; and O & R suggests that it will be helpful to distinguish three aspects of regimes, namely the minimum elements a prisoner should receive by right ('the threshold quality of life'), 'appropriate opportunities' and 'privileges', with what were previously regarded as privileges being progressively incorporated into the basic threshold quality of life in prison.

O & R spells out its own conception of normalisation, which is seen to entail the provision of 'regimes which allow prisoners the opportunity to live as normal lives as possible and as may be consistent with the requirements of security and order', and points to the need to review practices in three areas, namely 'access to families', 'quality of life' and 'preparation for release'. O & R recognises the necessity of control but integrates this more clearly into its overall framework: control is in a sense subsumed within normalisation.

In terms of our framework, O & R represents, on the one hand, a confluence of normalisation and control discourses and, on the other, a fusion of bureaucratic and professional discourses. However, it fails to accommodate legal discourse, making few references to prisoners' rights or the means by which they can be enforced. In accordance with prevailing government ideology and normalisation, O & R emphasises prisoners' responsibilities, their need to make choices and to face the consequences of their decisions.

The definition of normalisation which is adopted in O & R (cited above), and its relationship to the provision of opportunities, also raises a number of problems. If the yardstick for living as normal a life as is consistent with the requirements of security and order is the kind of life the offender could lead outside prison, where few opportunities for personal development and self-improvement, education, training or employment may be available and where, in any case, little pressure may be exerted on the offender to take advantage of them, then this may not be consistent with the provision of opportunities and the encouragement which prisoners will need if they are to take advantage of them. In fact, the concept of normalisation may even be an impediment to the development of such opportunities. Indeed, whilst using a normalisation rhetoric, it is clear that in some important ways, and despite its protestations to the contrary, O & R is dragging the SPS back in the direction of rehabilitation. Some will see this as a failure, but for us, if we are allowed to be normative rather than analytical for a moment, it carries certain benefits. We shall expand on this in our conclusions.

While C & C reflects the confluence of bureaucratic and normalisation discourses and hence belongs in cell 2 of the matrix, A & C is the product of the fusion of bureaucratic and control discourses and therefore belongs in cell 3. O & R is more complex: it represents, on the one hand, a confluence of normalisation and control discourses and, on the other, a fusion of bureaucratic and professional discourses. It can therefore be seen to inhabit the space defined by cells 2, 3, 5 and 6. In our view this synthesis is not a source of weakness but is, rather, a source of strength. Moreover, we think it would be beneficial if this process of assimilation was extended to embrace the currently excluded forms of discourse. Two of the weaknesses of O & R are that it falls to give adequate expression to legal forms of discourse or to recognise the centrality of rehabilitation discourse to its own proposals. The future for the Scottish prison system (and other prison systems) lies in its ability to formulate policies and engender practices which occupy the space defined by all nine cells of the discourse matrix.

CONCLUSION

We have shown, we hope, how useful our framework has been in the analysis of one substantive area of decision-making and the broader domain of penal policy-making in Scotland. We are well aware that to some our approach could be seen to be rather classificatory: a quasi-anatomical exercise in sorting and placing into boxes. This is indeed *one* of the things we have been doing. However, we believe that there are other dimensions to our work, and we should like to conclude by pointing these up.

First, we have shown how useful our approach can be to the study of fairly detailed decision-making. Further evidence on this will be forthcoming in our analysis of other areas of day-to-day administrative decision-making which, for reasons of space, we do not describe in this chapter.

Secondly, our approach has been exceptionally enabling in the study of social change. One of the things that was said to us quite often as we carried out our fieldwork was that we were studying Scottish prisons at a bad time, since so much was changing and it was far from clear what the final outcome would be. Our feelings were exactly the opposite: the fact of change enabled us to construct our framework, as we could see the processes at work very clearly. Further, we are able to see the system in a state of movement. Hence, the approach we offer is one that recognises social change.

Thirdly, change does not occur out of the blue. It relates to both 'internal' and 'external' social struggles. We have paid some attention to external policy development, but our main substantive focus has been internal. We see groups of social actors engaged in social struggles. During the course of these struggles, actors draw upon existing discourses but also inflect them in new directions depending on the current balance of social forces. Although we do not analyse such struggles in this paper we intend to do so in our forthcoming book *Power, Discourse and Justice*. Some have commented that this paints an over-conflictual portrait of the nature of the prison system. However, this is to misunderstand our view. Social life can be conflictual and still involve balance and accommodation between different groups. We do not imply a continuing war of all against all.

Finally, we believe that our approach enables us to formulate a clear position on the ends and means of imprisonment. The framework we have devised enables us not only to describe existing policy and practice and to account for recent changes within the prison system, it also enables us to formulate a clear normative position on the future of imprisonment. Unlike most of the participants in this debate, we do not champion a single set of aims or a particular set of procedures for achieving them. Each of the three ends discourses we have identified, and likewise each of the three means discourses, is 'coherent and attractive' (Mashaw, 1983) and has much to offer. Furthermore, the various discourses are not 'mutually exclusive' but are, rather 'highly competitive' (ibid.). Thus although 'the internal logic of any one of them tends to drive the characteristics of the others from the field as it works itself out in concrete situations' (ibid.), the task for policy makers is to try to produce an optimum balance between these different discourses. This balance will be different in different concrete situations but the goal for the Scottish Prison Service is to produce a synthesis of what is best in each of the discourses we have identified.

In adopting this normative position, we wish to make it clear that we are not merely arguing for a pluralism in which the discourses characterised by each of the nine cells in our matrix all coexist with each other and in which each discourse holds sway over some limited domain. Thus, for example, a rehabilitation strategy might be applied to certain groups of offenders (in particular, those convicted of sexual offences and other crimes of violence); a control strategy might be applied to others (for example, those who are unable to settle into a prison regime and those who get involved in violent incidents within the prison); while normalisation applied to everyone else. Likewise, some decisions might call for the development and application of bureaucratic rules and procedures, others for the exercise of professional judgement, while a third set called for the development of legal forms of adjudication. Although such an approach would have its attractions, and might indeed be preferable to the current position in which the dominant forms of discourse have tended to drive other discourses out, it is based on a very simplistic view of prisoners and the appropriateness of prison procedures. The approach that we are arguing for, in which each form of discourse is always present albeit to a different degree, is, in our view, based on a more realistic understanding of prisoners and the complexity of prison procedures. It is, of course, much more difficult to achieve but it holds out the prospect of far greater success by seeking an optimum balance between the competing claims of several intrinsically persuasive forms of discourse.

REFERENCES

Adler, M. and Longhurst, B. (1989), 'The classification of long-term prisoners in Scotland', in E Wozniak (ed.), *Current Issues in Scottish Prisons: Systems of Accountability and Regimes for Difficult Prisoners*, Scottish Prison Service Occasional Papers, no. 2 (Edinburgh: Scottish Prison Service) pp. 21–45.

Adler, M. and Longhurst, B. (1990), 'The future of imprisonment in Scotland: a critique of policy', in A. Brown and R. Parry (eds), *The Scottish Government*

Yearbook, 1990 (Edinburgh: Unit for the Study of Government in Scotland) pp. 226–42.

Adler, M. and Longhurst, B. (1991), 'The future of imprisonment in Scotland: a great leap forward?', in A. Brown and D. McGrove (ed.), *The Scottish Government Yearbook, 1991* (Edinburgh: Unit for the Study of Government in Scotland) pp. 209–16.

Adler, M. and Longhurst, B. (forthcoming), *Power, Discourse and Justice: A New Sociology of Imprisonment* (London: Routledge).

Cohen, S. (1985), *Visions of Social Control: Crime, Punishment and Classification* (Cambridge: Polity).

Cohen, S. and Taylor, L. (1979), *Prison Secrets* (London: National Council for Civil Liberties, and Radical Alternatives to Prison).

Foucault, M. (1977), *Discipline and Punish: The Birth of the Prison* (Harmondsworth, Middx: Penguin).

Garland, D. (1985), *Punishment and Welfare: A History of Penal Strategies* (London: Gower).

Home Office (1979), *Report of the Committee of Inquiry into the United Kingdom Prison Services* (May Report), Cmnd. 7673 (London: Her Majesty's Stationery Office).

Hudson, B. (1987), *Justice Through Punishment: A Critique of the 'Justice' Model of Corrections* (London: Macmillan).

King, R. and Morgan, R. (1980), with J. P. Martin and J. E. Thomas, *The Future of the Prison System* (London: Gower).

Longhurst, B. (1989), *Karl Mannheim and the Contemporary Sociology of Knowledge* (London: Macmillan).

Mashaw, J. (1983), *Bureaucratic Justice* (New Haven, Conn.: Yale University Press).

Richardson, G. (1984), 'Time to take prisoners' rights seriously', *Journal of Law and Society*, **11**(1), 1–32.

Scottish Prison Service (1988a), *'Custody and Care': Policy and Plans for the Scottish Prison Service* (Edinburgh: Scottish Office).

Scottish Prison Service (1988b), *Assessment and Control: The Management of Violent and Disruptive Prisoners* (Edinburgh: Scottish Office).

Scottish Prison Service (1990), *Opportunity and Responsibility: Developing New Approaches to the Management of the Long-Term Prison System in Scotland* (Edinburgh: Scottish Prison Service).

4 Security, Control and Humane Containment in the Prison System in England and Wales

ROY D. KING and KATHLEEN McDERMOTT

The media coverage given to the prison protest and riot at Strangeways in April 1990 – the most serious disturbance yet seen in the prison system of England and Wales and which coincided with the writing of this chapter – threw the questions of security, control and humane containment into stark relief. But the relationship between these matters is a complex one that has frequently been misunderstood; it almost certainly changes over time as one or another element is singled out for special attention. The research reported here was intended to provide a clear description of the present relationship between these variables in England and Wales and to set down some benchmarks against which future developments in the system might be measured.

The task of providing reliable and valid benchmarks is much easier said than done, for there is no ready litmus test to be applied to any of the phenomena we are concerned with here. In much of what follows we have relied on a combination of objective, quantitative indicators of performance and subjective, but systematic, qualitative assessments provided by staff and prisoners. And wherever possible we have sought to give meaning to these measures through the time-honoured comparative method: comparisons are made with past performance; with what is achieved in other prison jurisdictions; with the aspirations of the prison service; and with the standards laid down by penal reform groups and partly enshrined in the Council of Europe Prison Rules.

Some measure of the increasing emphasis given to security and control in the prison system of England and Wales can be obtained from the most cursory examination of the annual reports on the work of the prison service. In the first report following the transfer of responsibility for prisons from the Prison Commission to the Home Office in 1963, 'escapes' and 'discipline' were dealt with in a single paragraph. Following the famous escapes of Wilson in 1964, Biggs in 1965 and Blake in 1966, which led in turn to the enormously consequential reports by Mountbatten (Home Office, 1966) and Radzinowicz (ACPS, 1968), prison security got a subheading of its own. But there was remarkably little space devoted to control

– indeed, for some years there was no mention even of assaults on staff except in the statistical appendices.

All this changed dramatically with the demonstrations organised partly in conjunction with PROP (the Preservation of the Rights of Prisoners group) in 1972. In that year security and control were given a chapter to themselves and subsequent reports gave more or less systematic accounts of 'concerted acts of indiscipline', roof climbing and hostage-taking as well as escapes. Even so, it is hard to tell how far this increased reporting reflected real changes in either the quantity or quality of such incidents. In 1986–7, by which time the annual reports had been completely redesigned as vehicles for impression management rather than the conveyance of information, 'Custody and Control' took pride of place as the uncomprising title for the first chapter.

Had such a growing concern been at the expense of the humanity of the system and the quality of prison regimes? Mountbatten explicitly indicated, both in his report and subsequently (Mountbatten, 1972), that he did not wish to see any reduction in rehabilitative efforts – even where these might appear to threaten security as with hostels and working-out schemes. The Department's Annual Report for 1967 (Home Office, 1968, p. 5), however, reported reluctant but unavoidable curtailments of prisoner activities as a result of implementing the security changes – although in the following year the Prison Department was claiming that the gloomy predictions about the impact of security on regimes had not been fulfilled (Home Office, 1969, p. 5). In virtually every subsequent annual report there are indications of new developments of one kind or another but it is impossible to produce a systematic picture of the changes from this kind of source – and the belief that regimes had deteriorated continued to be widespread both inside and outside the service.

In attempting some analysis of these issues it is best to begin with some simple, common-sense definitions because the terms security, control and humane containment are ones which derive essentially from the official language of prison managers rather than the language of social science. By *security* we mean matters that relate directly to keeping prisoners physically in custody – the taking of reasonable measures to prevent escapes which are proportionate to the risks at stake. By *control* we mean matters that relate to the maintenance or restoration of social order within prisons when it is perceived to have been put under threat. We use *humane containment* in the sense that was widely adopted following the collapse of the rehabilitative ideal and the rhetoric associated with the treatment and training of offenders to describe the aspirations to provide decent conditions for prisoners in terms of physical facilities, regime activities, contact with families and so on.

One frequent problem of understanding has been the conflation of the concepts of security and control. This was most marked in the immediate responses to the series of dramatic escapes in the mid-1960s, particularly in the presumption that prisoners who may be serious 'escape risks' are also likely to be 'control problems'. Such a presumption was a major factor, for example, in the Radzinowicz Committee's rejection of Lord Mountbatten's recommendation that all the highest security-risk prisoners should be concentrated in a single maximum-security prison; and it was embedded in the subsequently adopted 'dispersal' policy whereby those prisoners were instead distributed more thinly around several maximum security prisons (see King and Morgan, 1980). The May Committee (Home Office, 1979) and the Control Review Committee (Home Office, 1984) – the former responding in passing and the latter specifically to the problems of disorder that had dogged the dispersal system throughout the 1970s and early 1980s – belatedly acknowledged that the concepts of security and control are not the same, and that action to deal with one is not necessarily appropriate for the other (see King, 1985). It was becoming clear, and was to become clearer, that while prisoners as well as staff have a vested interest in well-ordered institutions, anyone who is detained against their will could potentially become a control problem without ever threatening the security of the establishment by attempting to escape. But while the concepts of security and control are analytically separable they are clearly not unrelated, not least because incidents where control is lost may constitute the occasion for escape attempts – planned or otherwise.

The connection between either or both of these concepts and humane containment is not nearly so obvious as might appear at first sight. It is, for example, too easy to suggest that the less humane the conditions the more likely it is that prisoners will try to escape from them. Clearly it is possible to imagine regimes which are so utterly inhumane that escape is not possible, and perhaps not even thinkable. At the other extreme, popular imagery about holiday camps notwithstanding, it is unlikely that even the most rewarding regime would be sufficient to keep prisoners inside were there not also powerful physical or psychological barriers to prevent escape. As far as control is concerned, it would be easier to argue that prisoners may be more likely to rebel against harsh conditions had it not actually been the case – until Strangeways and the disturbances the previous year at Risley – that the worst incidents of loss of control in the prison system had mostly been in those institutions which were least crowded and best resourced. In fact, some degree of humanity in the system of containment is required before escape or rebellion is possible, but it would clearly be absurd to suggest that the more humane the regime the more likely become escapes or loss of control. Indeed, some versions of the currently fashionable concept of 'dynamic security' espoused by prison officials (see Dunbar, 1985), whilst it once again conflates the notions of security and control, invokes the constructive activities of prisoners and the positive involvement of staff in those activities, as the best prophylaxis for control problems.

To get a clearer sense of where these matters of security, control and humane containment presently trade off against one another we embarked on a study of five prisons, representative of all the levels of security and function in prisons for adult males, in the prison system of England and Wales. Fieldwork was conducted in Gartree (maximum-security dispersal prison), Nottingham (category B training prison), Featherstone (category C training prison), Ashwell (category D open training prison), and Birmingham (category B local prison) between 1985 and 1987. The prisons were all chosen from the Midland administrative region, partly as a matter of convenience but more importantly because we wanted to try to understand the relationship between the prisons as part of a system.

The research team spent at least three months in each prison observing virtually all aspects of the functioning of the establishment, at weekends as well as during the week, and in the evenings and at night as well as during the day. More than 300 prisoners and staff were interviewed, often on tape, and over 1000 prisoners and staff responded to our enquiries through self-completion questionnaires. Access was given to all areas of the prison, though this was in part conditioned by considerations of gender, and where required most documentary sources were also made available to the research team.

As it turned out, the potential significance of any benchmarks we were able to establish for the system would be much greater than we could have anticipated at the outset. Our fieldwork was completed just before the implementation of Fresh Start – the major reorganisation of shift systems for prison staff designed to end the dependence of the prison service on overtime working and to put prison officers on salaries which, it was hoped, would bring an end to the industrial disputes which had plagued the service for a decade. But Fresh Start was also conceived as part of the government's drive for economy, efficiency and effectiveness, and management consultants had advised that the reorganisation would produce 15–20 per cent savings, half of which could be ploughed back into the service to enhance prison regimes. Our data thus offers the opportunity for future researchers to evaluate the effectiveness of this major change and its impact on regimes. We were able to return to our prisons for a brief period after each of them had been 'Fresh Started' to begin that process (see McDermott and King, 1989; King and McDermott, 1990b).

Our research design also closely resembled that adopted in an earlier study (King and Morgan, 1976; King and Elliott, 1978) which involved five comparable prisons in the south-east and south-west regions between 1970 and 1972 – Albany (dispersal), Coldingley (category B), Camp Hill (category C), Ford (category D) and Winchester (local) – so that although the studies had somewhat different objectives, some directly relevant comparisons were possible with respect to regimes using hitherto unpublished data.

Finally, further comparisons were possible between Gartree and the maximum-security prison at Oak Park Heights in Minnesota which had been the subject of similar research (also funded by ESRC) in 1984 (see King, 1987, 1991).

HUMANE CONTAINMENT: THE DETERIORATION OF PRISON REGIMES

In 1982, responding to the widespread concern about the quality of life in prisons, the government committed itself to publishing a draft code of minimum standards. A year later, presumably fearing that the price-tag for sensibly defined standards would be too high and that to declare standards which it did not achieve would be to make a rod for its own back, the government withdrew from that commitment. Instead, it embarked on a policy of seeking to raise standards through a system of internal monitoring of what was delivered in each institution and then requiring prison governors and their regional directors to agree new annual targets that might be realistically achieved within existing resources. It was a strategy of pulling itself up by its own bootstraps.

In 1984, shortly before our research began, and as a first step in this process, the prison service set out a new statement of its tasks. There were four of them: first, to keep untried or unsentenced prisoners in custody and to present them at court for trial or sentence; secondly, to keep sentenced prisoners in custody for the duration of their sentence with such a degree of security as is appropriate; thirdly, to provide for prisoners as full a life as is consistent with the facts of custody; and fourthly, to enable prisoners to retain links with the community to which they will return (Train, 1985). The third task clearly recognises the trade-off between regimes on the one hand and the facts of custody on the other – but, in the absence of standards and with no further advice on how the facts of custody might be expected to condition regimes, it may do little more than provide a ready-made excuse for failure to deliver improvements.

Nevertheless, the statement does go on to amplify what is required of the prison service in providing a full life for prisoners: it has to make available 'the physical necessities of life; care for physical and mental health; advice and help with personal problems; work, education, training, physical exercise and recreation; and opportunity to practise their religion'. And these are elaborated further in an accompanying statement of the function of prison department establishments which was delivered to prisons as Circular Instruction 55 of 1984. It is around these statements of functions that we have organised our assessments of the delivery of regimes in the institutions we studied. In the absence of any official standards against which to compare performance we have used the standards developed for the National Association for the Care and Resettlement of Offenders (NACRO) by Casale (1984) wherever these seem appropriate.

The first 12 functions relate essentially either to administrative matters concerned with presenting prisoners at court, releasing them at their due date and so on, or to considerations of security and control. We shall return to some of these later. Functions 13 to 22 relate to the provision of services and facilities for prisoners, community links and preparation for release – the heart of what has been thought of as regimes or the humane containment of offenders. We cannot deal with them all in a short account of this kind, so our presentation here is necessarily selective. But if the institutions we studied in 1970–2 and those we examined in 1985–7 were at all representative of the system – and we have no reason whatever to doubt this – then *our evidence shows a massive deterioration in prison regimes* (see King and McDermott, 1989).

Function 13 for prison department establishments requires them to provide (in accordance with the statutory provisions and departmental instructions which themselves define few, if any, real standards of quality) accommodation, meals, facilities for personal hygiene and sanitation, clothing, opportunities for exercise, and access to privileges. We confine ourselves here to looking at accommodation and sanitation, if only because the best known 'facts' about the prison system are that it is overcrowded and too many prisoners have to 'slop out'. While that is still true, these comparisons offered prison administrators some modest comfort.

Only 38.1 per cent of the prisoners in our current study were accommodated according to the NACRO space standard of 60 square feet per prisoner, providing they are not locked up for more than 13 hours a day. In the earlier study, however, the figure was even lower, with only 21.9 per cent in accommodation which met the standard. This cannot be taken as indicating an improvement because these differences clearly reflect the particular architectural characteristics of the establishments concerned and the period in which they were built. In fact it was impossible to generalise on accommodation standards because each prison had such a variety, and space varied according to whether prisoners were accommodated one, two or three to a cell or in multiple occupation dormitories. But given the simplistic way in which these matters are often addressed, it is important to note that single-celling did not guarantee adequate space and multiple occupation inadequate space. Ironically some of the worst accommodation – as far as space was concerned – was in single-celled new prisons and some of the best in single-celled Victorian prisons. Nevertheless it was true in 1970, and remained true in 1987, that crowding was worst for prisoners in local prisons, which tended to be nineteenth century in origin.

The impact of crowding, however, depends very much on the length of time prisoners actually spend in their cells and on the provision of, and most crucially the access they are allowed to, other services and facilities. In terms of facilities for personal hygiene and sanitation – the actual provision of WCs, washbasins, baths or showers – there appeared to have been a genuine improvement resulting from the refurbishment programme in recent years. Thus Birmingham, even allowing for its prodigious overcrowding, met proposed standards in these areas whereas Winchester 15 years earlier had failed them. The real problems arose because, for a variety of reasons including lack of time, poor organisation and poor maintenance, prisoners did not actually have sufficient access to them while they were in a usable state. As a result prisoners were often unable to use running water for brushing their teeth but had to collect it and take it to their cells: and with so many sharing cells for such long periods, prisoners sometimes resorted to wrapping faeces in their underpants and throwing them from the cell window – both as a means of avoiding living with the stench of the chamber-pot and a mechanism for getting back at the authorities for imposing such conditions of deprivation.

Function 17 is the one which most closely addresses the question of regimes. It requires establishments to provide 'a balanced and integrated regime, which may include work, education, physical education, access to libraries and individual and collective leisure activities'. No standards are set against which performance is to be judged although there is a carefully worded intention that these activities should occupy prisoners 'as fully as possible throughout the whole week'. The use of the permissive 'may include' rather than the prescriptive 'must include' makes the content of 'a balanced and integrated regime' a matter of judgement.

Once again we have to be selective, but it is appropriate to begin with work, education and training activities, for in our society the expectation is that these not only fill the greater part of our lives but serve also to define the kinds of people we are. We had some difficulty in deciding on appropriate measures to apply for these comparisons because the NACRO standards do not cover prison work. Rule 28(i) of the Prison Rules for England and Wales was evidently drafted for a different era when it required convicted prisoners 'to do useful work for *not more* than ten hours a day' (our emphasis). The European Prison Rules speak only about keeping prisoners occupied for a 'normal working day'. But what is a normal working day? In the earlier study we assumed this to be 7.5 hours for all prisons. It typified the aspirations of most trade unionists outside prisons and it was widely accepted by prison managers in those days as an unspoken target inside the prison system. But it seemed perverse to use the same standard for the current study when the Prison Department in its report for 1986–7 had declared targets of six hours for training prisons and four hours in locals (Home Office, 1987), even though these seemed to us to be unduly low. We show our results in Table 4.1.

TABLE 4.1   *Maximum daily hours in work or similar activities*

Prison	Hours in work	Suggested standard
Dispersal		
Albany (1970–2)	8.0	Pass
Gartree (1985–7)	5.0	Fail
B Training		
Coldingley (1970–2)	8.0	Pass
Nottingham (1985–7)	4.5	Fail
C Training		
Camp Hill (1970–2)	7.5	Pass
Featherstone (1985–7)	6.0	Pass
D Training		
Ford (1970–2)	7.5	Pass
Ashwell (1985–7)	6.5	Pass
Local (convicted)		
Winchester (1970–2)	5.5	Fail
Birmingham (1985–7)	2.5	Fail

In every comparison much less time was spent in work or similar activities today than had been the case fifteen or more years earlier. All of the training prisons then met the more stringent standards: now only Featherstone and Ashwell could remotely claim to provide a full working day. Prisoners in the best of the training prisons today spend less time in work than those in the worst of the training prisons in the earlier study. Even more strikingly long-term prisoners in the higher-security prisons today spend less time in work than convicted prisoners once did in the local at Winchester. Winchester in fact would have easily met today's targets for local prisons and would only just miss those for training prisons.

It is important to point out that within this overall decline there has also been a change in the nature of activities. Work as such, particularly work in workshops, has been markedly reduced. In 1986–7, for example, 42 workshops were closed as part of a general retreat from the policy of developing prison industries which had been in place since the 1960s. To some extent · this shortfall has been taken up by an increase in the provision of day-time education and vocational and other training courses as part of the search for more balanced regimes. Our evidence suggests that this changing balance has largely been welcomed by the prisoners involved, who saw prison work as mindless activity of little benefit to anybody, whereas education and training courses are seen as more constructive. But it also seems to be the case that day-time education has grown (there was none at the time of the earlier study) at the expense of evening education (of which there used to be a lot) so that education now reaches fewer prisoners than formerly.

In part, the decline of evening education reflects probably the most important change between the two studies: *the astonishing shrinkage of the unlocked day.* The amount of time prisoners spend out of cells conditions both the adequacy of the space they have whilst locked up and their access to regime activities. Our data are given in Table 4.2.

The NACRO standards call for 11 hours out of cells which provide a minimum of 60 square feet, and longer where this space standard is not met. When one looks at the comparisons in this table there are simply no improvements to be seen: the best that can be said is that at least the time out of cells for remand prisoners in Birmingham is not worse than it was in Winchester – but when prisoners already spend 22 hours locked up there is not much scope for further deterioration. Only Featherstone and Ashwell now meet the NACRO standards for time out of cell, but in both cases prisoners there spent more time locked up than had been the case in Camp Hill and Ford. Convicted prisoners in Birmingham were much worse off than their counterparts in Winchester. But the biggest changes were in the high-security prisons: prisoners in Gartree and Nottingham now spend

TABLE 4.2   *Hours locked and unlocked*

Prison	Hours in	Hours out	NACRO standard
Dispersal			
Albany (1970–2)	9.75	14.25	Pass
Gartree (1985–7)	15.00	9.00	Fail
B Training			
Coldingley (1970–2)	10.00	14.00	Pass
Nottingham (1985–7)	14.50	9.50	Fail
C Training			
Camp Hill (1970–2)	11.00	13.00	Pass
Featherstone (1985–7)	13.00	11.00	Pass
D Training			
Ford (1970–2)	9.00	15.00	Pass
Ashwell (1985–7)	10.00	14.00	Pass
Local (Convicted)			
Winchester (1970–2)	15.00	9.00	Fail
Birmingham (1985–7)	18.50	5.50	Fail
Local (Remand)			
Winchester (1970–2)	22.00	2.00	Fail
Birmingham (1985–7)	22.00	2.00	Fail

more of their time *locked up* (over 60 per cent) than their predecessors in Albany and Coldingley used to spend *unlocked* (58 per cent). Indeed, on this, as on several other matters, the regime in Gartree and Nottingham most closely resembled what used to prevail for convicted prisoners in Winchester local prison. It needs to be repeated that the comparisons we have been making are not of the same prisons over a period of time, but of two small groups of similar prisons studied at different times. Nevertheless, if these prisons are representative – and we believe they are – then the message is inescapable: *there has been a major deterioration in regimes in all types of prison since the early 1970s, and the deterioration has been most marked for prisoners in higher-security prisons and for convicted prisoners in local prisons.* There are many prison officers who, having locked prisoners away for the night at a time usually applied to pre-school children in outside society, subscribe to the view that 'happiness is door-shaped'. And there are certainly many prisoners who find it easier to do their time 'behind the door'. But there can be little doubt that the growth in the amount of time spent 'banged up' has so restricted the opportunities for prisoners, and reduced the job satisfaction of staff, that both groups are less able to cope with the tensions generated when prisoners *are* unlocked.

How can these changes be explained? Certainly the most familiar excuse for the plight of the prison service – being starved of resources – lacks credibility. The May Committee noted that as far as prisons in England and Wales were concerned, capital expenditure compared favourably with that on other services (Home Office, 1979, para. 6.95), though it nevertheless regarded prisons as a special case and since then capital expenditure on prisons has outstripped that in most other fields. Is it perhaps the case, then, that a hard-pressed staff, facing worsening staff–prisoner ratios, are simply unable to unlock the ever-rising numbers of prisoners? Quite the contrary. Over the prison system as a whole, during the period covered by our researches, the prison population grew by less than one-fifth, while the numbers of staff increased by more than two-thirds. These changes alone, taking no account of the enormous increases in overtime which amounted to the equivalent of a further 1000 officers, produced a 70 per cent improvement in the staff–prisoner ratio between 1971 and 1986. There are many local factors that bedevil comparisons of staffing in the particular establishments we studied, though as it happens the fairest comparisons would be between the dispersal prisons at Albany and Gartree and the local prisons at Winchester and Birmingham. Gartree had almost twice as many uniformed staff per prisoner (and working longer periods of overtime) as did Albany earlier, in prisons of nearly identical design and serving substantially the same population. When all grades of staff were taken into account, there were actually more staff than prisoners in Gartree. Yet Gartree had a far more improverished regime than Albany. Birmingham had three times as many uniformed staff as Winchester and only just over one and a half times as many prisoners, resulting in a hugely improved staff–prisoner ratio – yet it had a much-reduced regime. It has to be borne in mind, however, that only about one-eighth of the population in Winchester were remand prisoners whereas in Birmingham the proportion was about two-fifths.

In Table 4.3 we present the summary findings from this part of our research: the percentage changes in time in work and similar activities, in hours unlocked, and in uniformed staff–prisoner ratios for each of our pairs of prisons.

What these findings seem to show is that the major improvements in staffing had simply been absorbed by other duties. In the case of the dispersal prisons, such duties almost certainly had to do with enhanced security and control measures which almost certainly also curtailed

TABLE 4.3   *Differences in regimes and staff ratios for study prisons, 1985–7 compared with 1970–2 (%)*

Category	Locked up		Work		Staff Ratio	
	More	Less	More	Less	Better	Worse
Dispersal	53.8			37.5	93.8	
B Training	45.0			43.8	2.5	
C Training	18.2			20.0		2.6
D Training	11.1			13.3	75.7	
Local convicted	23.3			54.5	68.8	
Local remand	Same		Same		68.8	

regimes. In the case of the local prisons, the increased staff was probably absorbed by both security and control on the one hand, and the major growth in the commitment, arising from the increase in remand prisoners, to escorting prisoners to and from the courts on the other.

The prison service set great store by Fresh Start as an attempt to develop a more effective use of staff resources and to redress falling standards. But when we went back to our five prisons, some three months after they had been 'Fresh Started', only ten of the 397 staff we contacted believed there to have been *any* improvements in the regimes for prisoners. Our own measures did show a number of instances where things had got better – but we found twice as many examples where things had got even worse. If anything, the changes widened the differences between the best and the worst regimes rather than narrowed them (McDermott and King, 1989). Moreover, while there had been some undoubted improvements in the organisational structure and most staff approved of the changes to pay and hours, a clear majority felt that job satisfaction, relations with management, training and promotion opportunities had all seriously declined (King and McDermott, 1990b).

SECURITY AND CONTROL

Function 11 requires each establishment 'to maintain a level of security appropriate to the prisoners who are or may be held at the establishment'. At the time of our research prisoners were still essentially categorised according to the security categories laid down by Mountbatten: category A – prisoners whose escape would be highly dangerous to the public, the police or the security of the State; category B – for whom the very highest conditions of security are not necessary but for whom escape must be made very difficult; category C – prisoners who cannot be trusted in open conditions, but who do not have the ability or the resources to make a determined escape attempt; and category D – who can be trusted in open conditions. But the logic of sending prisoners to prisons closely attuned to their defined security needs had been eroded by the dispersal policy. As a result, the security terminology relating to prisons is confusing: the maximum-security dispersal prisons are technically category B prisons to which category A prisoners may be dispersed. Once there, the category A prisoners face a number of additional restrictions – concerning cell location, frequency of moving cells and of cell searches, and visits. They will also be 'on the book' – a system which requires prison officers to accept responsibility for their whereabouts by initialling a book which follows each category A prisoner around the prison.

This leaves category B (non-dispersal) and category C training prisons as closed facilities, and category D open training prisons. All local prisons are category B, many with a capacity to house category A prisoners both direct from the courts and on periodic transfer from the dispersal system. In addition, two of the special security wings, which date from before Mountbatten and were the emergency response to the escapes of the 1960s, continue at Leicester and Parkhurst, albeit in modified form.

There has been continuing concern that too many prisoners may be held in high-security conditions. In the early days of the policy the dispersal system contained prisoners from all security categories (see King and Elliott, 1978), although, as the control problems of the 1970s developed, lower category prisoners were either transferred to other prisons or else 'recategorised' as B and left where they were. After the May Committee wondered whether the Home Office had got the balance of security right (see King and Morgan, 1980, ch. 3), a working party recommended that greater use of the lower security categories be made (in part to fill up the underused open prisons). In 1983 the Chief Inspector of Prisons argued for the separation of security categorisation procedures from allocation decisions in order to prevent the tendency to define prisoners as suitable for the spaces available; and for the need to review a prisoner's security category as the risks diminished in the course of his sentence. More recently the Control Review Committee suggested that consideration be given to the adoption of a more objective system of security classification, akin to that used in the US Federal Bureau of Prisons, to reduce the risk of 'over-categorising'.

Since our research there have been further developments in security procedures to which we shall return in our concluding comments. But it is appropriate to begin with some brief statement of the population in the different security categories in each of our prisons at the time of our study. Birmingham local prison was the main, though not the only, allocating prison from which the training prisons in our study received their prisoners. Since the population of Birmingham turned over fairly rapidly there is little point in recording its composition in security terms. But it is important to note that much of the security categorisation – apart from category As which were decided at headquarters and a number of prisoners already categorised but passing through Birmingham – was carried out in the Observation, Classification and Allocation Unit at Birmingham. Although matters such as current offence, sentence length, previous convictions and so on properly played a major part in determining security categorisations, we were left in no doubt that the perceptions of staff in the OCA unit, both of the prisoners they dealt with and the prisons to which they could send them, were profoundly influential in categorisation and allocation decisions. In particular, OCA staff tended to distinguish between 'good' and 'bad' prisoners and 'good' and 'bad' prisons when making their dispositions.

OCA staff saw Gartree as a 'bad' dispersal, in contrast to the available alternative at Long Lartin which was seen as 'good', and allocated 'eligible' prisoners accordingly. It seems likely that the perception by OCA staff of Afro-Caribbean prisoners as potential troublemakers may account for the higher proportion of these prisoners at Gartree (14.9 per cent) than Long Lartin (8.9 per cent) – and at the same time illustrates the tendencies to conflate not only security and control, but also categories of 'black' and 'anti-authority', when it comes to making decisions on the ground (McDermott, 1990).

In terms of security proper, 45 prisoners in Gartree, or nearly 15 per cent of the population, were in category A – one of the highest concentrations of such prisoners then to be found in the system. Amongst the category A prisoners a distinction was drawn between those receiving 'high-risk' visits under close observation – some ten prisoners virtually all regarded as 'politicals' involved in Irish or Arab organisations of one kind or another – and the remainder who had normal visits along with other prisoners. The great majority of prisoners, over 83 per cent, were in category B and a further 2% – one of the smallest proportions in the dispersal system – were category C prisoners servicing the prison in various jobs that required a degree of trust.

Nottingham prison was the only category B non-dispersal prison in the region and so questions of reputation hardly arose in allocation decisions. Even so it was clear that a group of prisoners involved in an incident in Stafford – a category C prison – had been transferred to Nottingham on control rather than security grounds. Exactly two-thirds of the Nottingham population were in category B with almost a third in category C and just under 2 per cent in category D. In addition, there was a hostel outside the grounds which, by definition, catered only for category D prisoners.

Featherstone was undoubtedly seen as one of the good category C prisons for the region. As far as allocation from Birmingham was concerned, it received the 'best' of the category C prisoners whilst Stafford received the 'worst'. Featherstone also had a reputation for quickly 'shipping out' to other prisons any prisoners who misbehaved. All the prisoners in the main prison at Featherstone – including some 40 life-sentence prisoners – were category C security, although many staff claimed that the population was getting 'worse' as they received some prisoners, formerly in dispersals, who had been recategorised. At the same time the governor was under pressure, in the light of the working party and the inspectorate reports, to recategorise prisoners as category D wherever possible and send them on to open prisons. In his annual report he claimed only very limited scope for implementing this policy, no doubt in part because of the conflicting demand to maintain the level of activity in the extensive workshops. Indeed within Featherstone, but separate from the main prison, there was also a short-term unit populated by category D prisoners who worked on the prison farm, and it was often difficult to keep this up to strength.

All the prisoners in Ashwell, including 17 life-sentence prisoners, were in category D. But whatever the difficulties in recategorising prisoners for open conditions, there was a feeling amongst some staff at Ashwell that the prison was ceasing to be a 'true' category D prison. It was perhaps inevitable that when Ashwell received the occasional draft of up to 20 prisoners from a category C prison, staff should see them as not 'really' category D prisoners – not in the way that persons originally classified as such in the OCA units were 'real' category Ds. However, it is important to note that the governor reported no change in the number or quality of incidents in the prison that could be regarded as a consequence of the increase in 'lifers' and 'recats' in the Ashwell population.

We asked prisoners whether they regarded their own current security categorisation as appropriate. Only 60 per cent accepted that the way they had been categorised reasonably corresponded to the risks they posed to the public, the police or the state. Not surprisingly, the higher the security category – or more strictly, the higher the security of the prison they were in, for that was more important in practical terms – the less likely were they to regard it as reasonable. Thus nine out of ten prisoners in Ashwell thought this was about right for them, compared to about two-thirds in Featherstone, one-half in Nottingham and only just over one-quarter in Gartree. For most prisoners, as far as they were aware, their security category had not changed in the course of their sentence. But about one-third had been recategorised downwards and nearly one in ten had been recategorised upwards: for two-fifths of them the change of security categorisation had not been explained and did not make any sense.

In order to get a staff perspective on this, we asked officers to say what proportion of the population in their prison should more properly be housed in higher or lower security prisons. Although staff in Nottingham, and especially Featherstone, where there was anxiety about receiving prisoners who had been recategorised, reported that some prisoners should be housed in higher-security prisons, overall these data provided some support for the over-categorisation view – and from a surprising quarter. Thus virtually all our respondents in Gartree thought that some of the prisoners in their charge could be safely housed in less-secure conditions: 64 per cent of officers said that up to a quarter of the population could be decategorised, and 25 per cent thought that up to a half could be at a lower security establishment! In Nottingham nine out of ten officers felt some prisoners could be down-graded: 71 per cent thought this applied to up to a quarter of the population and 18 per cent thought this applied to up to a half. In Featherstone 83 per cent of staff saw scope for transferring up to a quarter of their prisoners to open conditions. In Ashwell over half our respondents thought that some of their prisoners did not need to be in prison at all: 47 per cent applied this to up to a quarter and a further 6 per cent to up to a half their population.

It is hard to summarise our other data in relation to security in any simple way, but it is probably fair to say that the majority of staff and prisoners felt that the level of security – in terms of staffing levels, hardware, closed-circuit television, dog patrols, frequency of cell searching, body searching and so on – was broadly appropriate for the type of prisoners *intended* to be in that prison (as distinct from those whom we have seen were thought to be inappropriately categorised). There was, however, a tendency for prisoners to think it sometimes over the top, especially in Gartree; whereas staff, particularly in Nottingham and in Ashwell, would have liked a somewhat tighter security.

Given the variation in the published average costs for keeping a prisoner for one year in our research prisons – Gartree (dispersal) £24,284; Nottingham (cat. B) £13,312; Featherstone (cat. C) £9724; Ashwell (cat. D) £9256; and Birmingham (local, whose unit costs, of course, were much reduced by overcrowding) £11,024 – it is quite important to get security allocation decisions right. Since the research was completed the latest figures for these prisons show the differential costs between high and low security to have widened still further.

Function 12 requires prison department establishments to 'maintain good order in the interests of the operation of the prison, and to take such steps as are necessary for the safety of its staff and inmates'.

We asked all our respondents whether they rated their prison as safe or dangerous, from the point of view of prisoners and from the point of view of staff. Two general tendencies could be discerned in their replies. First, staff typically perceived their prison to be safer for the prisoners than for themselves, whereas prisoners saw their prison to be about equally safe – or dangerous – for staff as it was for prisoners. Secondly, the proportions of both staff and prisoners who saw their prison as dangerous increased with the security level of the prison. There were, however, some exceptions to these tendencies and the differences between the highest and lowest perceived levels of safety were very marked indeed.

Thus Ashwell and Featherstone, the two lowest-security prisons, were seen as almost universally safe for everyone by both staff and prisoners. At the other extreme Gartree was clearly seen as a dangerous prison. Over half the prisoners saw it as dangerous for themselves and almost as many saw it as dangerous for staff. Nearly half the staff also saw it as a dangerous for prisoners but almost three-quarters of them saw it as dangerous for themselves and fellow officers. Nottingham and Birmingham were generally between these extremes, although we found that there were nearly as many staff in Birmingham who were anxious for their own safety as there were in Gartree. This was probably because Birmingham had the highest level of recorded violence, and also because staff believed that the prison housed large numbers of mentally disturbed offenders.

Although the levels of perceived danger varied widely from prison to prison there was considerable agreement as to which were the most dangerous times and places: unlock, 'slop out' and meal times were seen in all prisons as the times when violent incidents were most likely to occur; and the recesses, which for reasons of delicacy are minimally supervised, and the workshops, because of the ready availability of weapons, were seen as potentially the most dangerous places. There is an additional theme, not found amongst the staff at the lower security prisons in Ashwell and Featherstone, but repeated throughout the higher-security prisons, that staff feel unsafe when out of sight of other officers. Prisoners, everywhere, felt most safe in their own cells: staff, everywhere, felt most safe in their own offices.

At the time of our study, staff at Gartree had recovered considerable confidence following the most recent disturbances in the prison's troubled history as a dispersal prison. The closing-off of parts of the landings to provide emergency exits for staff had contributed to their greater sense of security but there was a continuing uneasiness about supervising certain areas of the prison – particularly the upper landings, darkened TV rooms and so on – which was often handled by joking references of a 'mock macho' kind. Thus a new principal officer told his staff as he left the wing office after discussion of 'no-go' areas in prisons: 'Right, I'm going to the 4s, and I'm going to check the recesses, then I'm going to do that on all the landings, and then I'm going into the TV room and change the channel.' Such a remark would have been unthinkable for a member of staff in Oak Park Heights, a so-called 'new generation' maximum-security facility in Minnesota, with which at this point it is appropriate to draw some comparisons.

Although Oak Park Heights serves as a last-resort institution in a comparatively small state prison system, it houses a population substantially similar to that in Gartree. In recent years it has also successfully contained some of the most 'difficult' prisoners who have been 'boarded out' in Minnesota from the most notorious of United States federal penitentiaries at Marion, Illinois. Oak Park Heights was designed to give a high priority to the safety of staff and prisoners, through the ease of supervision of relatively small groups of prisoners housed in eight 52-bedded units which provide self-contained living, working and recreational accommodation. Identical questions asked in the two prisons revealed that Oak Park Heights was seen to be safer, more secure and more trouble free than Gartree, even though prisoners were out of their cells for 15 hours a day compared to the 9 hours achieved in Gartree. Moreover, Oak Park Heights prisoners enjoyed a much fuller and more highly rated programme of treatment, industry and education, as well as much more effective contact with families and the outside world. In spite of the obvious security features of the design in Oak Park Heights, it was prisoners in Gartree who were the more likely to see security and control measures as 'over the top' (see King, 1991).

It is apparent from these findings that both the design of buildings and the organisation of specific aspects of the daily routine may play important roles in the maintenance of good order and discipline within the prison system. But given that prisons basically involve holding relatively large groups of people against their will under the supervision of relatively small groups of staff, good order also depends fundamentally upon the quality of relationships sustained between these two groups, and a variety of measures that are available to deal with situations when working relationships break down. Our findings in these areas are too complex to summarise here although we have discussed elsewhere some of the stratagems that staff and prisoners deploy to deal with the problems they encounter in their daily concern to survive on the landings (McDermott and King, 1988); and the resort by staff to the use of administrative measures for dealing with so-called 'subversive' or 'control problem' prisoners (King and McDermott, 1990a).

But prisons also have an organised system of rewards and punishments which are intended to help motivate prisoners towards what the authorities consider to be appropriate prison behaviour, although the Control Review Committee questioned whether these actually sent 'the right signals' to achieve their purpose (Home Office, 1984). About three-quarters of all staff and three-quarters of prisoners thought that the system of rewards and punishments was reasonably effective, but this masked some major differences between prisons. The pattern of staff response seemed to reflect particular problems in their own institutions whereas prisoner responses clearly reflected their position in the security hierarchy: almost all our prisoner respondents in Ashwell thought the system was effective compared to four-fifths in Featherstone, two-thirds in Nottingham, and three-fifths in Gartree. On closer examination it seemed to be the case that those who considered the system to be ineffective were responding to the perceived loss of privileges that accompanied a downgrading of security status – thus supporting the reasoning of the Control Review Committee. One of the most important complaints was that prisoners who in higher-security prisons had acquired a place in more-privileged work assignments expected to find themselves in the least-privileged jobs on transfer to lower-security prisons. Regardless of whether they thought the system of rewards and punishments effective or not, there was widespread contempt for both governors' adjudications and Board of Visitors' adjudications – fewer than one in five prisoners regarded the former as fair, and less than two in five thought the latter fair.

CONCLUSIONS

In this study we have explored some of the interconnections between security, control and humane containment. There seems to be little doubt that in many respects the containment offered by the prison system now is less humane than it was two decades ago, and that there has been a widespread deterioration of regimes across the board. This deterioration cannot simply be explained by lack of resources because it has been accompanied by a major growth in staffing. The fact that the staffing increases have occurred mostly in the higher security prisons, including the local prisons, suggests that additional staff have largely been absorbed by the increased demands of security and control on the one hand, and by the court commitment for increased numbers of remand prisoners on the other. There seems reason to believe, moreover, that the measures taken to increase security since the Mountbatten Report, and the use of greater restrictions in an attempt to improve control in the dispersal system since the implementation of the Radzinowicz Report, have themselves contributed directly and indirectly to the deterioration of regimes, without necessarily increasing the sense of safety of either staff or prisoners. Our data suggest that both the design of buildings and the reorganisation of daily routines at unlock, slop out and mealtimes in particular, but with regard to other activities also, may have a considerable part to play in the maintenance of good order and discipline within the prison system. Since our research began the Prison Department has begun to incorporate elements of 'new-generation' thinking – on the design of living units and the circulation of prisoners around the prison – into its prison design briefing system and this is finding its way into the building programme although, ironically, not in maximum-security establishments, which is perhaps where it is most needed. The implications of better-organised routines for good order and discipline remain to be taken up.

The introduction of Fresh Start – primarily a package of new working arrangements for staff – was intended also to produce savings which could then be ploughed back into enhanced regimes to increase the value for money spent on the prison service. Our preliminary return to the five prisons some months after they had been 'Fresh Started' revealed twice as many examples of further deterioration of regimes as it did of improvements and pointed to new sources of difficulty between prison officers and the Home Office. These must be overcome before a properly professional staff can be expected to develop systematically the kinds of relationships with prisoners which are sometimes evident in some parts – and not necessarily the most obvious parts – of the system.

As events transpired, Fresh Start coincided with what might turn out to be two further twists of the downward spiral that links security and control to humane containment – though in itself it can hardly be held responsible for them. First, in April and May 1986 the Prison Officers' Association called for industrial action as part of its strategy to put pressure on the Home Office over the introduction of Fresh Start. There were serious disturbances in many prisons which marked the extension of 'control problems' from the dispersal prisons, where for the most part they had previously been confined, to the lower-security training prisons. By the time Fresh Start had been introduced and we returned to our study prisons, the open prison at Ashwell had been fenced and was described to us as 'low' category C prison; and Featherstone was in the process of becoming a 'high' category C prison. Secondly, on 10 December 1987, some months after Gartree had been on Fresh Start and only one day after we completed our return period of fieldwork, two prisoners escaped by helicopter. There followed a series of immediate measures – from the provision of a new high-security exercise enclosure, through randomised access to outside recreation, to a member of staff assigned to plane-spotting – which applied not just to Gartree but throughout the dispersal system. All these changes had consequences for the regimes.

It should not be thought that all the changes will necessarily be for the worse, because the knee-jerk response to troubles in the prison system and which prevailed through much of the 1970s, while still powerful, is tempered by the thinking enshrined in the report of the Control Review Committee, some of whose recommendations continue to be implemented. Thus, any tightening of security and control procedures in lower-security training prisons has been to some extent off-set by an extension of privileges in an attempt to 'send better signals' as to what the system is about. Similarly, the longer-term response to the Gartree escape is a plan to reduce the size of the dispersal system to six prisons by the mid-1990s, each with a greater concentration of category A prisoners. Meanwhile refinements have been introduced within the category A classification limiting the allocation of certain prisoners to those dispersal prisons with the best security. One consequence of this in Gartree has been that the number of prisoners on restricted visits has doubled as some 'gangsters' have been added to the list of 'politicals'.

Ironically, the 'siege of Strangeways' occurred in a prison which had had one of the worst regimes, and which was just beginning to experience some modest improvements as a result of Fresh Start. It was almost certainly too little and too late.

No one should suppose that getting the balance right between security, control and humane containment can ever be an easy matter. But if the prison service is to emerge from its present crisis into a well-ordered future with a realistic prospect of avoiding trouble, then action is required on three fronts. First, a commitment by the government and the courts to the minimum-use-of-custody principle, which would bring the prison population more closely into line with resources, is a precondition for the establishment of humane regimes – at least in our local prisons. Secondly, a commitment by the prison service to the minimum-use-of-security principle could and should lead not merely to a major reduction in the resort to expensive high-security custody but give scope for changing the attitudes of staff; this would permit the development of more satisfying roles for prison officers.

And thirdly, if some future ESRC research initiative is not to record still greater deterioration in prison regimes, there must be a commitment to legally enforceable standards of custody that would ensure that resources for the prison system are maintained at levels appropriate for the task.

REFERENCES

ACPS (1968), *The Regime for Long-Term Prisoners in Conditions of Maximum Security*, Report of the Advisory Council on the Penal System (Radzinowicz Report) (London: Her Majesty's Stationery Office).

Casale, S. (1984), *Minimum Standards for Prison Establishments* (London: National Association for the Care and Resettlement of Offenders (NACRO)).

Dunbar, I. (1985), *A Sense of Direction* (London: Home Office).

Home Office (1966), *Report of the Inquiry into Prison Escapes and Security* (Mountbatten Report) (London: Her Majesty's Stationery Office) Cmnd. 3175.

Home Office (1968), *Report on the Work of the Prison Department, 1967* (London: Her Majesty's Stationery Office) Cmnd. 3774.

Home Office (1969), *Report on the Work of the Prison Department, 1968* (London: Her Majesty's Stationery Office) Cmnd. 4186.

Home Office (1979), *Report of the Committee of Inquiry into the United Kingdom Prison Services* (May Report) (London: Her Majesty's Stationery Office) Cmnd. 7673.

Home Office (1984), *Managing the Long-Term Prison System*, the Report of the Control Review Committee (London: Her Majesty's Stationery Office).

Home Office (1987), *Report on the Work of the Prison Service, 1986–7* (London: Her Majesty's Stationery Office) Cm. 246.

King, Roy D. (1985), 'Control in prisons', in M. Maguire, J. Vagg and R. Morgan (eds), *Accountability and Prisons* (London: Tavistock).

King, Roy D. (1987), 'New generation prisons, the prison building programme, and the future of the dispersal policy', in A. E. Bottoms and R. Light (eds), *Problems of Long Term Imprisonment* (Aldershot: Gower).

King, Roy D. (1991), 'Maximum security custody in Britain and the U.S.A.: a study of Gartree and Oak Park Heights', *British Journal of Criminology*, 31(2), 126–52.

King, Roy D. and Elliott, K. W. (1978), *Albany: Birth of a Prison – End of an Era* (London: Routledge & Kegan Paul).

King, Roy D. and McDermott, Kathleen (1989), 'British prisons 1970–87: the ever-deepening crisis', *British Journal of Criminology*, 29(2), 107–28.

King, Roy D. and McDermott, Kathleen (1990a), 'My geranium is subversive: notes on the management of trouble in prisons', *British Journal of Sociology*, 41(4), 445–71.

King, Roy D. and McDermott, Kathleen (1990b), 'A Fresh Start: managing the prison service', in R. Reiner and M. Cross (eds), *Beyond Law and Order* (London: Macmillan).

King, Roy D. and Morgan, Rod (1976), *A Taste of Prison* (London: Routledge & Kegan Paul).

King, Roy D. and Morgan, Rod (1980), *The Future of the Prison System* (London: Gower).

McDermott, Kathleen (1990), 'We have no problem: the experience of racism in prison', *New Community*, **16**(2), 213–28.

McDermott, Kathleen and King, Roy D. (1988), 'Mind games: where the action is in prisons', *British Journal of Criminology*, **28**(3), 357–77.

McDermott, Kathleen and King, Roy D. (1989), 'A Fresh Start: the enhancement of prison regimes', *Howard Journal of Criminal Justice*, **28**(3), 161–76.

Mountbatten, Lord (1972), Interview with Dr Bolt, *Prison Officers' Magazine*, **62**(8), 86–7.

Train, C. (1985), 'Management accountability in the prison service', in M. Maguire, J. Vagg and R. Morgan (eds), *Accountability and Prisons* (London: Tavistock).

5 Researching the Discretions to Charge and to Prosecute

ROGER LENG, MICHAEL McCONVILLE and
ANDREW SANDERS

Prominent miscarriages of justice such as the Confait affair and the cases of
the 'Guildford Four' and the 'Maguire Seven' have focused public attention
on the processes by which alleged offences are investigated and alleged
offenders prosecuted. These cases raise serious doubts about the ability of
the criminal trial to expose the faults and errors which may be built into a
case by the very processes of investigation and prosecution. They further
suggest that the problem is not generated simply by corrupt or illegal
practices of police and prosecutors, but rather that miscarriages of justice
may arise also through currently *lawful* practices. Miscarriage of justice
thus may be seen as an inherent feature of our present adversarial system,
in which control of a case in its early stages is vested in well-resourced state
agencies whose function is to prepare and present a case for the prosecution.

This point was recognised by both the Inquiry under Sir Henry Fisher
which considered the Confait case and the Royal Commission on Criminal
Procedure which followed in 1981. The reforms inspired by the Royal
Commission's Report – the Police and Criminal Evidence Act 1984 (PACE)
and the Prosecution of Offences Act 1985 (POOA) – were presented as
introducing fairness, openness and accountability and as strengthening the
rights of suspects whilst at the same time enhancing police powers of arrest,
detention, search and seizure. The underlying assumption was that criminal
justice personnel, and the process itself, would be responsive to changes in
the law. The system, it was thought, could be changed by legal reform.

As well as seeking to minimise future miscarriages of justice, the reforms of the 1980s sought to address two other major concerns. First, that
prosecutions were instituted too readily. This led to weak cases reaching
court and forced many people to undergo trial on insufficient evidence,
wasting the time of police, lawyers and courts, and having knock-on effects
such as increasing pre-trial delays. Secondly, that the police rarely consider
alternatives to prosecution even though prosecution might have adverse
consequences in starting an offender on a criminal career, and even though
the objectives of deterrence and rehabilitation might be achieved by other
measures, such as cautioning.

The principle that an individual should be prosecuted only where it is in the public interest to do so (that is, where there is no acceptable alternative) was expressed in guidelines issued by the Attorney General in 1983, and repeated in guidelines on cautioning issued by the Home Office in 1985 and in the Code for Crown Prosecutors issued by the Director of Public Prosecutions in 1986. The responsibility for not prosecuting weak cases and for operating the public-interest criterion is shared between the police and the Crown Prosecution Service (CPS), with the CPS acting as ultimate gatekeeper by virtue of its power to veto any prosecution.

THE RESEARCH

A full assessment of the prosecution process would focus on whether or not its checks and balances are effective to avoid miscarriages of justice; on whether weak cases are weeded out before trial; and on whether cases are diverted where there is no public interest in pursuing a prosecution. The more general theoretical question concerns the relationship between legal rules and the behaviour of officials to whom those rules relate: specifically, how far police discretion is, and can be, constrained by legal and other rules (for instance, on the prosecution of weak or cautionable cases); and how far police control of the prosecution process can be attenuated by creating institutions like the CPS. This was the policy and theoretical context for our study.

It built on earlier research which indicates that prosecution decision-making is largely determined by 'working rules' of the police which are geared towards particular policing goals. Cases are constructed by the police, in the sense that the police choose their suspects, choose to collect certain evidence and have choice over the questions asked at interview. The police then have control over the way the resulting evidence is presented and interpreted (McBarnet, 1981). This measure of control allows the police to anticipate and determine later decisions by prosecutors (McConville and Baldwin, 1981; Sanders, 1985). McBarnet (1981) has argued that if this degree of police control is unhealthy, then it is the permissive structure of legal rules that is at fault, rather than police policies as such: the police, she argued, only do what the law allows them to do. The specific aims of our research were to assess: the actual 'working rules' (Smith and Gray, 1983) which guide the police, and their relationship to legal rules; how far the new guidelines on evidential standards and cautioning policy changed police charging practices; and how far the CPS is independent of the police.

The fieldwork began in 1986. With the co-operation of three English police forces and the CPS we took random samples of non-motoring arrests and reports for summons in six police stations until a total of 120 adult and 60 juvenile cases per station was reached (producing a total sample of 1080 cases). We had access to the case files at every stage, and also interviewed all the officers involved where possible (achieving success rates of 91.4 per cent for arresting officers and 48.4 per cent for custody officers). Where cases went to court or were otherwise dealt with by the CPS we interviewed all prosecutors handling the case. This research methodology enabled us to test official accounts against those which police and prosecutors gave us in interview and to uncover the motivations of the various actors and the process of case construction.

WORKING RULES AND LEGAL RULES

The law does not tell the police which criminal laws to enforce, which people are suspects, which areas to patrol, which citizen complaints and reports to act upon or which alleged offences to prosecute. In relation to each of these matters the police have broad discretion with which the courts have declined to interfere on the principle of 'constabulary independence'. Research on police discretion (for example, Smith and Gray, 1983; Dixon *et al.*, 1989) shows that the result is the opportunity for the police to set their own priorities and follow their own hunches. The legal limits on discretion are vague. Stop and search on the streets, and arrest, for example, may be done only on the basis of 'reasonable suspicion' (PACE, ss. 1, 24). This concept is so notoriously vague that even the Royal Commission, which commended it, could not define it (para. 3.25).

Similarly broad discretion is conferred upon the police and CPS in relation to prosecution decision-making. The official guidelines provide two main criteria. The first is evidential sufficiency: prosecution should only take place when there is a 'realistic prospect of conviction'. The second is that, even if there is sufficient evidence, there is no presumption in favour of prosecution: it should only take place when in the 'public interest'. This is indicated by various criteria, including seriousness of offence, previous record, interests of the victim and particular characteristics of the offender such as age or illness (Sanders, 1985).

Because the discretion allowed to the police within the law is so broad, we were aware of the pitfalls of seeking to explain police behaviour purely in terms of the legal rules and official criteria, despite McBarnet's (1981) argument (to which we shall return in the Conclusion). Instead, by analysing officers' own accounts of their actions and decisions, we attempted to discover the social or working rules which routinely inform their decisions without dismissing the influence of legal rules and official guidelines. It was the *relationships* between official rules and police working rules which particularly interested us.

Other research has suggested that police discretion is substantially influenced by the demands of citizens. Thus, police work is seen as being essentially 'reactive' to citizens' complaints, rather than being 'proactive' in the sense of self-motivated work to seek out crime and criminals (Shapland and Vagg, 1988). However, our research demonstrates that the fact that a lot of police work is reactive does not prevent the operation of police working rules: even where the police react by attending an incident at the behest of a citizen, their freedom of action thereafter is unfettered. For example, it is well documented that where the police are called to incidents of 'domestic' violence, they reserve the right to make decisions about arrest and prosecution according to particular values and standards of their own (Hanmer *et al.*, 1989).

Since we discuss working rules systematically elsewhere (McConville *et al.*, 1991), our purpose here is to set out some major determinants of police behaviour, their consequences for prosecution decisions, and their relationship with legal and other official rules. One major working rule was expressed by an officer in this way: 'When you get to know an area, and see a villain about at 2.00 am in the morning, you will always stop him to see what he is about' (Case AH-A115). 'Previous' is sometimes all the police have as the basis for a stop or arrest. In other cases, the knowledge of 'previous' makes the officer follow the suspect to see if crime or suspicious acts are committed. In Case AT-A047, for instance, the police were in a street market looking for pickpockets when 'up walks this chap who we knew was one of the suspects . . . you tend to follow the ones you know'. In very serious cases, such as a rape investigation taking place in Area AT (one of our six police stations) many suspects were arrested purely on the basis of 'previous' in order to verify alibis and take blood samples.

Another important working rule is that order and authority be maintained. This has been documented in earlier research (Sanders, 1985), but our research shows that the power of this working rule has not been diminished by official guidelines. Thus the arresting officer in Case AT-A053 said of the defendant:

> He had to be Jack the Lad and wanted to be put down. So I put him
> down. . . . I grabbed him and arrested him.
> RES: On what basis?"

AO: Well, it's hard to explain. . . . You get him off the streets and make the residents happy.

There are numerous similar examples from other areas: 'We can't have people going around pushing police officers when they feel like it' (Case CC-A085); '. . . refused his details and challenged me to arrest him, so I did' (Case CE-A983).

Victims play an important role in relation to the citizen initiation of crime detection which we discussed earlier. However, police working rules distinguish influential from non-influential victims, and the concept of the victim is itself often a matter of police construction (McConville *et al.*, 1991, ch. 2). The more powerful and 'respectable' the victim, the more likely it is that his or her interests will be reflected in the action taken by the police. Quite minor cases of disorder or alleged dishonesty would result in arrest and charge where they concerned powerful victims, typically businesses. Purely inter-personal disputes not involving influential victims, typically cases of domestic violence, would be far less likely to result in arrest and charge. The differential treatment of these two categories of case could not be justified either on grounds of seriousness or of evidential sufficiency. Consider the following two cases, the first of which resulted in a prosecution, the second in a decision to take no further action.

Three youths were involved in a dispute about the size of their bill in a restaurant. The manager summoned a police constable who arrested the youths after they refused to pay the sum demanded by the restaurant. The youths were prosecuted but the case was later dropped because of lack of evidence of dishonesty. Commenting on the case the arresting officer said that: 'I feel that this matter would not have gone this far if [the defendants'] attitudes towards Pizza Hut staff and the police had been different.'   (Case CC-A074/75/76)

A man had been drinking and was threatening his girlfriend in public. He had already struck her and, said the arresting officer: 'She had a swollen face, I believe she had a black eye, and she was in a very distressed situation.' As the officer explained, when the officer arrived, the man ignored police advice, became 'threatening towards the police . . . abusive and started fighting with police officers and had to be arrested for his behaviour (including damage to the police car)'. He had an extensive criminal record for assault, among other matters.   (Case CC-A052)

This officer's account in the second case implies that the man would not have been arrested merely for the assault on his girl friend had he not behaved badly towards the police. Moreover, the custody officer did not feel that he should have been arrested anyway. He decided within 20 minutes that no further action would be taken against the man on the basis that this was a domestic incident which was 'just a flash in the pan . . . would have calmed down on its own . . . . When he stood in front of me [he] was quite reasonable.'

As Case CC-A052 shows, prosecution decisions do not automatically follow on from arrest decisions. In fact, around half of all arrested persons are not prosecuted (40 per cent of adults, and 65 per cent of juveniles). Some – juveniles in particular – are cautioned, but in many cases there is a formal police decision to take no further action (nfa). The evidential threshold for arrest – reasonable suspicion – is less stringent than that for prosecution (the 'realistic prospect of conviction'). Thus, even where there are real grounds for suspicion justifying the arrest, further evidence may be required before a prosecution can be brought. As our research discloses, many arrests are made on hardly any evidence at all, for example, all of the arrests made in the rape inquiry in Area AT. In many such cases no further action is the expected and inevitable outcome. In many instances the police are sure of the suspect's innocence, the arrest being only a convenient way of holding the suspect whilst verifying this.

There are other reasons, though, for non-prosecution. Where suspects are arrested because they are 'known' to the police, 'deals' are particularly important. The police frequently allow 'little fish' to escape prosecution in order to catch 'big fish'. In Case BK-A114, for instance, D, who was an informant, admitted stealing from a fellow lodger. According to the officer in charge, no further action was taken 'in view of the fact that he could be useful to us' in the future. This was revealed to us in interview, but was not the 'official' reason recorded on the file. This case well demonstrates the need to look beyond the official guidelines and the official record in order to discover the reasons for police action.

The irrelevance of official rules also becomes apparent in this context. Many suspects who escape prosecution through 'deals' are cautioned instead, particularly for drugs offences. When the police raid premises looking for drugs they seek the conviction of 'dealers' rather than mere 'buyers'. In both Areas AT and CE, those buyers who were prepared to give evidence against the 'dealers' were cautioned or nfa'd. Yet the cautions did not fit the official guidelines in any way, for the police did not consider offence seriousness, previous record or other personal characteristics. Cautions were used as bargaining counters. Also, in these and other cases, the police did not secure confessions to the offences cautioned despite very clear preconditions in the guidelines to this effect. Sanders and Bridges

(1990) found a similar example of a youth accused of deception who had 'form as long as your arm' who was cautioned in exchange for information. Again, these reasons were rarely recorded on paper, and could only be ascertained through interview with the officers involved.

A reason for non-prosecution in many other cases is that prosecution serves no police interest. Sometimes this is because the arrest was made simply to mollify the victim (especially in 'domestics'), and sometimes because a suspect who failed to respect authority on the street became more contrite as a result of arrest. Thus in Case CC-A052 (above) the domestic violence was not considered to warrant prosecution, and the suspect's disrespectful street behaviour was overborne by his later co-operative attitude to the custody officer. The suspect was therefore nfa'd. When arrests are made to satisfy entrepreneur-victims, the 'need' to prosecute is reduced if the suspect pays the victim back. Thus in Case BK-A014, the arresting officer said: 'We did a deal. He had £10 in his possession and agreed to take it down to the garage', hence there was nfa. And when arrests are made to mollify domestic victims, cautions are given for injuries which would, in other circumstances, lead to prosecution.

The same is true for positive prosecution decisions. Rather than systematically applying the tests set out earlier, in adult cases the police simply operate a presumption in favour of prosecution, despite the official guidelines' presumption against it. Thus both evidentially weak and policy-weak cases are frequently prosecuted. This can be demonstrated in many ways. For current purposes one illustration of each must suffice.

First, well over half of the cases dropped by the CPS were identified first as weak by senior police officers reviewing the case after the custody officer charged; these cases were, in other words, weak from the start. Prosecutors were frequently scathing about police standards in this respect (McConville *et al.*, 1991, ch. 8). Thus in Case CC-A118 the prosecutor expressed regret to the police at dropping the case. He explained: 'It's all PR. It's another way of saying "You should never have charged this man in the first place".' While the charging of some of these cases was simply error, some cases were prosecuted in full knowledge of the evidential weakness. This was occasionally done to punish the 'criminal'. In an alleged unlawful sexual intercourse case where the evidence was very weak but where the defendant had been in custody for several months, the officer in charge said: 'If he did it he's had some punishment. If he did it, of course, it's not enough. But it's some.' More often it is done in the hope of securing a guilty plea to the original or lesser offence.

Secondly, the Code for Crown Prosecutors suggests that cases in which absolute or conditional discharges are likely are, *prima facie*, suitable for caution. A total of 31 out of 288 sentenced adults (10.8 per cent) were so sentenced. Over half of these were judged by us to be cautionable. Yet we found that police officers rarely considered cautioning adults. When they did, it was usually in the types of circumstance discussed earlier which are not envisaged by the guidelines. The inconsistent applications of the 'public interest' guidelines are only inconsistent in terms of official criteria. In terms of police values there is no inconsistency.

At first glance it might appear that the presumption in favour of prosecution does not operate in juvenile cases: 37.8 per cent of our juvenile sample were cautioned or warned, as against 35 per cent who were prosecuted. However, the police operate an informal tariff by which prosecution normally follows for juvenile suspects who have previously been cautioned either once or twice. The power of the tariff is demonstrated by the fact that for more than one-third of the juveniles who were prosecuted, the decision to charge was made without any reference to special juvenile liaison procedures. Home Office guidelines encourage consultation with other agencies and consideration of personal factors in all juvenile cases, but the police regard all this as irrelevant in cases where *they consider* prosecution to be the only option. Thus, high rates of cautioning do not indicate that presumptive prosecution has been displaced in favour of individualised discretionary decision-making. Rather, the presumption in favour of prosecution is simply deferred rather than being abandoned.

THE ELEMENTS OF THE CONSTRUCTED CASE

The discussion so far has treated as unproblematic the notion that cases may be 'evidentially weak' or 'cautionable'. But this is not the case. Neither the strength of the evidence nor factors indicative of caution are inherent, objectively ascertainable features of a case which wait to be revealed by either prosecution or defence. Rather, both the evidence and the existence (or not) of factors indicative of caution are products of police work in constructing the case. The techniques of case construction include seeking out (or not) particular types of evidence, accepting or rejecting evidence which is offered to the police by suspect or witness, the generation of evidence by asking particular questions in interview, and the evaluation of facts. These techniques apply equally to evidence which tends to prove an offence and evidence which relates to the issues of whether or not it is in the public interest to prosecute.

To describe a case as a 'construction' is not pejorative and does not imply criticism. Case construction is not peculiar to the police and is necessarily a feature of a system for adjudicating or resolving disputes (Nelken, 1983). In an adversary system in which each side must pursue just one side of the story, case construction inevitably becomes a partial and partisan process. In what follows we seek to describe and illustrate some of the techniques of case construction which we observed.

Confession Evidence

Interrogation is the principal investigative strategy employed by the police (McConville and Baldwin, 1981). In order to maximise confessions, the police seek to control both interrogations *per se* and the broad environment in which interrogations take place. This means securing automatic detention following arrest, control over access to solicitors, control over written records of custody and interrogation, and manipulating unsupervised interrogation – in the car, in the cell and so forth – rather than relying upon the formal recorded interrogation (McConville *et al.*, 1991, chs 3 and 4; Sanders and Bridges, 1990). Interrogation takes place on police territory, on police terms, and at the pace of the police. As the PACE Code of Practice governing detention states, a police officer is 'entitled to question any person from whom he thinks useful information can be obtained. . . . A person's declaration that he is unwilling to reply does not alter this entitlement' (Code C, Note 1B).

The police use many different 'tactics' to ensure confessions (Irving, 1980). Trickery, deception, fear, 'Nice-Guy/Nasty-Guy' methods and so forth are all common. Even where the interrogation is not 'oppressive', so as to render any confession inadmissible (PACE, s. 76), the conditions are created for directly pressuring suspects into speaking. Thus the Royal Commission accepted that the concept of the 'voluntary' confession was meaningless. Very large numbers of suspects are either silent or deny the alleged offence(s) initially, but then make partial or complete confessions. Pressure is inevitable, for the essence of interrogation is to overcome the suspect's unwillingness to speak. Some officers accept this: 'Sometimes it's necessary to shout at people, especially the ones who are abusive and you know are restless, and the heat's on and you have to keep up the pressure' (Case CC-A003). The primary purpose of police tactics of pressure and trickery in interrogation is to induce true confessions. However, precisely these tactics may also generate false confessions (as in the Confait and Guildford cases) or, more commonly, statements which are misleading in that they reflect a prior police view of what happened rather than the suspect's own recollections.

Psychologists have distinguished two types of false confession. A 'coerced-compliant' confession occurs where the suspect confesses for some instrumental purpose such as obtaining bail or to relieve the pressure upon him or her, but knows throughout the falsity of the confession. A 'coerced-internalised' confession occurs where the suspect confesses because he has been persuaded that he really is guilty of the crime (Gudjonsson and Mackeith, 1988). But our research suggests an important third category: the 'coerced-passive' confession. Here police questioning induces suspects to adopt the confession form without necessarily understanding the legal significance of what they are saying or accepting. The police rarely ask simple information-seeking questions; rather, questioning is usually directive in nature, and aimed at proving the case. For example, 'the suspect was alleged to have damaged a car windscreen. He had been drinking heavily. He said that in the course of a row, he had swung his arm out "and hit the windscreen and it broke" ' (Case CC-A002).

POLICE: Did you intend to smash the windscreen?
SUSPECT: No.
POLICE: So you just swung your hand out in a *reckless* manner? [emphasis supplied]
SUSPECT: yes, that's it, just arguing.
POLICE: Why did you hit the window in the first place?
SUSPECT: Just arguing, *reckless*, it wasn't intentional to break it . . . [emphasis supplied]

The suggestion of recklessness is first implanted by the police as a favourable, exculpatory alternative to the defendant, who accepts it as such and then adopts it. However, recklessness is a term of art. It is part of the definition of the offence with which the man was charged (criminal damage), which is why the police sought the defendant's acceptance of this description of his actions, even though he was not using the term in the technical sense, but rather was using the term colloquially to support a plea that the breakage was accidental. In providing him with the terminology in which to press his 'excuse', the police constructed a key element of the case. Having made this key strategic gain, the officer does not explore the matter further, for to do so would be to run the risk of showing that the man had used the term 'reckless' in a sense quite different from that contemplated in law. Here is another example:

POLICE: How did you take it?
SUSPECT: I just put it in my shopping bag.

POLICE: Then what did you do?
SUSPECT: Walked out of the store.
POLICE: So you stole the bag. Is that correct?
SUSPECT: Yes!

Again, once the suspect has agreed to some act or acts, the police attribute the necessary state of mind and any other legal requirements of guilt by a 'question' which purports to *summarise* the legal effect of what the suspect has related: '*So* you stole . . . '.

There are many other examples which we could give (McConville *et al.*, 1991, ch. 4). The point, though, is that the 'facts' which supply 'strength' or 'weakness' are themselves created by questioning. This is recognised by official actors, as in this request from the CPS to the police: 'Please proceed as charged – theft. But could someone please advise [the store detective] not to say "I believe you forgot to pay" when apprehending shoplifters' (Case CC-A069). Such questions from store detectives create weak facts (the defence that the theft was not deliberate), rather than evidential strength. The choice of what types of fact to create lies with the police and other enforcement agencies.

Exculpatory Evidence

Many suspects deny allegations and provide an alternative story. The police sometimes check these stories, but usually only when they are genuinely undecided about whether to arrest and charge in the first place. The purpose of interrogation is to provide support for the police case, not to elicit the suspect's side of the story. Thus lines of defence provided by suspects are considered irrelevant and are ignored or argued away.

> The suspect was named as a person who was involved in disorder in a town centre on a Saturday evening following a football match. When arrested he told the police that he had spent the evening in a neighbouring town, had gone to the cinema and then returned home. He also named two people who were visiting his mother who could vouch for the fact that he had returned home at 9.50 pm and he also offered to describe what both films were about. The interviewer ignored his offer to describe the two films. The man was charged with threatening behaviour. At trial no evidence was offered after it became apparent that the two named alibi witnesses would support his story.   (Case CCA-A043)

In several acquittals the weakness in the case related to evidence initially offered by the suspect in interrogation but which was not followed up by the police. So not only do the police create strength in cases, they also (by omission through laziness, overconfidence or whatever) create weakness. The resources of the defence are, however, limited. Defendants cannot always follow up their alibis. Some leads are therefore just not checked out. So in one case where the suspect claimed that he did not take part in the offence, and cited two onlookers who could back him up, no one produced the onlookers and the defendant was convicted.

Frequently there is no clear line to be drawn between exculpatory and mitigatory statements. The claim that damage was accidental or that articles were taken when under stress could be both exculpatory (denial of criminal intent) or mitigatory (excuses provided but no legal justification). The latter often provide the basis for cautioning on 'public interest' grounds. Consequently, police interrogation methods which aim to create the strongest possible police case, and to avoid encouraging or checking up on excuses, create not just confessions but also negative any public interest in non-prosecution. Thus in most minor prosecutions it is impossible to judge the cautionability or otherwise of the case because the relevant information is simply not provided in the file. Prosecution becomes inevitable in such cases.

Unverified Police Evidence

Verifiability has been central to many of the problems of criminal justice. Prior to PACE, the police were not required to record interrogation precisely, and confessions were usually contained in the form of written statements by suspects. Allegations of fabrication were frequent. In an attempt to reduce both fabrication and the allegations, PACE and the Code now require contemporaneous recording (by hand or tape) of formal police station interrogations. However, the Code does not forbid 'questioning' in certain informal settings (at time of arrest; in the police car, and so on) and our research found that many conversations with accused persons in the police station are not recorded because the police choose not to characterise them as formal interviews.

Because the police may still rely in evidence on things said by a suspect in an informal setting, the scope for 'verballing' the suspect (attributing to him or her an admission which was not actually made) remains. It is notable that in our research sample the police often alleged that admissions had been made at the time of arrest where the suspect either completely denied the offence in formal interview or said nothing.

A further means of ensuring the creation of evidence favourable to the police case is the practice of using informal 'chats' with a suspect as a means of structuring the interview in advance. Such 'off-the-record' meetings between police and suspect are restricted by PACE, which requires the custody officer to refuse informal access to the suspect and to record all meetings which do take place. However, officers whom we interviewed indicated that such informal contacts were a regular part of police work and a vital tool in the interrogation process. This is confirmed by Sanders and Bridges (1990). The significance of these informal chats is that inducements and deals may be made which could not be made on the record or perhaps with a solicitor present, and that by preparing the way for the formal interrogation, the officer can anticipate and avoid the possibility of the suspect suggesting any form of defence on the record.

There are many other opportunities which the police have to construct evidence. Some were given to us in this interview:

> The officer told us that for threatening behaviour the police would always say that women and children were present, as someone had to be likely to be afraid for the charge to succeed. He said: 'If we know they're guilty we make sure they are.' If he saw a car with a smashed window and a man walking down the road ahead with a radio which he dropped when he saw the police, and if he also denied carrying the radio when apprehended, he (the officer) would say in his evidence that he saw the man break into the car and take the radio. The man, he said, would inevitably say that he had found the radio on the street: 'That might be true but it would be 99 per cent certain that he'd broken in and taken it.' (Case AT-A107).

Implications

When we use terms like 'weak' and 'strong' we generally accept that there is a subjective element in these evaluations. However, it is not just evaluation of evidence that is subjective, but its very creation. Confessions and incriminating statements are created through questions aimed at those results. Exculpatory and mitigatory statements are not created, or are undermined, with the same sense of purpose. And when no confessions are made, or they are unsatisfactory in some way, the police can 'verbal' suspects to fill the gaps. When other evidence is needed the police can often provide that too.

The Royal Commission hoped to deal with these problems by requiring the police to record everything they did. However, it is the police who record everything that the police do. This is fraught with danger, and the written record takes on an existence and evidential quality of its own. If a defendant says he was visited in a cell by an officer, this is hard enough to prove in the face of denials from the officer. If the custody record does not record such a visit, proof is made harder still. Similarly, police statements about what they claimed to see suspects do, whether they were drunk or not, or insolent or not, all have stronger evidential value when written at the time the events in question allegedly occurred.

If weakness and strength are created by the police through written files there is a further implication: later decision-makers vetting those files for weakness and strength, and cautionability or otherwise, will have to do so on the basis of the evidence which has already been constructed for specific purposes by the officers in the case. Cases which fall at later hurdles would, then, be expected to be not those which are intrinsically weak or cautionable (if we can talk in such terms); rather, they would be cases which are constructed poorly. In our research we looked at the work of senior officers who reviewed cases, juvenile liaison bureaux who decide whether or not to caution, and the CPS who decide whether or not to continue prosecutions initiated by the police. Here there is only space to discuss the CPS, but the first two are discussed elsewhere (McConville *et al.*, 1991, ch. 7).

THE ROLE OF THE CROWN PROSECUTION SERVICE (CPS)

The CPS possesses the power to veto any prosecution and is, therefore, the ultimate gatekeeper of the criminal courts. The CPS is formally independent of the police, but is completely dependent in the senses that the police are its sole client and are its only source of information about a case.

The CPS can seek to justify its existence by pointing to the large number of cases which are dropped on the basis of evidential weakness. However, it is in fact rare for the CPS to drop a case following their initial review where the police wish to prosecute. Thus, in many dropped cases the evidential weakness had already been signalled by the earlier review by the police. In Case CC-A085/6/7, for instance, the police reviewer commented: 'I cannot see how the theft charge can be pursued'; and in Case CC-A074/7/6: 'I am not happy with the evidence.' A reluctance to drop cases with which the police wished to proceed was apparent in many cases. Thus, in Case BW-A013 following the defendant's acquittal the prosecutor admitted to us that this was not unexpected because the evidence was a bit 'thin' although there was a case to answer. Here is a similar case:

> The CPS reviewer described the evidence in a public order case as a 'bit thin'. He speculated that the defendant was arrested just to get him off the

street, and expressed sympathy for the police in difficult public-order situations. He prosecuted, but the defendant, not surprisingly, was acquitted. (Case CC-A027)

There are several reasons why the CPS is willing to prosecute cases it perceives to be weak. One, revealed in the case above, is that the CPS empathises with police working rules and therefore avoids undermining them. The CPS also pursues weak cases because, while weak cases which are contested *may* end in failure, *all* dropped cases by definition end in failure. Thus in Case AH-A020 the prosecutor complained bitterly to us about poor police investigation. He expected to lose the case, but in fact the defendant was convicted.

Another reason is that so many defendants plead guilty. Rather than dropping *weak* cases, the CPS drops cases that are likely to *fail*:

The CPS reviewer wrote that the charge was very weak. He advised that the case be dropped if the defendant pleaded not guilty. (Case AT-A109)

The CPS suggested that if the defendant pleaded not guilty, they bargain over compensation instead of proceeding with prosecution. (Case BW-A083)

No cases in our research sample were dropped on public-interest grounds alone, apart from those in which the defendants were already being prosecuted for more serious offences or were already in prison. Yet, even according to the Code's own indicator of cautionability – a nominal court penalty – many cases should have been so dropped. Most of the time it did not occur to prosecutors to drop cases on the grounds of cautionability. One prosecutor explained that prosecutors start from the position that people should be prosecuted if there is sufficient evidence. Thus, the pro-prosecution presumption of the police is maintained by the CPS. On one very rare occasion when a prosecutor did suggest dropping such a case the police objected so strongly that that prosecutor's senior overruled him and personally decided that the case should be prosecuted.

The police anticipate and control review by the CPS by the control which they exercise over case construction. Thus, as discussed above, the police routinely regard exculpatory evidence as irrelevant and rarely follow up defences suggested in interviews or by other evidence. A consequence of this is that at the time when the prosecutor determines whether there is a realistic prospect of conviction it may not be apparent that a defence may be raised. Similarly, with the question of public interest: the Code requires prosecutors to consider such matters as the defendant's attitude to the offence, whether he or she was ill or under stress, or was provoked. But in terms of police objectives there is no reason to collect this information, or, if known, to include it in the file. In many cases in the research, information relevant to cautionability was known to the police but not recorded, and the CPS approved of the decision to prosecute in total ignorance of it.

Since the CPS tends to identify with police values, as embodied in police working rules, the police rarely find it difficult to persuade CPS to prosecute cases which may be otherwise dubious. Here is another example:

> An 18-year-old took a bulb from the civic Christmas tree. He was charged with theft. The police told CPS that 'It would be nice if publicity could be given to the matter with a view to deterring others from acting in the same manner.' This told the CPS that what might, in normal circumstances, be too trivial to prosecute was, in its context, relatively serious. The CPS prosecuted.   (Case BW-A083)

The CPS is essentially reactive. Rather than setting its own prosecution policy, it sees its job as to carry out efficiently police prosecution policy. Thus, in Case CC-A108 a woman was charged with criminal damage for smashing a social services office window. She explained to the police that she did this because they would not find her a new home. She had left her former home as a result of being raped by her landlord. Not only did the CPS not regard this as an extenuating circumstance justifying dropping the case on 'public interest' grounds, but the reviewer did not consider asking the police to investigate the rape allegation. In this case, as in many others, the reviewer – when asked – assumed that the police had good reasons for acting in the way they did. In reality it does not matter to the CPS what the police's reasons are. As long as there is sufficient evidence, a conviction can be recorded.

CONCLUSION

The assumption underlying the reforms of the 1980s is that police and prosecutors are susceptible to control by law and administrative guidelines, and that the practices of these agencies may be changed by tightening the law and increasing the scope of administrative guidance. Thus, it has been assumed that national policies on diverting offenders from prosecution and not prosecuting weak cases can be operationalised by Home Office cautioning guidelines and the Code for Crown Prosecutors. Similarly, it is assumed that the problem of miscarriages of justice can be addressed by tightening the legal regulation of police investigation and by requiring the police to respect and enforce certain protective rights conferred on suspects.

Our major finding is that these assumptions are wrong. Legislators and government policy-makers have ignored the powerful working rules, linked to the particular goals of the police, which shape police conduct and decision-making. Where legal rules and working rules conflict, the latter will prevail unless there is both a real possibility of being discovered and effective sanctions for breach of those legal rules (Smith and Gray, 1983). Without these possibilities, legal rules become merely presentational devices which inform the police how their decisions must be presented in order to be in apparent conformity with the law.

The law therefore facilitates police conduct and decision-making according to police working rules, by providing a means of both obscuring what actually occurred and of justifying police action. Thus, the working rule that all arrestees may be detained for interview is facilitated by the legal rule which tells the police that detention is lawful provided that the custody officer writes a certain verbal formula on the custody record. The conflict between the legal rule that all interviews with a suspect must be recorded and the working rule that interviews should be preceded by an informal chat is similarly resolved. The informal chat is simply not noted on the custody record as having taken place. This bypasses the need to record what was said. Custody officers are willing to break the law routinely in these ways because the power to make these decisions is conferred on them by law, with no system of effective review and no sanction for abuse of the discretion which they exercise.

As it is assumed that the police will respect the laws which regulate them, so it is assumed that the conduct of prosecutors will be governed by the principles laid out in their Code. This ignores both the relative dependence of the CPS on the police and the influence of the prosecutors' own working rules. Decisions about evidential sufficiency and public interest can be anticipated and controlled by the way in which the case presented to the CPS is constructed by the police. Thus, the evidence of witnesses which contradicts the police case *may never be seen* by the prosecutor. Where the police have decided that a prosecution is appropriate they have no motivation to seek or include information which might support caution or non-prosecution.

For prosecutors the primary working rule is a presumption in favour of prosecution, at least in those cases in which the police have indicated that they wish to proceed. They are content to proceed with weak cases unless the weakness is so blatant that there would be absolutely no question of a conviction, and questions of public interest rarely intrude on their decision-making. This failure rigorously to apply criteria of evidential sufficiency and public interest arises from the absence of any incentive to do so, or sanction for failure to do so. For a service which judges itself, and expects to be judged by others, according to its conviction rate (Crown Prosecution Service, 1989; National Audit Office, 1989) there is no reason to drop provable cases simply on public-interest grounds. In relation to evidentially weak cases, again there is no incentive to drop on that ground alone. It is the experience of prosecutors that weak cases commonly produce a guilty plea. Where a guilty plea is not offered spontaneously, it may often be procured by offering inducements such as a reduction in the number of charges or agreeing to proceed on a less-serious charge. Because weak cases may produce convictions, there is no reason to drop a case when it is first reviewed purely on grounds of weakness. It pays the prosecutor to bide his or her time, and to consider dropping the case only if it appears that the defendant intends to plead not guilty and is not willing to bargain.

Ten years ago, Doreen McBarnet analysed the detailed rules and practices of the criminal justice system to determine how the state obtained convictions (McBarnet, 1981). Her conclusion was that the law did not live up to its rhetoric of 'due process': rules and procedures which were presented as protecting standards of proof, in fact operated in the service of crime control to ease the functions of investigation and prosecution and deliver convictions. She argued that because the law itself facilitated crime control there was little need for police illegality to secure convictions.

Our research supports McBarnet's view that the legal environment in which the police operate facilitates crime control. However, she draws the focus of enquiry away from police practices and towards an examination of what the law permits; and away from the motivations of institutions and individuals towards the structure of the law. We have shown that successful pursuit of crime-control objectives depends upon a variety of police practices. Even when these practices are not illegal or contrary to official guidelines they are not *prescribed by* the law; rather, they are *allowed by* it. The role of law is not to prevent illegality, but to obscure and validate it. Equally, we argue, the key to understanding the criminal process does not lie in the extent to which the law facilitates crime-control practices, but rather in the working rules of the individuals and institutions involved in crime control. To understand why the criminal justice system works in the way it does we need to give equal emphasis to the behaviour of officials and to the legal framework in which they operate.

This research illustrates how meaningless it is to pass laws without attending to the goals and occupational culture of those whom these laws are supposed to control. Dixon *et al.* (1989) reached similar conclusions in relation to stop-and-search powers. The research also suggests that review bodies cannot effectively review earlier decisions or processes of other agencies without access to the raw material which those agencies considered, or – at least – submissions from agencies other than those which they are reviewing. This is why the CPS finds its role so difficult to fulfil, and raises similar questions about similar bodies (for example, the Police Complaints Authority). This also means that any expectation we may hold about the role of the CPS or custody officer in reducing miscarriages of justice will have to be radically revised.

REFERENCES

Crown Prosecution Service (1989), *Annual Report 1988/89* (London: Her Majesty's Stationery Office).
Dixon, D. *et al.* (1989), 'Reality and rules in the construction and regulation of police suspicion', *International Journal of the Sociology of Law*, 17, 185.
Gudjonsson, G. H. and MacKeith, J. (1988), 'Retracted confessions', *Medicine, Science and the Law*, 28(3), 187–94.
Hanmer, J. *et al.* (1989), *Women, Policing and Male Violence* (London: Routledge).
Irving, B. (1980), *Police Interrogation* (London: Her Majesty's Stationery Office).
McBarnet, D. (1981), *Conviction* (London: Macmillan).
McConville, M. and Baldwin, J. (1981), *Courts, Prosecution and Conviction* (Oxford: Oxford University Press).
McConville, M., Sanders, A. and Leng, R. (1991), *The Case for the Prosecution* (London: Routledge).
National Audit Office (1989), *Review of the Crown Prosecution Service* (London: Her Majesty's Stationery Office).
Nelken, D. (1983), *The Limits of the Legal Process* (London: Macmillan).
Sanders, A. (1985), 'Prosecution decisions and the Attorney-General's guidelines', *Criminal Law Review*, 4–19.
Sanders, A. and Bridges, L. (1990), 'Access to legal advice and police malpractice', *Criminal Law Review*, 494.
Shapland, J. and Vagg, J. (1988), *Policing by the Public* (London: Routledge).
Smith, D. and Gray, J. (1983), *Police and People in London* (London: Policy Studies Institute).

6 Ethnic Minorities, Crime and Criminal Justice: A Study in a Provincial City

TONY JEFFERSON, MONICA WALKER and
MARY SENEVIRATNE

INTRODUCTION

The issues posed by race and criminal justice in Britain are contentious, none more so than the longstanding conflict between the police and black people. Though this achieved its most dramatic exemplification in the riots of the 1980s, the warning signs had long been in place. Much has been written about the issue, and who, or what, is to blame. Factors such as the 'lawlessness of black youth', 'deprivation' and 'police racism' are just the three most prominent ascribed causes in a wide-ranging debate (cf. Benyon, 1986). Less dramatically, other moments in the criminal justice process – the decision to caution or to charge, for example – have also come under critical scrutiny.

The truth is, however, that the resulting picture remains contradictory in parts, blurred or missing in others and, perhaps in consequence, highly contested. Reiner (1985), for example, has drawn attention to the way observationally based findings contradict the 'discriminatory pattern [of policing] suggested by the quantitative work' (p. 171); and Walker (1987) to the latter's methodological problems. The result is that you can find similar evidence (for example, that Blacks are more likely than Whites to be stopped, arrested, and so on) given different interpretations. Our study is an attempt to clarify matters.

In making the decision to do a comparative study of Afro-Caribbeans (hereinafter called Blacks), Asians (from the Indian sub-continent) and Whites, we were following a common methodological approach designed to uncover any differences in treatment, since these are one possible indicator of discrimination. Within this broad strategy, we intended to tackle five main problems raised by studies of this sort. The first concerned the issue of 'over-representation': were Blacks over-represented (in relation to their numbers) in any part of the statistics produced by the Criminal Justice System? The second was that of interpretation – if so, why? (cf. Reiner, 1989).

The Metropolitan Police (MPD) has consistently found, over many years, Black over-representation in London's arrest figures. In 1986, for example, 17 per cent of those arrested were black though they constituted only 5 per cent of the general population (Home Office, 1989). Moreover, Stevens and Willis (1979) have shown this over-representation applies to all age and offence groups. However, the meaning of this over-representation was unclear since no controls for the social and economic factors which might explain it had been made. We felt this could be rectified by comparing arrest rates of those living in the same (small) areas which broadly share similar social and economic environments. This would require recording the race of each person arrested and the enumeration district in which he lived, and then comparing rates within areas.

As for the outcome of arrest in terms of cautions, convictions and sentences, the picture was unclear. First, there was little data on those released without prosecution or acquitted. Secondly, the sentencing data, which suggested that Blacks and Whites with similar offences and criminal records have the same chance of a custodial sentence (see, for example, Mair, 1986) seemed confusing when set against the over-representation of black people in custody (see, for example, Home Office, 1986). Thirdly, the cautioning data was similarly confusing, with Landau's finding in London of black juveniles being less likely to be cautioned (see, for example, Landau and Nathan, 1983) contradicted by the work of Farrington and Bennett (1981), who found no racially based differences in cautioning rates. Once again there were methodological problems, with class and factors such as whether parents were prepared to accept the caution inadequately considered.

Some of these difficulties, we felt, might stem from the tendency to focus only on a particular, isolated moment of the criminal justice process. We decided to tackle this by following through (statistically) our sample from arrest to sentence, and by supplementing this with observations conducted at key decision-making sites (for example, cautioning/sentencing) in the process, and interviews with relevant participants.

Fourthly, there was the issue of 'London bias'. Since all the published arrest data, and much of the other, referred to London, this did pose the question of the provincial experience. We decided, in consequence, to focus upon Leeds as a sort of check on the generalisability of the London experience.

Finally, there was the general problem of comparability. In 1983, the Policy Studies Institute (PSI) published its survey of the general population of London (Smith, 1983). One of the issues it raised was the relationship between experiences of the police and attitudes towards them. Though these were found to be correlated, it was also found that experiences of being stopped could not by themselves account for the more hostile attitudes of black youth (Smith, 1986). We wanted to see if similar results would emerge in the provinces, and whether controlling for area, as did Tuck and Southgate (1981) in their Moss Side, Manchester, survey, would make any difference. In other surveys the samples have been representative of those living in large areas (populations of over 100,000) so that many of the white sample came from areas containing more in the higher social classes. The comparison with non-whites has been therefore between those living, in the main, in different circumstances.

In order to obtain more meaningful comparisons our survey concentrated on black, Asian and white males living in the areas of Leeds where most of the non-white people live. These are the areas which have more than 10 per cent of the population non-white, and contain about 58 per cent of the Blacks in Leeds, 55 per cent of the Asians, but only 6 per cent of the Whites. This enabled us to compare the experiences of the police of those living in the same small areas and to relate these to attitudes. The sample was clearly not representative, particularly of Whites in Leeds. However, comparisons were between groups living in similar circumstances. In every part of our research we confined ourselves to the group most involved in the criminal justice system, namely, males aged 10 to 35.

In the following sections we describe the methodology and results of the five main aspects of our research. These are (1) arrest data, (2) stop data, (3) outcome of arrest, (4) observation and interviews, (5) survey. In the main, only statistically significant results will be mentioned. These are followed by a summary and our overall conclusions, the latter discussed in the light of the five problems identified above.

Arrest Rates

With the co-operation of the West Yorkshire Police we obtained the race (as perceived by the police), sex, age, offence and address of every person stopped or arrested in Leeds for six months in 1987.

To compare arrest rates within areas we recorded the enumeration district (e.d. – about 150 households) where each person arrested lived, and the base population of each race in each e.d. The best estimates we could get of the latter were from special tabulations from the 1981 census which gave us the numbers where the head of household was born in the Caribbean or Africa (expected to be black), the Indian sub-continent (expected to be of 'Asian' appearance) or elsewhere. The age groups available were 5–15 and 16–29 in 1981. We thought this would provide reasonable estimates of those aged 11–21 and 22–35 in 1987. Since many of the numbers involved were very small or zero, it was necessary, in carrying out the analysis, to group together e.d.s and, in many of the areas not near the centre of the city, to use whole wards in order to obtain enough non-whites. (For details of the problem and assumptions involved, see Walker, 1992.)[1]

An initial examination showed that Blacks were over-represented, with an arrest rate of 7 per cent as against only 3 per cent of the whole population (not nearly so large a difference as in London, however, with 17 per cent as against 5 per cent). Asians were roughly proportionately represented, as in London, and Whites slightly under-represented. Blacks and Asians tended to have higher proportions arrested for violence and theft, whereas Whites had more for burglary and damage (for full details, see Walker *et al.*, 1990).

A breakdown by age-group showed a similar picture, with Blacks having a higher rate than Whites in both age groups. As would be expected, rates are higher for the younger group (see Table 6.1).

TABLE 6.1   *Race distributions and arrest rates by age group (all wards together)*

	Age 11–21				Age 22–35			
	Black	Asian	White	N = 100%	Black	Asian	White	N = 100%
Population (%)	3.5	5.3	91.2	37165	3.1	3.7	93.3	51245
Persons arrested (%)	5.7	3.4	90.8	2669	6.0	3.7	90.3	1590
Rates (no. arrests per 100 pop.)	11.7	4.7	7.2	7.2	6.3	3.1	3.0	3.1

In our analysis controlling for areas, we classified all e.d.s according to whether they contained less or more than 10 per cent non-white households.[2] For convenience these are called 'whiter' or 'blacker' areas, and the arrest rates for the two groups are given by age and race in Table 6.2. In the blacker areas we found Whites had higher rates than Blacks and Asians, in the younger age group, but in the whiter areas Blacks had a higher rate than Whites in both age groups. (These differences were statistically significant.)

A more detailed analysis of the black and white rates (summarised in Table 6.3) revealed that the black rate decreased with increasing 'blackness' whereas the white rate increased. It was also found that the white rate was significantly correlated with the unemployment rate and the percentage

TABLE 6.2　Arrest rates^a by age group and area type

Ratio[b]	Age 11–21				Age 22–35				All males: 11–35	
	Black	Asian	White	All	Black	Asian	White	All	Population	%
< 10%	15.0	5.0	6.9	7.0	8.9	3.2	2.9	3.0	79,235	90
> 10%	8.9	4.4	13.3	9.9	4.4	2.4	3.9	3.7	9175	10
All areas	11.7	4.7	7.2	7.2	6.3	3.1	3.0	3.1	88,410	100

NOTES

^a Rate = (total number arrested in all relevant areas/total estimated population in these areas) × 100.
^b Ratio = (all black households + all Asian households)/all households.

TABLE 6.3　Arrest rates^a related to census variables (Blacks and Whites)

	Arrest rates				Census data					
	Age 11–21		Age 22–35		% Privately rented		% Unemployed		No. of households	
Ratio[b]	Black	White	Black	White	Black	White	Black	White	Black	White
< 2%	16.5	5.4	6.1	2.4	5	4	7	18	420	90,900
2–10%	11.1	8.3	9.0	3.2	15	13	25	19	1055	76,820
10–33%	9.5	12.6	4.1	3.6	10	27	21	27	500	4460
> 33%	7.8	14.4	4.6	7.3	3	26	41	39	915	1340
All areas	11.7	7.2	6.3	3.0	9	9	24	19	2890	173,520

NOTES

^a Rate = (total number arrested in all relevant areas/total estimated population in these areas) × 100.
^b Ratio = (all black households + all Asian households)/all households.

of privately rented households of Whites in the area, and this was not the case for Blacks. For Asians none of these variables was significant. Whites had significantly more in privately rented accommodation (one indication of a more transient population) than the Blacks, and the correlation with the arrest rate is in keeping with an earlier finding in Sheffield (Baldwin and Bottoms, 1976). So, for Whites there was a fairly comprehensible relationship between certain indices of poverty and deprivation and the arrest rate. However, since this was not the case for Blacks, another explanation for these arrest rates is needed. (Data on social class from the census were not sufficiently accurate to be useful, as they were based on a 10 per cent sample.)

There is no doubt that the high black rates in the whiter areas are difficult to explain, but it is worth pointing out that these are very large areas (mainly wards with over 6000 households). In the wards with less than 2 per cent non-white the number of blacks was small and only 49 Blacks were arrested. This means that any misperception of race by the police or miscoding disproportionately amplifies percentage differences. Moreover, if there has been even a small change in the black population since the 1981 census data on which our estimates are based, this too will have had a disproportionate effect on our figures. However, as we saw earlier (note 1) the changes we know of suggest only a higher black arrest rate. Having said that, a personal investigation by the researchers into the areas where those arrested lived revealed that both white and black arrestees in the whiter areas lived in poor-quality housing in small groups in large 'white' wards.

What this analysis shows is that it is necessary to examine areas of residence in detail before any conclusion can be drawn either about a tendency of the police to discriminate against black people or about black people being more 'criminal'. However, explanations of the differences found remain to be explored. The characteristics of the three races are different in some respects even though they live in the same small areas. The survey (see below) in the blacker areas confirmed that more white people lived in privately rented accommodation and showed that they had lived in the area a shorter time. But they also appeared to have fewer in social classes 4 and 5 than the blacks, and had higher educational attainments. This was the case even when students were excluded from the analysis. These demographic characteristics make the higher white arrest rate in the blacker areas even more striking.

It has to be remembered that the arrest data reflect all the factors affecting the perception and reporting of offences by the public, and the police decision-making involved – factors that for many years were regarded as making any interpretation of 'official' statistics dubious. In the present context, for example, an explanation of the comparatively low black arrest rate in the blacker areas could, perhaps, be ascribed to the possibility that many offences are intra-racial and Blacks may be more reluctant to report them to the police. This latter tendency emerged from our survey, which revealed that whilst Blacks had a slightly lower victimisation rate than Whites, they also reported a lower proportion. It could also be that the police are more reluctant to record intra-racial offences, though we have no evidence on this point.

Stop and Search

While arrests by the police arise, in the main, as a result of the reporting of offences by the public, 'stop and search' is entirely due to police proactive behaviour.

The Police and Criminal Evidence Act (PACE, 1984) requires a record to be made of every compulsory stop and search carried out; in West Yorkshire the numbers appear fairly small. For example, while in London about 7.6 'stops' (persons and vehicles stopped and searched) were made per 1000 population, the corresponding figure in West Yorkshire was about 0.8 (1987 data). This suggests one significant difference between London and a provincial force.

We obtained details of all stops (323) recorded in the six sub-divisions of Leeds in the same six-month period as for arrests. There were cases involving 303 males where the race was recorded, 18 of whom were black, 14 Asian and 271 white. Over half the stops were in one police sub-division (Chapeltown), which has a high non-white population, and nearly two-thirds involved a search for drugs. About a quarter of those stopped were arrested (for all races) and these accounted for about 1 per cent of all arrests.

Overall, the analysis in relation to residence revealed that blacks were over-represented in the whole city (blacks 7 per cent; Asians 3 per cent; whites 90 per cent), to about the same extent as for arrests. Further analysis also showed a similar pattern. The black stop rate, for all ages and areas together, like the arrest rate, was about double the white rate. Young males had a higher stop rate than older males; and for both age groups in the 'blacker' areas whites had a higher rate than blacks and Asians, whilst in the 'whiter' areas blacks had a higher rate than whites and Asians (see Table 6.4).

TABLE 6.4　*Stop and search rates*[a] *(males)*

Ratio[b]	Age 11–21			Age 22–35			All		
	Black	Asian	White	Black	Asian	White	Black	Asian	White
< 10%	8.1	3.6	3.5	4.3	2.5	1.6	6.0	3.0	2.2
> 10%	4.4	0	9.9	2.5	0.9	6.5	3.3	0.5	7.6
All	6.1	1.6	2.6	3.3	1.6	1.8	4.6	1.6	2.1

NOTES

[a] Rate = (total no. stopped and searched in relevant areas)/(no. resident in areas)
　　× 1000.

[b] Ratio = (all blacks households + all Asian households)/all households.

The results of our survey, in the blacker areas, are described later but it is worth pointing out the correspondence between both sets of data (see Table 6.7). Though we asked for the (higher) number of car and street stops (not only searches) in the previous 12 months, none the less differences between races were of the same order.

Outcome of Arrest

We intended to follow up all non-Whites and a sample of Whites (total about 1500) arrested. This involved inspection of returned police files. Unfortunately, only about half had been returned during the time available for inspection. As the files of cases where there was no further action (NFA) and for those cautioned would usually be returned quickly, we think we have good estimates of these. We decided it was important, however, also to obtain accurate estimates of the numbers (and outcome) of those dealt with in the Crown Court, and we were able to obtain this data from the Probation Service. The data of the remaining cases – just over one-third of all adults – are those tried in the magistrates' courts.

Our analysis of juvenile files revealed that on average about 8 per cent had 'no further action' with no difference between races. After removing them, however, it was found that a higher proportion of Asians – 72 per cent – were cautioned for all offence groups (see Table 6.5). Although these were juveniles, as many as 14 per cent of Blacks were tried in the Crown Court, with Asians and Whites having significantly less at 7 per cent – which still seems high (see Table 6.5). A detailed examination of the

TABLE 6.5   *Outcome of arrest (juveniles)*

	Black	*Asian*	*White*
Intended sample	95	56	280
% no further action	9	4	8
Total dealt with	86	54	261
Of these:			
% cautioned	31	72	41
% Magistrates' Court trial	54	20	52
[followed up]	[11]	[9]	[19]
[not followed up]ᵃ	[43]	[11]	[33]
% Crown Court trial	14	7	7

NOTE

ᵃ These figures are estimates and probably include a few cautioned or having no further action whose files had not been returned by July 1988 (see text).

records showed that six of the 12 Blacks were probably arrested in one incident, and some of these were charged with robbery and public-order offences. In this and the other cases it was not clear if there was a co-defendant aged 17 or over which would justify trial in the Crown Court.

The pattern for adults was not dissimilar (see Table 6.6). In this case Asians had significantly more (at 15 per cent) with 'no further action', though the cautioning rates of the remainder (on average 6 per cent) did not differ between races. (This figure was considerably lower than that for the whole of West Yorkshire, which was 15 per cent.) Once again, as for juveniles, significantly more Blacks were tried in the Crown Court. These findings are consistent with that of a study of the London courts (Walker, 1988, 1989).

TABLE 6.6 *Outcome of arrests (adults)*

	Black	*Asian*	*White*
Intended sample	255	126	756
% no further action	7	15	9
Total dealt with	237	107	687
Of these:			
% cautioned	4	5	7
% Magistrates' Court trial	57	66	62
[followed up]	[21]	[30]	[23]
[not followed up]ᵃ	[36]	[36]	[39]
% Crown Court trial	39	29	31
% acquittal rate (all courts)ᵇ	12	6	4

NOTES

[a] These figures are estimates and probably include a few cautioned or having no further action whose files had not been returned by July 1988 (see text).

[b] Owing to the incomplete follow up of magistrates' court cases these figures may be inaccurate (and probably under-estimates).

This research did not undertake a sentencing study because necessary details (for example, number of charges, offences taken into consideration, and so on) were not incorporated. So only a selective overview will be given.

Since only 8 black, 5 Asian and 43 white juveniles were sentenced in the magistrates' courts, a detailed analysis was not carried out. Altogether 19 (or 34 per cent) had a custodial sentence; the offences sentenced covered the whole range, with theft predominating. Of the 30 sentenced in the

Crown Court just half the Blacks and Whites received custody, and three of the four Asians.

For adults in the magistrates' courts, data on previous convictions were available. We found that Blacks and Whites averaged approximately three whereas Asians averaged under one. There were corresponding differences in the proportions with no previous convictions. However, in the Crown Court proportionately more Blacks than Whites had no previous convictions. A regression analysis of sentences, taking into account offence type and previous convictions, found that the type of sentence for the three groups did not differ significantly in either court, nor did the length of custodial sentences.

Overall the proportions given custodial sentences in the Crown Court did not differ significantly and averaged 60 per cent. It was mentioned earlier that for adults (as well as juveniles) a greater proportion of Blacks were tried in the Crown Court. This was the case for each main offence group. Offences were examined in detail to see if these would explain this difference. Only a small percentage (7.5 per cent) were indictable-only and had to be tried in the Crown Court. This was the same for each race. Triable-either-way offences are either tried in the Crown Court because magistrates feel they are too serious to try or because the defendants elect for jury trial. However, we found no differences between races, with 25 per cent of defendants electing for Crown Court trial and 75 per cent being sent by magistrates.

It seems, then, that there is no obvious reason why there are proportionately more Blacks tried in the Crown Court, though there are slightly more indictable-only, slightly more where magistrates decide and slightly more where the defendant so chooses. But the fact that more black defendants are tried in the Crown Court, where the chances of a custodial sentence are higher, can help to explain the increasing over-representation of black people in prison. The percentages receiving immediate custody in the Crown Court were not significantly different and were similar to a national figure of 52 per cent. In the magistrates' courts the national figure (1987) for indictable offences given custody was 7 per cent – a figure slightly higher than ours.

Acquittal rates in our study do not appear to be consistent with London figures, particularly in the Crown Court. At 12 per cent for Blacks in both the magistrates' courts and the Crown Court, this was significantly higher than Asians and Whites in both the magistrates' courts (where they averaged 5 per cent) and in the Crown Court (3 per cent). In London, by contrast, in both courts Blacks had only slightly more acquitted (by about 1 per cent). The magistrates' courts figures are similar to those for London

(7 per cent; Walker 1989), but the Crown Court figure for London is far higher than the Leeds figures, being nearer to 25 per cent. Once again, these differences may be pointing to significant regional differences.

Observations and Interviews

Analysing statistical data reveals certain facts requiring explanation – in our case, the differences found between the races in arrest rates, juvenile cautioning rates, adult 'NFAs', acquittal rates and Crown Court trials. Searching for possible explanations may involve collecting and analysing new statistical data or utilising other forms of data, such as observations and interviews. During this aspect of the research, we were able to observe 135 cases of non-white and matched white defendants in court, and to interview ten of the solicitors involved who had some dealings with non-white clients. We observed a Case Referral Panel (which decides on the cautioning of juveniles) in action, and also interviewed panel members. The hope was that this supplementary data might help to explain some of our statist-ical findings, such as why Asian juveniles were more likely to be cautioned and Blacks more likely to go to Crown Court and to be acquitted.

We observed the Chapeltown Panel in action on four occasions, and witnessed 23 cases being discussed; 12 blacks, 8 whites and 3 Asians. Nothing in our observations, nor in the subsequent interviews, revealed any evidence of racial bias in the decision to prosecute or caution. Panel members were certainly aware of the problem of racism and thought it might be operating elsewhere in the criminal justice system. But all felt that their own Panel did not discriminate, and our own observations – limited though they were – support that.

A similar finding emerged from our court room observations and follow-up interviews. We observed 135 cases (about half being non-white, mainly black) in the magistrates' courts; very few (of any race) involved contested trials. The overall impression was that the bureaucratic routine predominated; that is, that cases proceeded (usually after one or several adjournments) according to an invariant formula and produced predictable outcomes. 'Interruptions' to this bureaucratic routine took the form of comparatively harsh or comparatively lenient benches (harshness or lenience being a subjective impression of the observers when judged against the mundane 'norm'). For our purposes, the important point was that such 'interruptions' to the routine happened regardless of race; a harsh bench remained harsh for the duration of its sitting whoever happened to be in front of it – and the same was true of lenient benches.

The ten solicitors (one Asian) interviewed did not say anything to disturb these impressions substantially. Some individuals thought the courts 'bent over backwards' to be fair to racial minorities, others that Blacks are more likely to plead 'not guilty' – both of which, if true, point towards an explanation of the higher black acquittal rate. We shall return to this question later, in our concluding discussion. But, overall, the feeling was that there was no systematic bias in the courts, even though the sample thought black clients tended to feel they were being discriminated against – a viewpoint which connects with some of our survey findings, to which we now turn.

The Survey

The aim of the survey was to investigate and compare the experiences of the police of Blacks, Asians and Whites, and to relate this to their attitudes to the police and to crime in their areas. The main survey was of males aged 16–35 but we included a sample of boys aged 10–15 for comparative purposes.

To make our comparisons more meaningful we confined our sample to those living in areas (enumeration districts) with 10 per cent or more non-White households, based again on the 1981 census. We achieved interviews with 171 black, 199 Asian and 271 white adults, and 64 black, 117 Asian and 44 white boys.[3]

It should be borne in mind that the respondents cannot be regarded as representative of Blacks, Asians and Whites in the whole of Leeds, since the areas sampled contained 58 per cent of Blacks in the city and 55 per cent of Asians but only 6 per cent of Whites. However, comparisons between races are between those living in the same small areas and differences which exist therefore are more likely to be due to race *per se* than to differences in environment. Because of our sampling design we would expect our adults to be different from those of other surveys, mainly in London, which have sampled very large areas. This obviously affects the usefulness of making other than very general comparisons with other surveys.

We shall anticipate the detailed results which follow by drawing attention to the finding that *in these areas* Blacks and Whites were similar in many respects in their experiences of the police, but were consistently different from Asians. However, Blacks tended to disapprove of the police more than Whites, and Asians were much more approving. The overall impression is that attitudes to the police of both the Blacks and Whites tended to be negative or hostile. As far as the boys were concerned, although many of the differences were not statistically significant, there were indications that responses and differences between races were similar to the adults'.

EXPERIENCES OF THE POLICE

There were two main types of experience of the police, respondent-initiated – such as phone calls to the police asking for help or reporting a crime – and police-initiated, where police suspected the respondent of an offence, for example. We shall examine the latter, more important group first.

Four types of police-initiated contacts were investigated: persons being stopped in a vehicle; persons being stopped when on foot (in the street); house searches; and arrests. People were asked about whether any of the first three events had occurred in the last 12 months, and about arrests in the last five years. For any of these events there was a follow-up questionnaire.

It was found that Whites (50 per cent) had significantly more who had had at least one type of contact than both Blacks (35 per cent) and Asians (28 per cent). The total number of such contacts was also higher for Whites. We also looked at the number of *different* types of contact ('STOPTYPES', ranging from 0 to 4) and found Whites had significantly more than Blacks who, in turn, had significantly more than Asians (see Table 6.7).

These results differ considerably from those of the Policy Studies Institute which found that Blacks were stopped considerably more often than Whites (Smith, 1983). This could be because the study was for the whole of London, while ours was only in the 'blacker' areas of Leeds, containing the more deprived Whites. Moreover, the London study was carried out before

TABLE 6.7 *Contact with the police (police-initiated)*

% experiencing one or more	Black	Asian	White
Car stop (one year)	21	17	24
Street stop (one year)	8	6	16
House search (one year)	5	1	4
Arrests (5 years)	14	6	20
Any of these	35	28	50
Mean number of stops, etc.	1.15	0.36	1.34
Number of different sorts of stops, etc. (0–4) (STOPTYPES)	0.50	0.30	0.65

PACE (1984) with its stricter requirements for recording stops. However, our results clearly do not show discriminatory stopping of Blacks.

The pattern for those initiating a contact with the police, by phone or otherwise, showed surprising similarity. The proportions contacting the police in the last 12 months were: Blacks 65 per cent, Asians 50 per cent and Whites 71 per cent. Again Asians had significantly less than Blacks and Whites (who did not differ). Full details are given in Table 6.8 where the percentages saying they were 'satisfied' with the contact are also given. Almost two-thirds in each category for each race said they were, except for 'approaches in the street' where less than half were satisfied.

Also given in Table 6.8 are the proportions who had been victims of offences and the proportions of those who had reported them to the police. (These would, in the main, be included in the earlier contacts.) Significantly more Asians than Blacks reported the offences, with Whites in between. Overall the proportion of all Blacks who reported being victims of offences was only 9 per cent, less than Whites (19 per cent) and Asians (22 per cent). In answer to other questions it was found that significantly fewer Asians had been annoyed with police or wanted to complain about them. Blacks did not differ from Whites in this respect.

In summary, Asians had fewer contacts of any type with the police and Whites more police-initiated ones, but also more satisfactory self-initiated ones. Blacks were less willing to report offences.

TABLE 6.8   *Contact with police (respondent-initiated)*

	Contacting police			Satisfied or v. satisfied (% of those contacting)		
	Black	*Asian*	*White*	*Black*	*Asian*	*White*
% made 999 calls	12	22	9	67	53	76
% made other phone calls	13	19	24	74	68	67
% called in at police station	26	24	28	67	64	69
% approached police in street	14	6	19	35	44	42
% contacted police any form	65	50	71			
Contacts (mean number)	1.4	2.7	2.5			
% of these ever dissatisfied	15	24	18			
% of these ever satisfied	45	53	58			
Satisfactory contacts (mean)	.38	.33	.55			
% victims of offence	23	37	42			
% of victims who reported to police	38	60	46			
% overall reporting victimisation	9	22	19			

ATTITUDES TO THE POLICE

There were several aspects of attitude to the police which were explored and we found consistently that Asians had a more favourable attitude than Blacks but were, in some responses, similar to Whites. On the other hand, in comparing Blacks and Whites, in some aspects Blacks had a less favourable attitude, while in others they were much the same.

Twenty-five per cent of Blacks thought there were too many police in their area – significantly more than Asians and Whites, who averaged 7 per cent. On the other hand, the percentages saying 'not enough' all differed significantly (Blacks 28 per cent, Asians 61 per cent and Whites 47 per cent).

We presented a set of statements about the police, such as: 'the police try to help the community'; 'the majority of police in Leeds do a good job'; 'there are quite a lot of dishonest policemen in Leeds', and asked respondents if they broadly agreed or disagreed. From this we obtained a score we called 'disapproval'. On the score, based on five items,[4] all the races differed significantly, Blacks being most disapproving and Asians least.

Several questions were asked about police malpractice (these items being the same as those of the Policy Studies Institute survey). Asked if some groups of people were particularly likely to be stopped by the police, about two-thirds of Blacks and Whites thought so, but only slightly over one-third of Asians. When asked which groups, two-thirds or more of these in each race said 'non-Whites' (Blacks 75 per cent; Asians 72 per cent; Whites 66 per cent). Similar results were obtained for answers to 'Are all people treated fairly and equally?', with even more (Blacks 80 per cent; Asians 76 per cent; Whites 74 per cent) of those answering 'no' to the question identifying 'non-Whites'.

Four other questions asked about perception of the police: whether they used pressure in questioning people; whether police took accurate records of evidence; whether they used unnecessary violence; and whether they made up evidence. On average just over half of both Blacks and Whites thought these types of malpractice occurred, but only a quarter of Asians. An overall score was obtained from these six items and was called 'perception of police': the score for Blacks and Whites was identical (3.5) and significantly higher than that for Asians (1.7).

Our last main item investigating attitude to the police concerned whether people thought they would report offences they had witnessed, help identify the culprit and give evidence in court, three such hypothetical incidents being described. We called this 'co-operation'. The incidents were a robbery, vandalism and a traffic accident. For the robbery, significantly fewer

Blacks said they would co-operate, at each stage, than Asians and Whites, who did not differ, and this was the case for each incident. Co-operation was consistently high for the traffic accident and lowest for the vandalism item. Only 48 per cent of Blacks would report the latter to the police, with 81 per cent of Asians and 66 per cent of Whites. Except on this item, Asians and Whites tended to have similar (and high) proportions willing to co-operate. Their overall scores did not differ significantly and were higher than that for Blacks. Full details are given in Table 6.9.

TABLE 6.9 *Co-operation with police (% yes)*

	Black	Asian	White
If you saw:			
someone knock a man down and take his wallet would you			
(a) tell police	75	96	92
(b) help identify culprit	64	90	87
(c) give evidence in court	51	80	83
youths smashing a bus shelter would you			
(a) tell police	48	81	66
(b) help identify culprit	41	74	61
(c) give evidence in court	35	65	53
somebody badly hurt in a traffic accident would you			
(a) tell police	95	99	98
(b) help identify culprit	85	94	96
(c) give evidence in court	73	86	93
Total score (0–9)			
co-operation	5.4	7.5	7.1
definite non-co-operation	1.1	0.6	0.6

We have pointed out that the three race groups have had different experiences of the police, so we investigated whether the several measures of attitude to the police were correlated with experiences. We found the best measure of police-initiated experiences was the number of different types of experience (called STOPTYPES) which varied from 0 to 4. The correlations were almost all significant – the greater the number of STOPTYPES, the more unfavourable the attitude. This is illustrated in Table 6.10. It can be seen that the attitude scores increase steadily for each race group for disapproval and perception (unfavourable) and decrease for co-operation,

TABLE 6.10 *Score related to number of types of stops, etc.*

No. of	% Distribution (STOPTYPES)			Disapproval score			Perception score			Co-operation score		
	Black	Asian	White	Black	Asian	White	Black	Asian	White	Black	Asian	White
0	65	75	50	17.6	15.2	16.0	3.1	1.5	3.2	5.6	7.7	7.2
1	25	21	38	18.1	16.7	16.6	4.0	2.3	3.6	5.9	7.2	7.3
2 or more	11	4	13	19.9	17.6	17.7	4.8	3.4	3.9	2.9	5.0	6.3
N = 100%	171	199	271									
Correlation	0.50	0.30	0.65	0.31	0.31	0.20	0.19	0.31	(NS)	−0.22	−0.32	−0.18
Mean All				18.0	15.6	16.5	3.5	1.5	3.5	5.4	7.5	7.1

as the number of STOPTYPES increases. However, it is interesting that for each line showing the number of STOPTYPES, differences between races are maintained. In particular, even when people have not been stopped at all, Blacks have higher 'disapproval' scores than Whites, who are higher than Asians; Blacks and Whites have a worse perception of police malpractice than Asians, and Blacks are less co-operative than Asians and Whites. It is clear that these attitudes and their differences cannot be 'explained' simply by whether or not the police had stopped them – indeed it would be surprising if they could.

A more detailed examination of the responses has been carried out using the follow-up questionnaires, and any expression of annoyance and dissatisfaction about police behaviour was scored. it was found that this was more highly correlated with the attitude scores than simply the number of stops and STOPTYPES, except for Asians, where the actual number of stops and so on was more significant. For Blacks and Whites, therefore, it wasn't so much the fact of being stopped that annoyed them as the way the police dealt with this – not everyone was dissatisfied who had been stopped. However, differences in the scores of disapproval and co-operation between Blacks and Whites were still significant, even controlling for these measures of dissatisfaction.

Examination of the details of why people had been annoyed by the police or wanted to complain revealed that of both Blacks and Whites a few had had very unpleasant experiences that could not be dismissed as minor insults. Very few of the unpleasant experiences of Blacks seemed to be related overtly to racism. Because of this it was interesting to note, as mentioned earlier, that nearly as many Whites as Blacks (on average about 45 per cent and 53 per cent respectively) thought the police discriminated against non-Whites.

DEMOGRAPHIC CHARACTERISTICS AND 'WAY OF LIFE'

We asked respondents about their age, occupation, how long they lived in the area, whether they lived in owner-occupied accommodation or whether it was rented (council or private). We also asked about their 'way of life', whether they had gone out each evening of the previous week, their transport, their destination and time of return. Many of these factors differed between race groups, and some were significantly correlated (but never highly) with the factors discussed earlier.

Asians went out on fewer evenings than Blacks and Whites (1.5, 2.6, 2.9 respectively), were home earlier (80 per cent by midnight, but only 48 per cent of Blacks and 57 per cent of Whites), tended to use cars and to visit friends or relatives (while Whites tended to have gone to pubs). Only for Whites did we find that those who had gone out more tended to have been stopped more. For all races, however, there was a significant correlation (of about $r = 0.20$) between number of evenings out and having been annoyed by the police.

The main findings regarding other demographic characteristics were that among Asians there were more married (42 per cent) than among Blacks and Whites (who averaged 26 per cent), and Whites had more single people who were not living with parents (56 per cent). This was partly accounted for by more being students, but even excluding these, Whites had more living in privately rented accommodation. This is consistent with the census data reported in subsection 1 above. Also linked to this is the fact that 52 per cent of Whites had lived in the area less than three years, compared with about a quarter of Blacks and Asians. For Whites and Asians, excluding students, those in privately rented accommodation tended to have a less favourable attitude to the police.

Whites had fewer in Social Classes 4 and 5 (semi-skilled and unskilled), with 44 per cent compared with 61 per cent of Blacks and Asians, while Blacks had more unemployed (42 per cent compared with a mean of 23 per cent for Asians and Whites). Whites tended to have more academic qualifications, nearly half having 'A' levels or above, compared with 15 per cent of Blacks and 24 per cent of Asians.

It is apparent, therefore, that there are many differences between the race groups regarding social status, but it is not easy to see how these would be linked to their experience of and attitude to the police. As they are living in the same small areas, differences in these variables seem more likely to be related to their race than to other factors.

The relationships between the percentage of non-Whites in the areas and various measures of attitude and experience were investigated. The only variable showing a trend with 'blackness' was 'co-operation'. Those living in 'blacker' areas tended to be less co-operative and this was the case for each race group.

CONCERN ABOUT CRIME

To obtain a wider picture we investigated experiences of crime as victims, feelings of safety in the streets, worries about particular crimes, whether these were seen as a problem in their area, and also, in the attitude questionnaire, opinions about crime and criminals.

In the main, Blacks showed less concern about crime. Only 10 per cent thought it unsafe to walk alone in the area after dark, compared with 31 per cent for Asians and 21 per cents for Whites (all differences being significant). Among the oldest in the survey, those aged 31–5, as many as 54 per cent of Asians thought it unsafe, but only 16 per cent of Blacks and 24 per cent of Whites. (Other studies including this item have usually included women and older people, both of whom tend to feel less safe.)

Respondents were asked if they thought that burglary, vandalism, street fights, mugging and 'crime' were problems in their area. On average (over five items) 30 per cent of Blacks, 37 per cent of Asians and 36 per cent of Whites thought these a big problem. However, for 'sex attacks on women' and 'women pestered', Whites had significantly more (averaging 24 per cent) than Blacks and Asians (average only 12 per cent).

Another question concerned worries about crimes: burglary, robbery and vandalism. In this case, more Asians appeared to worry (on average 53 per cent saying the items were 'a big worry'), Blacks and Whites were equal with about 36 per cent saying this.

The general picture, again, is that Asians differ from Blacks in their concern about crime, and that Whites are more concerned than Blacks on some items ('safety', 'problems') but are similar to Blacks regarding 'worries'.

SUMMARY OF MAIN SURVEY

Within our sample of areas with 10 per cent or more non-Whites, Blacks and Whites tended to be similar in many respects and Asians different. Whites had slightly more police-initiated contacts (stops, and so on) than Blacks, and Asians less. Blacks and Whites both had about 60 per cent who believed the police behaved badly, compared with 30 per cent of Asians. About half of Blacks and Whites thought the police discriminated against non-Whites.

For Blacks it was found that for all three measures of attitude to the police (disapproval, perception and co-operation) older people had a more favourable attitude than younger people. This was also the case for Asians (excluding perception) but not for Whites. However, Blacks overall had a more disapproving attitude to the police than Whites, with Asians, again, being less disapproving. Blacks felt less co-operative towards the police, regarding witnessing an offence; Whites and Asians did not differ in this respect.

Although all the measures of attitude to the police were related to stops and so on, and Asians were stopped less and Whites more than Blacks, differences between races on attitude were consistent regardless of the number of stops.

On the whole, Blacks were less, and Asians more, fearful and worried about crime than Whites.

THE BOYS

The boys' questionnaire was fairly short and was answered by 225 boys. Several items were of the same type as those given to the older group, and although few differences were statistically significant, they tended to be in the same direction as for the men, with Blacks tending to be least favourably disposed and co-operative, and Asians most. Direct experience of the police regarding stops affected just over a quarter in all races – perhaps surprisingly high, considering their age.

This small survey is of very considerable interest and suggests either that the attitudes found among the older group have been already implanted from their experiences while they were children, or that the older group have influenced the younger ones in their attitudes. The boys' actual experience of the police would be expected to be fairly slight, but may have had wider repercussions.

SUMMARY AND CONCLUSIONS

This study has shown that over the whole of Leeds black males (aged 10–35) have a higher arrest rate than Whites, with Asians being close to Whites. An analysis looking at two age groups (11–21 and 22–35) and area of residence of those arrested has revealed that there were differences between areas with more than 10 per cent non-White households (the 'blacker' areas) and those with less than 10 per cent (the 'whiter' areas). In the blacker areas Whites had a higher arrest rate than Blacks for the younger group, and for this group Asians had a lower rate than both Blacks and Whites. For the older group, differences between races were small in these areas. In the whiter areas Blacks had a higher arrest rate, with the Asian rate again close to that of Whites for both groups. The pattern with regard to 'stop and search', though less clear, was broadly similar.

The analyses of arrest outcomes showed that Asian juveniles received relatively more cautions than the rest, and more Blacks were tried in the

Crown Court. For adults, Asians had more with no further action, and Blacks had a higher proportion tried in the Crown Court and more acquittals. However, sentencing in the magistrates' courts and the Crown Court did not differ between races.

Observation and interviews relating to the processes involved did not reveal any obvious forms of discrimination.

The survey (in areas with more than 10 per cent non-Whites) revealed that Whites had slightly more negative experiences (stops and so on) of the police than Blacks, while Asians had less. However, Blacks tended to be more hostile to the police than Whites, although both groups thought the police discriminated against non-Whites. Asians tended to be more favourable to the police and more afraid of crime. The boys' survey to some extent revealed similar attitudes.

Finally, we need to go back to the problems identified at the outset and consider, briefly, whether our results have clarified matters and what still needs to be done.

Over-representation

For our purposes, the most important point to emerge is that when arrest rates are related to area of residence, the question of 'over-representation' becomes very complicated. This alone vindicates our decision to compare 'within-area' rates. In the blacker areas, it would appear to be the high white arrest rate that needs explaining. Since this was also correlated with certain indices of disadvantage and deprivation (high unemployment, high numbers in privately rented accommodation), the explanation might appear to be straightforward: more deprivation, more offenders, more arrests. And, indeed, the greater transience of the white population – that is, more living in private rented accommodation, and for shorter periods on average, than the black – is in line with this sort of explanation. However, arrest rates are a complex product of offending behaviour, reporting and recording practices and, in the case of proactive crimes, levels of police activity. Taking police activity: we know that areas with high rates of recorded offences tend to attract more police attention than those areas with relatively low rates – which is to say, simply, that we know police attend more to 'crimes of the poor' than to 'crimes of the powerful'. So could the high white arrest rate be explained, at least partially, in terms of levels of police activity? Unfortunately, our arrest rates were based on *where suspected offenders lived*, not *where offences took place*. So, unless these coincided in Leeds, with areas containing large numbers of offenders also having high offence rates (which has been found elsewhere, cf. Baldwin and Bottoms, 1976), our particular study could not shed light on the role of police activity, even supposing, with our purely statistical approach, we were in a position to do so.

We could, of course, approach this from the 'other side' and seek to explain the comparatively low black arrest rate in these same areas. It should first be emphasised that, in a strict sense, the two groups are not commensurable since these areas contain over 50 per cent of the Blacks and Asians living in Leeds and only 6 per cent of the Whites. However, Blacks in these areas were generally more disadvantaged in terms of unemployment, class and educational attainments; that is, they had more 'offender-related' characteristics, except for the greater transience of the white population. That suggests we need to look to differences in reporting behaviour by the public and/or differences in police recording and reporting activity. It could be that Blacks are reluctant to report crimes committed by other Blacks – a possibility that ties up with our survey finding that Blacks report less crime. On the other hand, police may take crimes against Blacks less seriously and therefore fail to record them as offences; or they may be more circumspect generally with Blacks in these areas, preferring – in the interests of better community relations, for example – informal resolutions to arrests. Singly, or together, these sorts of explanations are compatible with the notion of black 'no-go' (to the police) areas.

The other side of this particular equation is the notion of whiter areas being 'out of bounds' to Blacks. This could only begin to explain the high black arrest rate in the whiter areas (if this was not simply attributable to certain methodological limitations mentioned earlier) if such areas were also those where the offences were committed (which we do not know). This needs to be seen in conjunction with stereotypes of the criminal since, otherwise, we might expect higher Asian rates too in 'whiter' areas. Our evidence is not sufficient to decide such matters. But what is clear is that the relationship between crime, policing, race and arrests needs far more careful unravelling than it usually receives. The fact that Asians were *not* over-represented in any areas only endorses the need to make careful distinctions.

Outcome of Arrest

The outcome-of-arrest study revealed that Asians were more likely to be cautioned (juveniles) and to have had 'no further action' (adults) and that Blacks had a higher acquittal rate and more tried in the Crown Court for each main offence group.

The higher acquittal rate for Blacks, together with the higher use of cautioning and NFAs with Asians, suggests a number of possible explanations. It may be that non-Whites are more readily arrested, on lesser evidence, and this is later 'rectified' by caution, NFA or acquittal. Or, in the case of Asians, it could be that the police decide, despite the evidence, that Asians are less in need, once arrested, of a 'deterrent' court appearance because of their more tractable disposition or because of a belief that offenders will be dealt with adequately in the community. Our survey evidence certainly confirms a more conforming set of Asian attitudes to the police. In the case of Blacks, we first thought that their higher acquittal rates might be connected with the higher numbers going on to Crown Court, since Crown Courts have higher acquittal as well as custodial rates. However, since the higher Black acquittal rate holds true for both types of court, this cannot provide a sufficient answer. It may be, then, that their higher acquittal rates result from a more combative attitude in relation to the criminal justice system – a greater willingness to plead not guilty; or, it could be that Blacks are charged on the basis of weaker evidence; or it could be that, in order to combat any possibility of racism, the courts require a higher standard of proof to convict. The first and last of these possibilities were mentioned by some solicitors in interview. However, in the absence of further evidence at this stage, the matter must remain open.

The significance of Blacks having more Crown Court trials bears on the question of the importance of taking a processual approach, to which we now turn.

The Importance of a Processual Approach

Comparative sentencing studies, as we mentioned earlier, have shown virtually no differences in the sentences meted out to Blacks and Whites, once offence seriousness and previous convictions are controlled for. Our study confirmed this. But we also found significantly more Blacks being tried in the Crown Court. Since such trials are much more likely to produce custodial sentences, this fact, we concluded, must be implicated in the gradual build-up of Black prisoners. Additionally, we should not forget the significantly higher arrest rates for Blacks which must also contribute to this build-up. From our point of view, both show how important it was to look at the whole process. Had we focused purely on the moment of sentencing, the reason for the over-representation of Blacks in prison would have remained obscure. To shed further light on the matter, however, requires a closer look at two decision-making moments. First, we found no differences between the race groups in terms of the proportions of each taking the various routes to Crown Court trial: charged with fully indictable offences, sent by magistrates, election by defendant; this requires a closer examination of the various decisions underlying each route. Secondly, we need to take a closer look at an earlier stage – the decision to charge – to see whether, of those arrests leading to a charge, Blacks are likely to be charged on lesser evidence than Whites or Asians. Once again, though our study has identified the importance of this decision-making moment, it was not designed to go further.

London and Provincial Differences?

The picture in Leeds appears to be broadly similar to that in London, in that we found in the city as a whole some over-representation of Blacks in the police statistics for arrests and stops. However, we found that area of residence – a factor not utilised in the London studies – made a considerable difference. It may be that the comparatively low level of recorded stops in the Leeds statistics, mostly for suspected drug offences, and the comparatively high resulting arrest rate, suggest that stops are not generally used in conjunction with 'saturation' policing tactics in the way they clearly have been, on occasions, in London (cf. Scarman, 1981). Thus the notion of discriminatory stopping, so prevalent an issue for Blacks in London, appears, if at all, in a far more muted form in our provincial case-study.

Comparability, attitudes and equality

A full comparison with PSI and British Crime Survey data has yet to be tackled. Moreover, two differences between our study and that of the PSI should be noted. Our survey compared Blacks, Whites and Asians living in the same areas, whereas the PSI sample were from the whole of London. This suggests that the experiences of the three race groups in their sample were probably more dissimilar than those in ours, owing to overall very wide differences between the races in their social circumstances and areas of residence. Secondly, the PSI measure of attitude was the same as our measure of perception – which we found did not differ between Blacks and Whites. None the less, our findings – of more negative Black attitudes which could not be explained solely by experience – do echo those of the PSI. This suggests, possibly, a general, national dimension to Black antipathy to the police which is over and above particular, local experiences. This may also help explain the finding from our interviews with solicitors that Blacks feel discriminated against even when, to all intents and purposes, they appear to get similar treatment. This disjunction – between attitudes and experiences – raises difficult questions about what constitutes equality. Comparative studies of this sort are premissed – implicitly anyway – on the idea that equal, in the sense of similar, treatment is the desired policy goal. However, what the above suggests is that the depth of feeling – of oppression and injustice – may be so powerful in some disadvantaged ethnic minorities that the indignities, resulting from the bureaucratic indifference and a host of other interactional factors which befall most if not all of those caught up on the wrong side in the criminal justice system, are felt more keenly. It may well be the case that those processes contain a subtle (or not so subtle) racial dimension that the questionnaire and statistical approach, supplemented with observations of purely formal settings, is not equipped to pick up.

The result of all this may be that the goal of ensuring equal treatment should be replaced by that of appropriate treatment, a point Pinder (1984) makes in looking at the issue of race and probation work. In this case, it means taking attitudes of Blacks seriously on their own terms, not simply in terms of whether these 'truly' reflect their experiences, or whether their experiences – as judged objectively (that is, statistically) by others – are different from those of the majority population. The goal, from this perspective, is a turnaround in Black attitudes, from negative to positive. And this will only be achieved when the felt sources of discontent are fully identified and transformed. Finally, we should not overlook the very different, more positive attitudes of Asians. Given this, there can be no justification in studies of this sort for failing to distinguish between Blacks and Asians.

NOTES

1. Recent estimates obtained from a survey by the Leeds County Council indicate that our estimates of the white population in all areas and Blacks in the non-white areas are fairly accurate, but our estimates of Blacks in the whitest areas are too low. Asians appear to have been underestimated throughout.

2. This cut-off point was taken because it was anticipated that only areas with more than 10 per cent non-white would have large enough base populations of non-whites to enable arrest rates to be calculated sensibly.

3. For full details of the sampling scheme, response rate and numbers in the strata, and questionnaire, see Walker *et al.* (1990). The places of birth of the head of the 'Asian' households were: Pakistan 43 per cent, India 26 per cent, Bangladesh 5 per cent, others 26 per cent.

4. For full details see Walker *et al.* (1990). Items included in the 'disapproval' scores were developed by R. I. Mawby.

REFERENCES

Baldwin, J. and Bottoms, A. E. (1976), *The Urban Criminal: A Study in Sheffield* (London: Tavistock).

Benyon, J. (1986), *A Tale of Failure: Race and Policing*, Policy Papers in Ethnic Relations no. 3 (Warwick: University of Warwick).

Farrington, D. P. and Bennett, T. (1981), 'Police cautioning of juveniles in London', *British Journal of Criminology*, **21**, 123–35.

Home Office (1986), *The Ethnic Origin of Prisoners*, Home Office Statistical Bulletin 17/86 (London: Home Office).

Home Office (1989), *Crime Statistics for the Metropolitan Police District, Analysed by Ethnic Group, 1987*, Home Office Statistical Bulletin 5/89 (London: Home Office).

Jefferson, T. (1991), 'Discrimination, disadvantage and policework', in E. Cashmore and E. McLaughlin (eds), *Out of Order?* (London: Routledge).

Landau, S. F. and Nathan, G. (1983), 'Selecting delinquents for cautioning in the London Metropolitan Area', *British Journal of Criminology*, **23**, 128–49.

Mair, G. (1986), 'Ethnic minorities, probation and the magistates' courts: a pilot study', *British Journal of Criminology*, **26**, 147–58.

Pinder, R. (1984), 'Probation work in a multi-racial society', unpublished ms, University of Leeds, Applied Anthropology Group.

Reiner, R. (1985), 'Police and race relations', in J. Baxter and L. Koffman (eds), *Police: The Constitution and the Community* (Abingdon: Professional Books).

Reiner, R. (1989), 'Race and criminal justice', *New Community*, **16**(1), 5–21.

Scarman, Lord (1981), *The Brixton Disorders, 10–12 April 1981*, Cmnd 8427 (London: HMSO).

Smith, D. (1983), *Police and People in London. 1: A Survey of Londoners* (London: Policy Studies Institute).

Smith, D. (1986), 'West Indian hostility to the police in relation to personal experience', unpublished MS.

Stevens, P. and Willis, C. (1979), *Race, Crime and Arrests*, Home Office Research Study no. 58 (London: Her Majesty's Stationery Office).

Tuck, M. and Southgate, P. (1981), *Ethnic Minorities, Crime and Policing*, Home Office Research Study no. 70 (London: Her Majesty's Stationery Office).

Walker, M. A. (1987), 'Interpreting race and crime statistics', *Journal of the Royal Statistical Society*, A, **150**, 39–56.

Walker, M. A. (1988), 'The court disposal of young males by race, in London in 1983', *British Journal of Criminology*, **28**, 442–60.

Walker, M. A. (1989), 'The court disposal and remands of White, Afro-Caribbean and Asian men (London 1983)', *British Journal of Criminology*, **29**, 353–67.

Walker, M. A. (1992), 'Arrest rates and ethnic minorities: a study in a provincial city', *Journal of the Royal Statistical Society*, A (forthcoming).

Walker, M. A., Jefferson, T. and Seneviratne, M. (1990), *Ethnic Minorities, Young People and the Criminal Justice System*, main report to Economic and Social Research Council, Ref. E06250023. Centre for Criminological and Legal Research, University of Sheffield.

7 Talking about Policing

ROD MORGAN

INTRODUCTION

In 1981, following inner-city disturbances unprecedented in their ferocity, the government used a rarely invoked provision of the Police Act 1964: Lord Scarman was asked to conduct an inquiry into 'The Brixton Disorders of 10–12 April'. In November 1981 Lord Scarman delivered his *Report*. It was a seminal document, not because it offered an original analysis – the events to which it was a response were too highly charged and the aspects of policing it addressed were too fundamental to make that likely – nor because its recommendations were radical – the political minefields between which it had to steer made that an improbable outcome – but because with statesmanlike clarity, brevity and authority it diagnosed police–community relationships gone disastrously wrong and pointed to a politically feasible way forward.

Lord Scarman's *Report* was generally well received by the news media. It also became a best-seller. Most importantly, it was made the centrepiece of the government's programme for policing. Several of Lord Scarman's key recommendations were acted on. Principal among these was the setting up, first voluntarily and later in response to s. 106 of the Police and Criminal Evidence Act 1984 (PACE), of what are now often described as 'Scarman-type committees': police consultative committees (PCCs). The research which this chapter describes aimed to chart the implementation of this initiative. It also attempted to come to conclusions about the impact of consultative committees on both the streets of boroughs like Lambeth and the corridors of Westminster, which lie in uncomfortable physical proximity. We explored the consequences of the new 'talking about policy' which the existence of PCCs brought about.

The account which follows is necessarily brief: a fuller account will be available in a book.[1] Most of the data drawn upon were collected in 1984–8 during the period of two ESRC grants. However, the involvement of the research team in the operation of PCCs continued after the project had formally ceased. Police authorities are statutorily required to review their consultation arrangements from time to time and a good many have invited us[2] to assist them in that enterprise. This chapter is about a policy which is continuing to develop.

BACKGROUND: ILLS AND REMEDIES

It would be difficult to exaggerate the impact on the British body politic of the inner-city riots of 1981 (the 'uprising' as the title of one book on the subject subsequently described them). There had been rumblings and one major eruption (in St Paul's, Bristol, in 1980) before Brixton exploded, but the events which took place in 1981 were on an unprecedented scale. As Lord Scarman was subsequently to record: 'the British people watched with horror and incredulity an instant audio-visual presentation on their television sets of scenes of violence and disorder in their capital city, the like of which had not previously been seen in this century in Britain'. 'Mainland Britain' would have been more accurate. But the events in Brixton proved to be contagious. As the inquiry into their cause got under way further serious disturbances took place in Southall, the Toxteth area of Liverpool, Manchester Moss Side, Wolverhampton, Handsworth and Smethwick in Birmingham, Leicester, Bristol, Nottingham and on a smaller scale in many other cities.

Lord Scarman drew several unequivocal conclusions about the disorders in Brixton and elsewhere, conclusions which, rightly or wrongly, were taken by many observers to be generally applicable. Though young people, black and white, had been involved he found that the riots represented an 'outburst of anger and resentment by young black people against the police'. Their resentment stemmed in part from the adoption by the police of methods which did not command the support of the local community and which bore down particularly heavily on the ethnic minorities, so much so that they lost confidence in and respect for the police. Further, he interpreted the failure to maintain formal liaison between the black community and the police in Lambeth as both symptom and contributory cause of that withdrawal of consent which, he held, is vital to effective policing in a democratic society. This led him to the conclusion that 'a police force which does not consult locally will fail to be efficient'.

Given the anti-police nature of the riots, Lord Scarman naturally devoted a good deal of his *Report* to the police. They, he concluded, were becoming increasingly professional. The police have a highly specialised set of skills and behavioural codes of their own: 'they run the risk of becoming, by virtue of their professionalism, a *"corps d'élite"* set apart from the rest of the community'. Thus, 'if a rift is not to develop between the police and the public . . . it is in my view essential that a means be devised of enabling the community to be heard not only in the development of policing policy but in the planning of many, though not all, operations against crime'.

Readers unfamiliar with the constitutional framework for the governance of the police may find this statement surprising. The conventional method for enabling the public will to be reflected in the policies pursued by public services is through democratic political accountability, decisions being made by elected representatives at Westminster or in local government. Indeed, this is the method for which the Opposition argues. In the wake of the profound changes in the context and character of policing in the early 1980s the Labour Party committed itself to revising the Police Act 1964 to give the local police authorities, subject to 'minimum standards and guidelines set down by Parliament', powers to 'decide the nature of policing in their area' such that the 'chief constable's relationship with the authority would be similar to that of any other local council chief officer' (Labour Party, 1986). It is not so at present. Constables exercise original, not delegated, powers and chief constables enjoy a freedom from control by elected representatives which is unique in English public law. This is the doctrine normally referred to as constabulary operational independence (for a detailed discussion, see Lustgarten, 1986).

In a section of his *Report* which left-wing critics considered flawed, Lord Scarman endorsed the existing 'tripartite' arrangements for the governance of the police which underpins the operational independence of constabularies. He proposed that chief constables retain responsibility for the 'direction and control' of their forces, that police authorities continue with their budgetary supply task of ensuring forces' 'adequacy and efficiency' and that the Home Secretary continue to exercise his many powers and duties with a view to the 'efficiency' of all police forces. Moreover, he endorsed the situation in London where there is no locally elected police authority but where the Home Secretary acts in that capacity for the Met. Nevertheless, he judged that police authorities everywhere would 'act more vigorously' if they were given a statutory duty to organise consultative arrangements 'at police divisional or sub-divisional levels'. This was the participative mechanism on which he pinned his faith that policing would in future be more congruent with the wishes of people locally.

THE GOVERNMENT'S RESPONSE TO SCARMAN

The Home Secretary, then William Whitelaw, was initially cautious in response to Lord Scarman's proposal that PCCs be required by statute. The chief constables claimed that they were already doing informally what was proposed. Mr Whitelaw therefore considered that consultation might be achieved without legislation. In Lambeth he took immediate steps personally to resuscitate consultation by means of a committee which received considerable publicity nationally. In June 1982 the Home Office issued a Circular (HO 54/1982) (subsequently known as the 'guidelines') commending the formation of consultation committees everywhere. Many police authorities, most of them urged on by their chief constables, moved swiftly in response to the Circular. About a quarter had formal committees in operation by autumn 1982 and as many again had accepted the principle and planned to set up PCCs shortly. Indeed, some chief constables, as we subsequently discovered when we surveyed the growth of arrangements nationally, did not disguise their view that the best way of avoiding a statutory requirement was to keep several steps ahead of the political game.

In the event, the government decided on a compromise. When the first version of the PACE Bill was published in October 1982 it included a clause requiring consultation, but the clause was couched in such broad terms that it left the police authorities and chief constables with the widest conceivable degree of discretion. The provision, subsequently approved as PACE 1984 s. 106, required that arrangements 'be made in each police area for obtaining the views of the people in that area about matters concerning the policing of the area and for obtaining their co-operation with the police in preventing crime in the area'. Though police authorities were given responsibility for arrangements, nothing in the Act spelt out who was to be consulted, by what means, how often and about what. The government resisted calls for greater specification: the idea that policing is a matter for chief constables locally to determine, advised through mechanisms decided on jointly between police authorities and their chief constables to suit local circumstance, was carefully endorsed.

The government repudiated Labour proposals that police authorities be empowered to make policing policy. However, by acting resolutely on Lord Scarman's key recommendations, they demonstrated that they were not complacent about the need for the police conspicuously to be seen to carry the public with them. The police were to retain their operational independence but had now to make a more transparent show of good stewardship. This approach the government further endorsed by encouraging, through a Home Officer Circular, the introduction of lay visitors to police stations (another of Lord Scarman's recommendations). The government also pushed the development of performance indicators for the police and 'policing-by-objectives' planning cycles whereby chief constables and lower commanders announce their priorities and devise means for measuring their achievement. Finally, the government recommended 'partnership' schemes between the police, the public and the local authorities with a view to crime-prevention – neighbourhood watch, crime-prevention panels, the increased recruitment of special constables, crime-reduction committees, and so on. These partnership initiatives were subsequently to become a key component in the concept of 'active citizenship' which, when Home Secretary, Douglas Hurd made prominent in the late 1980s. All these developments provided the backcloth for the operation of PCCs.

THE RESEARCH PROGRAMME

The research, which involved three full-time workers, was conducted at four levels and involved the collection of very different types of data.

The National Picture

We were interested first in tracking the PCC initiative nationally. Where had the idea come from and how was it framed and implemented? We studied the Westminster and Whitehall process. We talked to ministers and senior civil servants and to representatives of the local authority and police associations. We read the speeches made during debates on PACE and by senior politicians elsewhere. We scrutinised correspondence sent out from the Home Office (recipients were generally more willing to show us this than were the authors). We traced those persons who had submitted evidence to the Scarman Inquiry. And we tracked the forays which Whitehall advisors had made to those parts of the country where good practices were said to be in operation. Finally, we conducted three national surveys (by telephone and correspondence) – in 1984, 1985 and 1988 – of every police force and authority in England and Wales, to see what they were doing by way of formal consultation in response to the successive urgings of the government.

By these means we gained a developmental picture of the policy. We concluded that though PCCs in a few localities represented a bottom-up commitment earnestly pursued in response to parochial relationship difficulties between the police and particular neighbourhoods or sections of the community, the policy writ large had classically top-down characteristics. It had been adopted by the government and promulgated from the centre. Further, as we shall see, we discovered that the rhetoric of local autonomy and flexibility – rhetoric so important for the constitutional doctrine that in Britain we have devolved policing locally accountable – was substantially belied by the reality of the Home Office-enforced implementation process. The blueprint for consultation which the government had disavowed and refused to incorporate in the Act had been imposed on the police authorities and forces by the back door. Though, arguably, the PCC initiative is not illustrative of policing policy generally, the story that unfolded provided evidence for the view that, *de facto*, we have a national police service locally administered.

The View at Force Level

On the basis of our first national survey in 1984, conducted before PACE came into operation, we discovered that different police forces were pursuing different consultative strategies. We selected six forces to represent the variety of policing environments, responses and police authority arrangements in the country. Two forces coincided with single county councils, two with combined county authorities and one with a former metropolitan county, now a joint board authority. Two forces were largely rural, one was almost wholly urban, three covered both major cities and rural hinterlands. None of the forces was a stranger to the policing controversies of recent years. Three had experienced major inner-city disorders during the period 1980–4. All had provided mutual aid in response to various crises and one was a major recipient of mutual aid during the 1984–5 miners' strike. One had been an early pioneer of PCCs (indeed its police authority chairman had chaired the Association of Metropolitan Authorities' (AMA) document which set out the model for committees which the government had adopted); three had responded positively (with different degrees of enthusiasm) to the first Home Office Circular; and two were resisting the pressure from Whitehall. Their chief constables, with the agreement of their police authorities, took the view that local police–community relationships were good, that existing informal consultative arrangements were adequate and that the formation of PCCs would constitute a needless bureaucracy.

After consulting the local authority associations and the Association of Chief Police Officers (ACPO), we approached each of the six police authorities and chief constables for permission to collect data on their patch. Five agreed. One chief constable, responsible for a rural force which had formal consultation in name only, refused. He gave no reason. We did not substitute his force.

Within each of our five forces we collected data reciprocal to those collected nationally. We were interested in how consultation arrangements were decided on locally. We interviewed senior officers, members of the police authorities and other community leaders. We read force policy statements and correspondence and police authority minutes. We tracked the interventions, if any, of Her Majesty's Inspectorate of Constabulary

(HMIC). By these means we were able fill in the national picture; explore the degrees of support and opposition to the PCC initiative; trace the patterns of pressure and resistance; unravel the degrees of understanding exhibited and will exercised by those who, according to the letter of the Act, were responsible for making the policy decisions.

Not surprisingly, we found variations between areas. But we also discovered certain common patterns. We found, for example, that the timing and shape of decisions about consultation depended heavily in most areas on the attitude of the chief constable. Except in the metropolitan area, where leading members of the police authority had been involved in the AMA deliberations referred to above, it was not the police authorities but the chief constables who took the lead or held back on PCCs. Further, in the one case where the chief constable unequivocally resisted setting up PCCs – a combined county authority covering two major cities and a large rural hinterland – he was able to carry his police authority with him and made a U-turn only when HMIC warned that failure to introduce committees would result in the force being found inefficient in terms of s. 106. Thereafter the police authority readily concurred with his revised view that PCCs were necessary. Committees were then introduced throughout the force on lines almost identical to those in the four other forces surveyed.

We also found that though most councillors could see no great need for PCCs locally, they thought they had little choice in the matter. The Home Office guidelines, which with minor amendments and some change of emphasis were updated in 1985 (HO 2/1985 – issued after PACE came into force) and 1989 (HO 62/1989, issued after our research and a Home Office review of arrangements had been conducted), were seen by most councillors and senior police officers not as advice but as instructions. Though the Act made no reference to PCCs, and might conceivably have been satisfied by, for example, beat constables continuing to liaise with parish councils and neighbourhood community associations (as had long been the practice in many areas) or periodic public opinion surveys (which several forces and local authorities were now conducting), the prevailing view was that committees were a requirement. This is scarcely surprising. Though the guidelines stressed that 'a uniform pattern . . . [of consultation] would not be sensible', the word 'arrangements' appeared always to be used interchangeably with 'groups'. The advantages of alternatives to formal groups were not canvassed. Quite the reverse. The circulars *assumed* the introduction of consultative committees: what the guidelines discussed, and what councillors assumed they had some discretion over, was the size of committees, their membership, their chairmanship, the frequency of their meetings, their terms of reference, their openness, their formality, their funding and their administrative support. Almost everyone assumed that they had no choice but to set up committees.

We found that most councillors were generally well-disposed towards the idea of formal consultation, though some were hostile, believing it to usurp their own role as elected representatives. Nevertheless they judged that committees were needed in at least a few areas within their force area. It became clear that the specific origins of the PCC initiative, in particular its ethnic dimension, were prominent in their thinking. A high proportion of councillors of all political persuasions saw PCCs as necessary in areas where a high proportion of residents were black. They thought them largely redundant elsewhere. Few were prepared publicly to voice these reservations. Indeed, the general consensus was that if formal consultation was to be introduced it had to be done uniformly. To do otherwise would be to risk accusations of racialism, partiality and inequity. Thus, though the Home Office guidelines spoke of the need for flexibility, in fact their implicit emphasis on committees was reciprocated by councillors' political instinct that consultation had to be introduced formally, comprehensively and uniformly. The result was that by the time we conducted our third national survey there was scarcely a police authority in the country that had not introduced PCCs throughout their force areas, usually by police sub-division.

The Committee Perspective

Within each of our five case-study forces we selected two committees (each based on a police sub-division), our overall selection determined by our wish to represent contrasting policing environs. We ended up with areas covering virtually the whole gamut of policing conditions to be found in the country: everything from an inner-city sub-division which had been the scene of a riot in 1981, to an affluent leafy suburb, to a depressed council estate built between the wars, to an industrial New Town, to an idyllic rural area of small market towns and hill farms invaded by tourists each summer. We were interested to know the degree to which the pattern of police community consultation is determined by the constitution for PCCs decided by police authorities or, rather, whether the process is shaped by the immediate locality within which they operate. We also wanted to know how PCCs fitted into the patchwork quilt of day-to-day consultation, formal and informal, in which the police had always maintained they were involved and which, we assumed, would continue, though possibly in modified form.

We collected data intensively in the sub-divisions. Using semi-structured methods similar to those employed at force level, we interviewed senior officers and as many members of each PCC as we were able. We observed committee meetings and studied their minutes and papers. Further, we plotted any activity which, according to the police, might be construed as consultation with the public. Some of these mechanisms were formal. For example, in a few areas there were local-authority-led crime reduction committees. Further, most police divisions had crime prevention panels, and in practically all sub-divisions one or other of the senior officers represented the police on a number of committees formed by a section of the local community or established to manage a local institution or activity. Other contacts were informal or *ad hoc*: in most sub-divisions the police attended council and other meetings when asked to or when there was something on the agenda which particularly concerned them. Clearly, it is difficult to distinguish consultation in particular from communication in general: so we sampled practically every form of contact between the police and the public that it is possible to chart, including correspondence from the public and police logs of messages received by the police in person or over the phone.

By these various means we were able to gauge the nature of PCC deliberations and assess their significance in the context of relations generally between the police and the public. However, before we discuss our findings we should first describe our fourth and final level of operation.

The View from the Grass Roots

Sub-divisions, at which level outside London the PCC initiative has largely settled (the Met has divisions as its basic unit), are relatively large administrative units. They typically cover a population of 50,000–120,000 people. They are each commanded by a superintendent. They normally employ more than 100 police officers. It follows that whatever a community is (the term has been used in a variety of ways in the social science literature), sub-divisions incorporate or cut across many of them. Given that the British public generally favours a system of neighbourhood beat policing, preferably on foot (this is now well established from public opinion poll evidence – see ACPO 1990, section 5), and given that most British people having contact with the police (in so far as they have contact at all), do so by asking a patrolling constable the way or the time (Southgate and Ekblom, 1984), we judged it important to study police–community relations at neighbourhood level. Within each of our sub-divisions we selected a neighbourhood – generally a beat or part of a beat – for even more closely focused scrutiny. As with sub-divisions, we selected neighbourhoods to represent the range of policing environs. We ended up with such contrasting beats as a shopping centre, a depressing complex of deck-access flats, part of a council estate, a major hospital and its surrounding streets, an industrial village and a group of rural upland hamlets.

In each of these neighbourhoods we accompanied on patrol the officer normally assigned to the beat. We asked him or her how he policed the beat, who he knew, who he talked to, which institutions he visited and above all which groups he regularly liaised with. We also sought out every community association we could discover in the neighbourhood and talked to their leading lights. We wanted to know at what level they had contact with the police, in so far as they had contact at all. We wanted to know what significance, if any, PCCs had for policing and police–community liaison on the ground. By these means we hoped to develop a picture of PCCs in operation from both above and below.

THE SHAPE AND OPERATION OF POLICE CONSULTATIVE COMMITTEES

We found that PCCs are generally rather different from that operating in Lambeth, the committee to which the news media has paid more attention. Lambeth has an open-ended forum. Any community organisation with a constitution and a minimum number of members can have a representative on it, meetings are frequent and open to the public and, because London has no locally elected police authority and because relations between the police and Lambeth Borough Council have been somewhat volatile historically, the forum elects its own officers and takes an independent line. This 'forum' model has been adopted in very few areas. Most parts of the country are covered by PCCs which are more akin to a formal local authority 'committee'.

Most PCCs are chaired by councillor members of police authorities, officers imposed from above rather than elected from within. Most committees meet relatively infrequently, generally every three months. Most have limited memberships, typically in the range of 15–30, a core of whom are appointed by the police authority and the remainder appointed by the core. Members typically include representatives of: county, district and parish councils; the principal statutory services (invariably education and youth services, sometimes social services, housing, leisure, probation, and so on); the churches; trades councils or chambers of commerce; ethnic minority associations; residents' and tenants' associations; neighbourhood action groups; and voluntary service organisations, particularly those for the aged. There is also a developing tendency for overlap with policing 'partnership' groups. Representatives of neighbourhood watch schemes are often included and in many areas PCC members are heavily drawn on to serve as lay visitors to police stations (see Morgan and Kemp, 1990). It follows that PCCs and their members operate within an increasingly integrated 'policing network' locally. There is a vertical relationship with the police authorities (usually through PCC councillor chairmen) and there are lateral links with other police monitoring and voluntary policing activities. As we shall see, this has consequences for the type of attitudes and experience represented within PCCs and the impact that committees make in relation to the objectives which they are said officially to serve.

PCCs generally meet on police authority or community association premises (though a few meet in police stations) and most meetings are open to the public. Attendance by the public is generally poor. This is not surprising. In most areas PCCs, like their parent police authorities, are provided with few or no support services and the publicity for their meetings is negligible. Most committees are provided with no more than a small annual budget to cover thè hire of halls and pay for agendas to be posted to members. The preparation of minutes is often a task undertaken by a volunteer member of the committee or a civilian police worker.

Most PCCs have a formal procedural style. The chairperson and the senior police officer present, almost always the sub-divisional commander, usually sit at a top table (on a raised dais, if there is one) facing the audience seated in rows. There is the customary sequence of approving past minutes, taking points arising and working through an agenda circulated beforehand. Agendas are typically short because members seldom notify secretaries of matters they wish to raise in advance, though they are repeatedly invited to do so. The principal items of business are generally the superintendent's report and a prepared topic on which a guest has earlier been invited to speak. Superintendents tend to speak for 10–15 minutes: they provide statistical or narrative digests of crimes which have occurred since the last meeting, report on any major staffing changes or unusual organisational events, and provide explanations of any changes in the law. These reports generally stimulate questions, which in turn prompt members to raise matters which concern them. This agenda item may, in the absence of a guest speaker, comprise virtually the whole of the meeting.

Guest speakers tend to be specialist police officers: representatives from the drugs squad, CID, schools-liaison or community-relations and crime-prevention departments are favourites. They are either invited to talk generally about their work or to address a particular issue about which members have expressed concern: popular themes are glue-sniffing or other forms of drug abuse, domestic burglary and its prevention, police relations with school pupils, the recruitment of ethnic minority officers, and the training of the police in race relations. A few representatives of other agencies also receive invitations: probation, social services, local authority youth and community services. Their talks, like those of the police guests, are used as the basis of a general discussion.

By these means the life of most PCCs describes a slow learning curve over a period of three to four years. Attendance rates typically settle down around the 50 per cent level. The members – over a third of them elected councillors of one sort or another, disproportionately male and middle-class (though not disproportionately white because considerable emphasis is placed on ethnic minority representation) and generally positive in their attitudes to the police when they join – gradually absorb information about police procedures and resources. They are provided with a conducted tour of their local police station and they get to know several members of police middle management. They become familiar with senior officers' views of the world (there is an important distinction to be drawn between what sociologists of the police refer to as the 'management' and the 'canteen' police cultures – see Reiner, 1985, for an overview) and they tend to become more sympathetic to them. Consciously or unconsciously, super-intendents' reports repeatedly underscore certain messages: that the police face a rising tide of crime (particularly serious crime); that the public is less deferential to authority than once it was; that police resources locally (manpower in particular) are either fewer now than they were in some past golden age or have seriously failed to keep up with the increased demands made on them; and that the police are handicapped by the duty to do more and more paperwork, much of it attributable to PACE.

Few PCC members have ever had adversarial contact with the police nor are they the sort of people who normally meet people who have. This is true even of councillors, persons who might be expected to receive representa-tions from members of the public unhappy about their treatment by the deliverers of local services. Most councillors report that the bulk of their constituency casework concerns housing, planning and education: seldom do members of the public bring specifically policing issues to them. It follows that most PCC members have little information or experience which runs counter to the police viewpoints of which they are made aware in what is often a socially congenial atmosphere. In many parts of the country PCC meetings are preceded or followed by tea and biscuits. Quite often the atmosphere in meetings is intimate. Because few members of the public or newspaper reporters attend superintendents often feel able to talk 'off the record'. Members are made to feel that they have been drawn into a privileged and responsible circle. It is perhaps not surprising, therefore, that after a few years they should tend to express even more positive views about the police and be more supportive of police arguments for increased powers or resources. Our findings in this regard have recently been confirmed by a survey of PCC members undertaken by the police staff associations (ACPO 1990, Section 5).

THE STATED OBJECTIVES OF CONSULTATION AND THEIR REALISATION

Analysis of the numerous political and administrative statements, oral and textual, issued by ministers and civil servants since 1981, suggests that PCCs are officially held to have four principal objectives.

First, they are to enable the consumers of police services to articulate and communicate to the police what it is that they want from the police. This follows from Lord Scarman's suggestion that the police, by virtue of their increasing professionalism and reliance on technology, are in danger of losing touch with public opinion. His message resonated with a powerful theme in public policy in the early 1980s: consumerism and the alleged insensitivity of public services to users. It meshed also with the implications drawn from analyses of the varied, contingent, diffuse and to some extent conflicting nature of the police mandate (see Bradley, Walker and Wilkie, 1986). Both standpoints led to the view that if the police are to be made more effective, then what are to count as the measures of police effectiveness must constantly be reappraised in the light of what it is that concerns the public, what the community considers policing priorities ought to be, and what police methods are generally considered by the public to be appropriate and legitimate. These things could only be learnt by giving users greater 'voice'.

Secondly, and the corollary of the first objective, is the perceived need to educate the public. The police provide what is in effect a generalised 24-hour emergency service. As a result, they are besieged with complaints and calls for assistance, many of which have little to do with crime. The police are also requested to respond immediately to events which cannot in the overall scale of things be considered emergencies, and about which, if they did respond immediately, they would be able to do nothing that could not be achieved later. Police services are also expensive. By one means or another they have to be rationed. It follows that the public have to be persuaded not to make unreasonable demands on the police. If the public are not to be alienated, then police rationing mechanisms have to be justified and explained to them. PCCs are to encourage two-way communication.

Thirdly, PCCs are designed to resolve conflicts. By definition, policing can never wholly be by consent. In the final analysis, policing involves coercive powers and the use of force against persons breaking the law. The doctrine of policing by consent depends rather on minimising force and maximising co-operation between the police and the policed. It is sustained by the police listening to the viewpoints of those in conflict with them, by their explaining their legal responsibilities, and persuading those against whom they use their powers that other more constructive dialogues are possible. By these means, it is hoped, confrontations will be defused and misunderstandings and deep-seated resentments avoided. PCCs are designed to build bridges.

Fourthly, it was hoped that PCCs would provide a springboard for partnerships to develop between the police and the public for practical crime-preventive effort. As we shall see, it is far from clear that this vision has ever been shared by all of the government's advisors in the Home Office. Nevertheless, it is clear that crime prevention was originally a core objective. Since the police are dependent on information and assistance from the public in order to know about and clear up most crime, then it follows that crime prevention has to be a joint process and the community must learn to shoulder its responsibilities for it. Once public trust in the police has been restored, once it has been demonstrated that the police and public are at one in their priorities, then, so the argument goes, PCCs can be used to launch and co-ordinate practical crime problem solving effort locally.

What have PCCs achieved in relation to these four broad objectives? It is not an easy question to answer. As we have seen, the introduction of PCCs has been only one of several policing initiatives of recent years. Formal consultation is part of a policy stream. The most that we can do is identify patterns of interaction and possible influence.

PCCs are operating country-wide. We estimate that there are at least 400 in England and Wales (they have not been introduced in Scotland) and about 10,000 people are at any one time committee members. Allowing for turnover, this suggests that at least 20,000 people in England and Wales have experience of membership. Many more people will have attended a PCC meeting. After operating in a relatively closed fashion in the early years, most PCCs have taken to the road, meeting in different venues around the sub-divisions and in some areas considerable efforts have successfully been made to attract the public. In some counties it is not unusual for 50 to 100 people to attend a consultative meeting in a village hall or community centre and in some inner-city areas PCCs have attracted even larger attendances, particularly when, to use the police jargon, the 'tension indicators' have been running high. However, even were as many as 500,000 people to have been to a PCC meeting (which we doubt), that is still less than 1 per cent of the population. Most committee members think that the public at large – probably more than 95 per cent of them – have not even heard of PCCs, a judgement with which researchers in the Home Office concur. It was decided not to ask a question about police–community consultation in the most recent British Crime Survey on the grounds that the proportion of respondents able to answer positively would be too small to make the exercise statistically worthwhile.

The failure to attract widespread public participation, and the fact that PCC members are disproportionately law-abiding (at least as far as having criminal convictions is concerned), male, middle-class and middle-aged, leads us to doubt their ability to represent the different views about policing that are to be found in the community. Of course, members may represent characteristics and views other than their own. And by the same token, since practically all PCC members formally represent wider constituencies, some of the messages they pick up will trickle down to others. But our data suggest that this is so to only a limited extent. Few PCC members report that they raise matters at meetings on behalf of others and most say that they seldom find much to report back to the organisations and groups they represent.

The same is true on the police side. PCCs are overwhelmingly attended by middle-management officers: few of the community beat constables in our survey neighbourhoods had been to a committee meeting and most were not sure who the members of their local PCC were, let alone what they had discussed. Few sub-divisional commanders, it appears, think it necessary to disseminate detailed information about PCCs to operational ranks. We found that the existence of formal sub-divisional consultation had had little discernible impact on the character of community policing.

For commentators this is either reassuring or disappointing, depending on one's viewpoint. We found no evidence to support the widely canvassed negative hypothesis advanced by many police officers that PCCs would absorb or displace the vital network of informal, immediate, day-to-day, grass-roots liaison which is generally held to be an essential ingredient of community policing. On the contrary, the evidence suggests that the introduction of PCCs has added to and stimulated further growth in the contacts the police have with people locally. Committees have not even displaced specific consultation arrangements with the ethnic minorities. In those sub-divisions where mechanisms were in place before the introduction of PCCs, they typically continue to operate, often now with representation of the PCCs. Further, because PCCs operate in the sub-divisional stratosphere as far as most communities are concerned (too far removed from the parochial concerns of neighbourhoods), they are often considered inappropriate vehicles to address the specific problems of a particular area. We came across several examples of more-localised consultation committees being spawned.

By the same token, we found little evidence to support the negative hypothesis advanced by some critics of contemporary policing that PCCs represent the latest increment in an advancing network of insidious police penetration *of* rather than *by* the community (greater surveillance, more intervention in domains previously regarded as private, and so on – see Cohen, 1985, for a broad statement of this thesis). PCCs do not deal in basic police intelligence nor, according to members, do they significantly increase the degree to which committee members have contact with officers between their typically infrequent meetings. We found that prolonged membership did not increase the likelihood that members either knew or had contact with the operational officers responsible for the neighbourhood where they lived. Though frequently invited to 'get in touch if you see anything untoward', very few members had thought it appropriate to take up the suggestion.

Equally disappointing, as far as Lord Scarman and the early Home Office policy analysts are concerned, are our conclusions that PCCs have achieved little (at least in the short run) in the way of conflict resolution and practical crime prevention. Young people, and certainly young black people, are conspicuous by their absence at meetings and it is in precisely those inner-city areas that were the scenes of rioting in the early 1980s that PCCs are often most moribund or effectively boycotted by the black community, particularly the Afro-Caribbean community. Committees are widely seen by those groups hostile to the police to be creatures of the police, toothless 'cons' which in the final analysis have no powers and whose views the police can ignore with impunity.

Nor during our extensive fieldwork and countryside surveys could we find more than one or two slender examples of committees claiming to have achieved anything practically to solve a local problem, change the way an area was policed, or stimulate a sub-committee or community group to tackle a concern identified during PCC deliberations. Indeed, as PCCs take to the road, meeting with new audiences in new locations each quarter, there is a tendency for committee members to take a back seat as the sub-divisional commander delivers set-piece presentations about the sub-division, his resources and priorities. The members have heard it all before many times and their decisions as to which venue should be visited next is generally dictated not by any analysis of where neighbourhood problems arise and need to be solved but where the message has not previously been delivered and the flag flown. Further, it is significant that in practically all the most recent crime-prevention initiatives to come out of the the Home Office, PCCs do not even figure. You will search in vain for a mention of PCCs in the publicity material put out by *Crime Concern*, the organisation which the government has funded to co-ordinate crime-preventive effort and the Home Office's own Crime Prevention Unit has concentrated its effort almost entirely on Crime Prevention Panels, neighbourhood watch, 'crimestoppers' and the like (see, Bottoms, 1990, for an overview).

Given this succession of negative findings, it may come as something of a surprise if we conclude that PCCs have had a considerable and largely unrecognised impact on the shape of policing policy in the late 1980s. The basis of this irony is that it is not the quantity but the quality of participation in PCCs which is of significance. Committees are for the most part made up of members of local community and political élites. Those members who are not councillors mostly hold offices in community organisations. They are part of the local 'great and the good', the municipal governmental 'inner circle'. As we have seen, they are overwhelmingly positive about the police when they join PCCs and they become more so with experience. It is not surprising, therefore, that though many police officers are wont to castigate PCCs as a 'bloody waste of time' (useless 'talking shops'), and though this is substantially true if committees are judged according to the official objectives which inspired their creation, middle-management officers actually devote a good deal of careful thought to nurturing them. They have done so because they have found them to be politically useful, a means by which sub-divisional messages can be delivered to police authorities and thus to headquarters.

Our experience is that in recent years the character of the politics of the police locally have changed profoundly. The battle lines on the police authorities have to a large extent been dispersed. Chief constables seldom stand now on their independent operational dignity, refusing to answer questions about policy. They take councillors into their confidence: share their operational dilemmas and resource constraints with them. And most councillors give their chief constables a more than sympathetic hearing. For through their membership of PCCs and lay-visiting panels they believe they have learnt about the reality of policing on the ground: they have not found blood on the walls and they have been persuaded by the accounts of their local superintendents that the police are hard-pressed and deserve more men, less paperwork and probably more legal elbow-room to tackle the anxieties which residents attending PCCs repeatedly bring to the police attention. From both ends of the political spectrum they tend to support their chief constables' claims for more resources. They have successfully been co-opted to the police standpoint. The enemy is now more often than not the Home Office and, by implication, the government holding down the police grant in particular and local government expenditure in general. Among Labour councillors there is diminishing support for plans to amend the tripartite arrangements for the goverance of the police. The police accountability debate has been relocated: it rests now not in the constitutional sphere but the realms of management and resources.

CONCLUSION

Some critics, particularly those supporting the view that police authorities should be empowered to determine broad policing policy, opposed the idea of formal consultation from the beginning. They favoured boycotting PCCs. In London several borough councils adopted this approach and refused to take part in them for several years. They argued that formal consultation was a sop designed to divert radical reform of the Police Act 1964 and shore up what they regarded as the discredited doctrine of operational independence. This oppositional stance gradually lost ground. It was a hostage to political fortune. It was redolent of anti-police attitudes, or could be interpreted as such by Conservative government ministers. Further, it was argued by 'realists' within the Labour Party and criminology, that whatever the merits of different models for police constitutional accountability, there was a need for grass-roots police–community consultation and this would remain the case even were police authorities empowered to make policy (Lea and Young, 1984). Direct parliamentary or local government responsibility for public services does not guarantee their sensitivity to users and in this respect the police are no exception.

We do not subscribe to the belief that the PCC initiative was a ploy deliberately pursued to subvert the radical plans of political opponents. Consultation equivalents of PCCs – in the fields of health, planning, education and housing – have been introduced by governments of very different persuasions for reasons not far removed from those which prompted Lord Scarman's recommendation, and we have no reason to doubt that the government genuinely hoped that committees would meet the objectives set out for them in the Home Office guidelines. The government was not complacent in the face of the manifest breakdown of confidence in the police which the riots and other events represented. Nevertheless, our conclusion is that the operation of PCCs *has* undermined the case for radical constitutional reform and that it may have done so without fundamentally repairing the policing practices that gave rise to the calls for reform. If that be the case then PCCs have served a symbolic as opposed to a substantive political purpose in spite of the intentions that inspired their creation. This almost certainly explains the effort currently being expended from the centre to ensure their continued operation in spite of the lack of evidence about their substantive effectiveness.

NOTES

1. Rod Morgan and Paul Swift (forthcoming), *Policing by Consent: Legitimating the Doctrine*.
2. In addition to the author, the research team comprised Dr Christopher Maggs and Mr Paul Swift. Their contributions were essential. Both have now moved on to other work. Whatever merit this research may have is attributable to their efforts. Whatever faults the interpretation of the data in this chapter betray are my own. Finally, I am grateful to the many police officers, councillors and community activists who gave so generously of their time helping us to undertake this study.

REFERENCES

Association of Chief Police Officers, Police Federation and Police Superintendents' Association (1990), *Operational Policing Review*, Section 5: 'The Public Survey: Consultative Committees' (Surbiton, Surrey: Joint Consultative Committee).

Bottoms, A. E. (1990), 'Crime prevention facing the 1990s', *Policing and Society*, **1**(1).

Bradley, D., Walker, N. and Wilkie, R. (1986), *Managing the Police* (Brighton, Sussex: Wheatsheaf).

Cohen, S. (1985), *Visions of Social Control* (Cambridge: Polity Press).

Labour Party (1986), *Protecting Our People* (London: Labour Party).

Lea, J. and Young, J. (1984), *What is to be Done about Law and Order?* (Harmondsworth, Middx: Penguin).

Lustgarten, L. (1986), *The Governance of the Police* (London: Sweet & Maxwell).

Morgan, R. and Kemp, C. (1990), *Lay Visitors to Police Stations: Report to the Home Office* (Bristol: Bristol Centre of Criminal Justice, University of Bristol).

Reiner, R. (1985), *The Politics of the Police* (Brighton, Sussex: Wheatsheaf).

Lord Scarman (1981), *The Brixton Disorders, 10–12 April 1981* (London: Her Majesty's Stationery Office).

Southgate, P. and Ekblom, P. (1984), *Contacts between Police and Public: Findings from the British Crime Survey* (London: Her Majesty's Stationery Office).

8 Crime and Criminal Justice in the Media

PHILIP SCHLESINGER and HOWARD TUMBER

INTRODUCTION

Our aim in this research project has been to explore how crime and criminal justice are handled in the British national media. We have tried to examine the whole communication process and therefore have studied the production of news and the content of newspapers, television news and current affairs programmes. To a lesser extent we have also examined some of the ways in which television audiences respond to programmes both factual and fictional about crime and criminal justice.

The relationship between crime and the media has been a matter of concern to social scientists for much of this century. The first studies on this question grew out of a broader concern with the role of the mass media in liberal democracies, originally prompted by the rapid growth of a popular daily press. Commentators in the early part of the century saw the popular press as abandoning its political responsibilities as a source of disinterested and accurate information and forum for rational debate. Instead, it was argued, it was becoming an arm of the burgeoning entertainment industry, using the techniques of melodrama to capture and keep its readers. The coverage of crime and justice could hardly avoid being a focus of debate, since it exemplified the new, questionable 'sensationalism'. In addition, it concerned an increasingly central area of state activity with far-reaching implications for public policy.

Alongside worries that coverage of crime might encourage or incite criminal activity by means of an 'imitation effect', there was a persistent anxiety that inaccurate or sensationalist reporting might create unnecessary public fear, leading to pressure for tough and immediate responses to given situations, thereby pre-empting more-considered initiatives, possibly with counterproductive results.

Concern over the role that the media play in fostering fear of crime still resurfaces periodically. For instance, research has been conducted into the contribution that news coverage might make to the upsurge of 'moral panics' about various forms of criminal or socially deviant behaviour. It has been argued that this contributes to a process of 'deviancy amplification', in which fear and negative stereotyping of groups judged socially threatening feed upon themselves, creating widely diffused anxieties amongst the public (cf. Cohen and Young (eds), 1973). In this general vein, at the end of 1989 a report was made to the Home Office's Standing Conference on Crime Prevention by the Working Group on the Fear of Crime chaired by Michael Grade, Chief Executive of Channel 4 Television. The report sought to identify some of the underlying causes and contributory factors seen as having a 'debilitating effect on the quality of life of too many of our citizens' (*Report of the Working Group on the Fear of Crime*, 1989, p. iii). It continued:

> The effect of crime reporting by the media is almost inevitably to increase fear. This becomes unacceptable when, as so often, crime is reported in an unbalanced way, with a strong emphasis on violent and unusual crimes, and on particular types of victim (notably young women and old people). The public receives only a distorted impression.   (Ibid., p. 2, para. 1.8)

When we conducted our research we could hardly be unaware of such perspectives. Although there was no provision for a study of public perceptions in the research budget, given our concern with how public knowledge and beliefs are constituted and given our awareness of current debates about crime and policing, we did think it important to begin exploring some possible links between crime coverage and fear of crime.

We were fortunate to be offered co-operation by the Special Projects Group of the BBC's Research Department, who allowed us to insert a limited number of questions into one of their regular 'Omnibus' surveys of the television audience during 1987. This survey covered a stratified national sample of the British public. Although this was a very limited exercise, it did allow us to gather relevant information on one central area of current debate: the dynamics of fear of crime.

The questionnaire responses revealed consistent relations between patterns of media consumption and respondents' fear of becoming victims of crime. Tabloid readers, heavy TV viewers and those preferring to watch ITV were more likely to say that they worried about becoming victims, and these relations were particularly strong where there was fear of being 'mugged' or physically attacked.

This may be partly explained by the fact that patterns of media consumption and patterns of fear may share certain common roots, but it also opens up the possibility that high consumption of 'popular' media may reinforce factors already present in people's existing situations and contribute independently to feelings of fear and insecurity. Certainly, our content analysis, in keeping with previous research on the topic, does show that 'popular' media tend to emphasise violent crimes against the person much more than do 'quality' media. We found, for example, that whereas almost half (46 per cent) of crime-related items in the daily tabloids that we sampled mentioned violent crimes against the person, the corresponding figure for the quality dailies was only 25 per cent, with mid-market papers falling almost exactly half-way between.

THE AIMS AND METHODS OF OUR RESEARCH

Fear of crime was not, in fact, the main focus of our research which centred on the workings of the daily and Sunday national press and television channels in London. Our study began in 1986 and we stopped collecting data in 1988. There have been several aims. Our concern with how news is produced has led us to examine the practices of relevant forms of specialist reporting and programme-making. This has become a well-established approach amongst sociologists of the mass media. However, we have also studied something much more unusual, and almost entirely neglected in previous British research, and that is how news sources *interact* with the news media. (To the best of our knowledge, the only other work along these lines has been undertaken in Canada (cf. Ericson *et al.*, 1989).) In pursuing this line of inquiry, we have been especially interested in how sources develop and use strategies and tactics of information management when dealing with journalists. A further major concern, reflected in our content analysis, has been to explore patterns of coverage of crime and criminal justice across the whole range of the national press and television.

Apart from the content analysis and the modest piece of audience re-search referred to earlier, full-length interviews were conducted with news sources in the crime and criminal justice fields. These included pressure and voluntary groups, trade unions and professional associations. Further in-formation was obtained through the collection and analysis of annual re-ports and accounts, publications, press releases and cuttings. Interviews were also conducted with the police, Home Office and HM Customs and Excise. We were also granted access to the Police College at Bramshill to conduct interviews with personnel in charge of media training courses. After gathering information on the activities of these groups, interviews took place with legal affairs, home affairs and crime journalists to establish their working briefs and their relationships with these various sources of information.

In our original research proposal we conceived of this study in terms of established models and empirical studies in the sociology of the media, to which we have ourselves contributed (Schlesinger, 1987; Schlesinger *et al.*, 1983; Morrison and Tumber, 1988). One of the most striking things about the tradition of research into news production, to which we have both adhered, is that the focus is upon the practices of newsrooms and news gathering. This has resulted in a great deal of new knowledge about how the media work, but at the same time it does have the shortcoming of neglecting the *interrelations* between media and the social institutions that they report. In our terms, then, it is 'media-centric'.

What has been both exciting and surprising for us is the way in which we have been forced to think again about these relationships by what we have discovered in the process of research itself. We have become increasingly aware of the need to develop a new analytical framework capable of handling the material emerging from the process of empirical investigation. Thus, as we continue to write about this study, we expect not only to discuss the new factual material that we have discovered, but also to contribute further to theoretical thinking (Schlesinger, 1988, 1989a, 1989b; Schlesinger, Tumber and Murdock, 1991).

NEWS SOURCES AND NEWS MEDIA

It is this novel aspect of our research on which we concentrate in the present chapter. Existing models have not been able to account adequately for the complexity of the relations between sources and media in the crime and criminal justice fields. Most work to date on this question has drawn upon one or other of two well-established positions.

First, there is a contemporary Marxist view that official sources are the 'primary definers' of the public agenda that is made available through the media (Hall *et al.*, 1978). In essence, what this line of argument suggests is that the power of politically and economically dominant groups in the society largely defines the contours of debate and ensures that their ways of thinking are reproduced, dominating the public agenda of discussion. Although there is much to be said for this line of argument, it does have some shortcomings and we have criticised it on a number of counts: in practice, it tends to lump together all official sources in an undifferentiated way, not recognising, for instance, how divergences within officialdom and the wider political class may lead to significant forms of competition over the definition of events and processes; it ignores the role of non-official sources in competing for space in the media, something we have found to be rather important in the criminal justice area; and it neglects informal methods of news management.

Alternatively, there is the empirical sociology of journalism which, despite offering many valuable insights into how the news is constructed, also has its shortcomings (Tunstall, 1971; Gans, 1979). This approach largely reconstructs its account of source activity from media practitioners' testimony. It tends to focus on single groups of journalists covering single institutional areas; it is pre-eminently concerned with the informal strategies of media, largely excluding those of sources; on the whole it avoids using models, working inductively according to the case in hand; and finally it pays little attention to non-official sources.

Because of their particular focuses, both these viewpoints are largely blind to the development of media strategies by news sources themselves, and it is the existence of such strategies that has been such a striking finding of our work. Because we chose to examine the activity of sources across the fields of crime and criminal justice, we have been obliged to take our distance from the media-centrism of the approaches identified above and to think again about the firm lines customarily drawn between pluralist and Marxist theories in the field of media research.

One objective, which has emerged as the study has progressed, has been to develop an analysis able to handle the activities of non-official sources without treating them either as theoretically irrelevant or simply viewing them from the standpoint of news gatherers and processors.

We have established new lines of inquiry by investigating how state institutions such as the Home Office and major police forces organise and develop information strategies towards the media. However, much more unusually, we have also asked similar questions about trade unions and professional associations such as the Law Society and the Police Federation, as well as pressure groups dealing with matters such as prison and penal reform, civil liberties and police accountability.

NEWS SOURCES IN ACTION

The first thing to consider is the extent to which any given news source is institutionalised, that is, how well established it is in the policy-making community. Obviously, in the fields of crime and criminal justice, the positions of greatest advantage are occupied by apparatuses of the state, such as the Home Office and the Metropolitan Police. These institutions engage in the routine dissemination of official information and have an enduring presence. As they frequently initiate activities, they may take advantage of the fact that they readily command attention for the release of information.

In the course of our research, an illuminating instance of how government ministers may make use of their institutional base came to light. During his first period at the Home Office as Minister for Home Affairs, David Mellor MP held a series of briefings every week on the Criminal Justice Bill (1988) for legal affairs correspondents. According to the journalists we talked to, this form of regularised briefing was a new departure. It had not been organised during the passage of the previous major piece of contentious law reform, the Police and Criminal Evidence Act (1984), Joshua Rozenberg, formerly legal affairs correspondent of the BBC (now home affairs correspondent), told us that every week Mr Mellor would say what would be coming up and

what we're going to be doing this week – it was while the Bill was going through committee in the Commons. And he [Mellor] thought this was wonderful from his point of view because he got quite a reasonable amount of publicity and coverage out of it both on radio and television. . . . If one is told 'David Mellor would be very pleased if you would come round and sit in his room and have a chat on a regular basis on a Monday afternoon and he will tell you what is coming up', and when he tells you it is something reasonably newsworthy, then you do so and it gets covered.

All the legal affairs journalists we talked to believed that Mellor had arranged these briefings partly for personal publicity. As one of them commented:

First of all he's fighting a fairly marginal seat; secondly, he's very ambitious; thirdly, he is well aware that the Prime Minister listens to the *Today* programme and is thus desperately keen to be on it because he needs to make progress in his own field; fourthly, he is one of those approachable members of the Government despite being reasonably wet in political terms . . . he realises the value to him of journalists in general and broadcasting in particular . . . he does not take the view that he must not tell the press anything ever.

Compared to state institutions, other news sources are relatively disadvantaged in competition for space in the media. However, even here not everybody competes on equal terms. At one end of the spectrum are long-term pressure groups such as Liberty (formerly the National Council for Civil Liberties, NCCL) and the Howard League for Penal Reform. At the other end are the least institutionalised organisations, namely, those brought into existence by very specific circumstances. These are *ad hoc* issue-oriented group or groups whose basis of support is narrow and weak, such as police monitoring groups.

A second important factor is the finance available to a given actor. The development of strategies to use the media has become increasingly common in recent years. Consequently, the extent to which access to the media is achieved has more and more become a crucial criterion of effectiveness. However, this can pose problems even for the best resourced: for instance, even where the Home Office and the police have invested in media monitoring and public relations, this has come up against internal budgetary limitations and has required explicit thinking about goals that might justify substantial expansion. Moreover, criteria for success are not clear-cut in ensuring that the attention desired is not just a matter of filling space and time but of achieving an impact, which is very difficult to assess.

Obviously, in the voluntary sector, where finance tends to be chronically shaky and activity is highly dependent upon low-paid idealists, the position is much more vulnerable. We have found that for such activists, it is difficult for a substantial and well-thought-out investment to be made in a media strategy. Furthermore, criteria of success tend to be rather vague and the range of media targeted to be much more restricted than in the case of state agencies.

More generally, it is important to note that the strategies for achieving media coverage are not always solely directed towards attempts to influence the policy agenda. Other reasons and motives may be discerned. For example, organisational imperatives such as the need to increase resources, to aid recruitment and, particularly in the case of professional associations and trade unions, the desire to boost membership morale. For voluntary and pressure groups media coverage can also enhance feelings of solidarity, dissipate isolationist tendencies and give a fillip to staff confidence. As Frances Crook of the Howard League said to us: 'a lot of members will say "Oh yes, you seem to be doing a lot. I've seen your name in the paper again." The higher profile we get, the more members we get.'

The National Association for the Care and Resettlement of Offenders (NACRO) has a number of aims which its information strategy attempts to fulfil. Paul Cavadino, the NACRO press officer, outlined their objectives in this way:

> On the general level we have got a duty to try where we can to get publicity for constructive approaches to crime, to dealing with offenders and preventing crime as part of public education because the media in any event have a lot about crime all the time, much of which is sensa-

tional, distorted, negative and unconstructive. If only to a small degree we can help to redress the balance by setting coverage of constructive ways of dealing with crime and offenders, then it is desirable to do that. On one level that is what we are aiming to do. On a more specific level, if you have got a scheme in a local area, particularly the sort of scheme that we run, and if they get a steady flow of reasonably good, sympathetic publicity for the work they are doing, then that obviously helps to build up goodwill in the area.

Paul Cavadino believes that it is possible to change attitudes, but it is important to be realistic about what can be achieved by the way of press publicity:

If people are totally hostile to what you are doing anyway then good publicity is not likely to change that. But if people are sympathetic but do not know very much about what you do but basically have their hearts in the right place or are neutral, then it is possible to put out material which reinforces that. Also, in an unpopular area like ours, that is the constructive treatment of offenders, what is important is that if people are in favour of what we are doing and of the sort of things we are saying, to try and make sure that they do not feel they are completely out of step with everyone else. If everything is of a hardline type and there is nothing positive being said in the media to counteract that, increasingly you can build up a climate where people feel that this is the norm and their own views shift a bit. You have got to try to make sure that people who are basically on our side keep seeing this said and that reinforces their own views and their own wish to see something better happen, something more constructive, some elements of decency injected into the way we deal with crime offenders.

Cavadino's comments illustrate the growing development of news source sophistication amongst pressure groups in the criminal justice area, where NACRO is in the forefront of such developments. The comments quoted above show both an understanding of the group's own needs and how these may translate themselves into a long-term campaigning strategy towards the media. Groups in the area of penal reform have traditionally been the poor relation of those in the social policy lobby. The Child Poverty Action Group has been seen as a particularly good model to emulate, and its strategy as an example to be followed and applied in other fields. The 'success' that has resulted is already evident. As a director of one of the prison pressure groups remarked:

It is remarkable that prisons are the issue that they are. I think that the ability of the various penal pressure groups to get stuff in the newspapers is astonishing given how marginal prison is to most people's lives and by comparison with the poverty lobby, the housing lobby, and indeed any other you wish to mention, our record is astonishing and very welcome.

The pursuit of an information strategy may also involve competition to raise a body's profile. A relevant example that we uncovered concerned HM Customs and Excise, who saw themselves as consciously competing with the police for media attention. But, as also became clear in the course of investigating this further, it is not necessarily the case that all strategies are aimed at the wider public.

HM Customs and Excise has raised its profile considerably in recent years because of concern about its public image. Due to past actions over Value Added Tax, officers felt that they had acquired an image of jack-booted men who visited during the night and kicked down the door. Secondly, even though the Customs were scoring major drug-busting successes as result of their investigations, their efforts were going largely unnoticed by both government and public because they did not have a very active public relations and press policy. As the Head of Information at Customs, Graham Hammond, told us:

> When we were in the arena bidding for money in competition with the National Health Service, the police and so forth, because our case wasn't in the forefront of ministers' minds we became neglected, and in fact the department suffered quite savage cuts in staffing as part of the government's review of Civil Service staffing. Subsequent to our higher publicity profile, I think it is no accident that we are getting more resources and more staff devoted to both tax collection and drug enforcement.

Graham Hammond had recently moved from the Ministry of Defence. His brief on arrival at Customs and Excise, he informed us, was totally at variance with that of his predecessors. The Commissioners of the Board decided that they wanted a more open publicity policy:

> Beforehand, the Customs and Excise had been an archetypical secret service with the press office considered to have completed a good job if they had kept the press at bay. As a result the department was not getting the resources that it felt entitled to, especially in contest to the police who at that time, compared to the Customs, were selling their cause fairly well.

In this perspective, the government was more disposed to give resources to the police because there was tangible evidence, via the media, of their effectiveness. Since the Customs have adopted a more open stance, the government, according to Hammond, 'has seen that there is considerable political advantage in being seen to be supporting a law-enforcement agency that succeeds'.

The Home Office has also operated in this way in order to secure extra resources, according to the Prison Reform Trust, who told us the following:

> Towards the end of the 1970s the Home Office wanted to embark upon a programme of prison construction. It saw one of the ways in which it could obtain resources for that was by putting pressure on the Treasury to open up the prisons to show just how decrepit they were. Hence the invitation to [a film-maker] Rex Bloomstein, to carry out his brilliant Strangeways [Prison] series for television. They [the Home Office] adopted a strategy of approaching journalists saying, 'Please come and see how awful our prisons are.' Previously, the Home Office had always discouraged journalists, kept them out of the establishments and would rarely tell them anything either on, or off, the record.

The police, too, have developed on these lines by considerably reorganising their information departments. These changes have taken place mainly in the large metropolitan forces where, with one notable exception, a more open and proactive policy has replaced a closed and reactive one. As Geoffrey Dear, at that time Chief Constable of the West Midlands, said:

> In the very best sense of the word we try and use the media. I don't mean manipulate because that would be wrong and they wouldn't allow it to happen anyway. By 'use' I mean we're in the business to inform the public, to create a position where the public are better-informed about what we're doing, to ask questions of the public through the media, and to use the media in the sense of running a story. For example, we have it in mind to move into some area of policing, or elevate or suppress certain profiles of policemen, and do they think it's a good idea or not. Handled the right way, and with the full co-operation and acknowledgement as to what's happening, you can measure public attitudes. It seems to me a very good vehicle to test public opinion in a way that you can't always test it through formally asking questions.

One of the contradictions of the Thatcher years is that while government and state secrecy has increased, the desire and need of the police for an improved image has steadily gathered momentum, requiring a semblance of openness. This image change, whilst initially involving a process of internal reorganisation and adjustment, later called for the dissemination of desired material through the media. Journalists, although welcoming this more open policy, have remained sceptical of some of its aspects.

For the police, it has been the crisis of confidence both inside the force and amongst the general public that has led them to redevelop their press and public relations operations. According to Kenneth Oxford, the then Chief Constable of Merseyside:

> Almost twenty years ago it was almost an indictable offence under the discipline code to talk to the media, which to me was counterproductive. And relating to my experiences in the operations field, I have always felt on balance that if you take the media along with you you're going to overcome a lot of unnecessary hurdles.

In the view of Stewart Tendler, crime correspondent of *The Times*, it was Sir Kenneth Newman, the former Commissioner of the Metropolitan Police, who was instrumental in further updating the policy of his predecessor, Sir Robert Mark, of opening up relations with the press. Mark's approach had originally been developed in the mid-1970s:

> What Newman did was to make it evident to his force that there is a lot to be gained from talking to the press and they have become a lot more open about what they are doing. . . . When I first started on Fleet Street the [Special] Branch did not seem to exist. If you rang up they denied who they were! Now there is no argument about it. So that's changed. . . . In general working they are a lot more realistic, a lot more apparently truthful. . . . It is the ethos that has changed, the availability of policemen to talk generally.

In 1986, a year before he left the Metropolitan Police, Newman also started briefings with crime correspondents and home affairs correspondents, an arrangement continued by his successor Sir Peter Imbert. The journalists have mixed feelings about these events. Some find them 'helpful' rather than 'useful'. Others are much more ambivalent, as is reflected in this comment to us: 'It's like all lobby systems, it's dangerous not to be part of it.'

The 1980s were not a very good time for the police in Britain. Their handling of the inner-city riots of the early years of the decade came in for heavy criticism in some quarters. Violent confrontations during the course of industrial relations disputes were also at the forefront of political debate: the most noteworthy cases were the coal miners' strike in 1984–5 and the print workers' disputes with newspaper owner Eddie Shah at his Warrington plant in 1983 and with Rupert Murdoch at his new Wapping plant in 1987. The shooting of innocent citizens in the course of operations caused great public concern, as did allegations of corruption and accusations of beatings in order to obtain confessions. All of these have contributed to a widespread shaking of public confidence and a diminution of support.

It is not surprising, therefore, that some large forces, such as the West Midlands, have spent considerable time and energy searching for a suitable model on which to base their PR operations. This search has spread as far as the United States, as well as seeking out 'best practice' in the British forces. The then Chief Constable, Geoffrey Dear, observed:

> I'm never too sure whether the media follow public opinion or pressure public opinion, but one thing in my philosophy is for sure: that unless you get accurate media coverage you're never going anywhere, and hopefully if you're doing it in the right way the accurate media coverage will be favourable media coverage.

Mr Dear went on to say that before he arrived at the West Midlands the force had low morale and the image was very poor. It had been misreported mainly because of the prevailing ethos of secrecy:

> If I was going to put anything right at all it had to be in the public arena, we had to tell the public that we were good, proud, professional, competent, and if we got it wrong we'd own up to it straight away, but that you, the West Midlands public, ought to recognise that you are being better served, and that obviously mattered, talking much more openly and forcefully and laying everything bare and hoping that they were objective in the way they reported it locally and nationally. And on all the indicators I think we are much better off than we were two years ago, morale is certainly much higher, the quality of service is higher, we get congratulating notices in many different newspapers, and certainly the results we're getting, measured in terms of crime going down and being held down against the national trend and detections going up, so at the moment we're moving.

(In August 1989, Chief Constable Dear disbanded the West Midlands Serious Crime Squad, amid allegations of serious misconduct over a number of years, and the West Yorkshire Police were called in to investigate these claims. Mr Dear himself has moved on to HM Inspectorate of Constabulary.)

The chief officers we spoke to all laid great store by the kind of press coverage their forces managed to achieve. In 1988 in a move aimed at boosting support for the Metropolitan police, the current Commissioner, Sir Peter Imbert, hired one of the best-known design consultancies and corporate-image specialists, Wolff Olins, to make a design audit of internal and external attitudes towards the force. The report on the corporate identity of the Metropolitan Police was entitled *A Force for Change*. It recommended the need for cultural change within the Met to support the recent organisational changes and the establishment of a clear collective vision. This cultural change, the report stated, should be made up from a series of developments, many of which were already taking place, affecting management systems, behaviour, attitudes, communication and visual identity (Wolff Olins, 1988). The designers' belief is that the proposed changes will produce more-favourable public opinion, resulting eventually in a changed impression of police effectiveness (whether genuine or not).

The main response to *A Force for Change* is 'The Plus Programme', a continuing series of measures drawn up by Deputy Assistant Commissioner Charles Pollard and Commander Alec Marnoch under the guidance of the Commissioner. Its strategy is to regard the public as consumers, the customers and paymasters of policing, not potential criminals and troublemakers. As Sir Peter Imbert stated: 'The Metropolitan Police has a strong tradition of service to the Public and our common purpose must now be to make the quality of that service even better' (*The Plus Programme – Making it Happen*, April 1989).

Many government departments have adopted high-street images to sell their services. After the General Election of 1987, the Department of Trade and Industry under Lord Young led the way in sales techniques. The contemporary emphasis is on business practice as a model for public-sector organisation and on entrepreneurship as the way forward for all. In keeping with this shift, public-sector organisations have adapted their public relations to commercial models in order to provide themselves with a more acceptable image. And the police have not been slow to follow suit, seeing citizens as customers to whom their activities have to be 'sold'.

Such image-building has characterised many of those involved in the crime and criminal justice field. It is a version of the mobilisation model, used by political leaderships to gain support for their objectives, which has spread to those on the outer rim of the policy-making circle. Unions such as the Probation Officers have completely revamped their internal and external communications. Other associations, such as the Bar Council, and firms of solicitors (who have only recently been allowed to advertise) have employed public-relations companies to look after publicity and relations with the press.

Some journalists at least, however, do retain a certain immunity from this kind of approach, as Malcolm Dean of the *Guardian* recounted:

> They call me, send press releases and what-not. . . . Every week you get about four calls from somebody you have not heard of at all. 'Oh, Gerry here, Malcolm, from PR Incorporate', and his only expertise is to offer these damn law firms that 'I'll fix you up lunch with Malcolm Dean'.

Talking of such lunches, Frances Gibb of *The Times* noted: 'I cannot think of a single instance where it's been any use.' Confirming this point, Terence Shaw of *The Daily Telegraph* stated:

> One still relies really on personal contact with barristers or individual members of the Bar Council because they do know the thing inside out, and public relations firms very often, unless they have one very good expert in it, tend to be channels [for pushing out material]. I could say the same in relation to government public relations departments; there are some who are pretty good but very often it is so much easier and quicker, and you get a much better understanding of the issue, to talk to some-body.

THE MEDIA AT WORK

The policy community dealing with crime and criminal justice has grown in recent years, added to which there has been the growing development of more-sophisticated media strategies by news sources, aspects of which we have outlined above. In response to these shifts, there have been changes in the organisation of specialist press and television reporting which we have sought to investigate in this study.

Journalists covering the areas of crime, law and justice can be divided into three groups: crime, home affairs and legal affairs. Although these three categories encompass the whole field, not all national newspapers have separate correspondents covering each area, as there are variations in the designations of personnel.

The five national 'quality' newspapers (the *Guardian*, the *Independent*, *The Times*, the *Daily Telegraph* and *The Financial Times*) all have legal affairs correspondents who, together with their BBC counterpart, constitute a fairly cohesive group. We have identified four main reasons for the growth in coverage of this specialism in the 1980s. First, the Conservative government introduced several major pieces of legislation such as the Police and Criminal Evidence Act (1984) and the Criminal Justice Act (1988). Secondly, proposed changes in the legal system (for instance, giving solicitors the right of appearance) served to focus the spotlight on this area. Thirdly, the major prosecutions in the 1980s of Sarah Tisdall, Clive Ponting and Peter Wright under official secrecy legislation has meant that newspapers required specialists to handle these stories' legal ramifications and could not rely solely upon home affairs or general reporters to cover them. Fourthly, with the launch of the *Independent* in October 1986, competition in the 'up-market' or 'quality' newspapers intensified, with battle joined for an audience that included solicitors, barristers and others working in the legal profession.

As Robert Rice, legal affairs correspondent of the *Independent* told us: 'One of the reasons [that] we have a law correspondent is because we think that lawyers are a very good market within our ABC1 group which we are trying to attract to this new newspaper. And so we decided at a very early stage that we would have to have law reporters to try and compete with *The Times*.'

Journalists have also increased their reporting of the European Commission on Human Rights in Strasbourg and the legal implications of industrial relations stories. Here, the miners' strike of 1984–5 was of signal importance, given the complexity of its legal dimension. The BBC's Joshua Rozenberg observed that the strike 'was being fought in the courts just as much as on the picket line and people were interested in what is a sequestrator or would Arthur Scargill go to prison for contempt of court'.

Given that amongst other things it addresses an opinion-forming élite, the 'quality' press has found it necessary to adapt to the increase in information being made available in the criminal justice field, particularly by state institutions. Malcolm Dean of the *Guardian* pointed to one example of this change: 'It's very interesting what has happened to the Lord Chancellor's department: four years ago there was no press officer, you just called his private secretary. . . . They now have three press officers, a chief information officer and two junior officers.'

The brief of the home affairs correspondents is not as easily definable as that of the legal affairs or crime correspondents, because they cover a wide area shaped mainly by the remits of the Home Office, which include police, civil defence, criminal law, penal policy, prisons, courts, broadcasting, gambling, immigration and nationality, community relations, voluntary services, data protection, fire service and electoral matters. Some home affairs correspondents cover all these, others concentrate upon just one or two areas. For example, broadcasting is now predominantly covered by media correspondents, particularly in the 'quality' press, whereas previously it was a subject for the home affairs correspondent.

The scope of home affairs, then, varies across the press. Apart from being largely anchored in the activities of the Home Office, it may also at times depend on the individual news editor's categorisation of a given story, with the previous experience and contacts of particular correspondents also playing a part in defining the brief. On occasions, the interest of a correspondent or an editor in a particular subject inevitably produces more coverage, which in turn sets off a relatively enduring pattern. The *Independent* has taken an interest in prisons from the outset. According to Sarah Helm, the newspaper's home affairs correspondent:

> That was something that was pushed right from the top, that was the editor's interest. When we first started it seemed to be his personal issue ... and it is a great social issue. I am very interested in it too but I would not have pushed it because on the whole it is not something that is easy to get people to read, it is not a very acceptable sort of subject. But it is all relative, it is very important and there is an endless wealth of material to write about in that area.

Traditionally, reform of the penal system has not been a subject at the top of the public agenda. The cynical view put forward by some of the pressure groups interviewed by us was that there were no votes to be gained by political parties or individual politicians by taking an interest in or championing reform. It has been viewed as having little audience or readership appeal. Hence, for a new 'quality' newspaper to be launched at a time when liberal and reformist views in Britain were under attack, and outlets for such views were perceived to be shrinking, was a boon for the voluntary and pressure groups working and campaigning in the criminal justice area. For the paper to take an active interest in prison reform was even more of a welcome bonus.

Crime, by contrast, is one of the biggest and most competitive areas in British journalism. Newspapers differ in the number of specialist crime correspondents and reporters they employ. The majority have one, while some have as many as three. The nature of coverage has altered considerably over the years and the type of journalist has also changed. Twenty-five years ago, crime coverage mainly concerned murder, jewel thefts and petty crime. It now encompasses drugs, terrorism, child abuse, rape, mugging, fraud, football hooliganism, and policy matters. As George Hollingberry of the *Sun* noted:

There is a multitude of stories which the crime reporter now has to cover, it is a very wide field indeed. . . . You have gone from smash-and-grabs and the odd murder story into this vast field of crime that's developed in the last twenty years. Where one thought in your last days of covering crime it would end up as a sinecure, you find that there is more and more crime to cover and many offices are increasing their coverage and their crime teams.

As a consequence of this increase, some crime correspondents specialise in particular sub-fields rather than attempting to cover the whole area. This marks a recent shift in the organisation of crime journalism. A number of factors can be identified as having contributed to the changing pattern of crime coverage. For example, the abolition of capital punishment has had an effect on the news value of a murder, lessening its impact considerably: As George Hollingberry pointed out:

In those early days . . . murder was a very dramatic affair because one knew that this was a capital offence and that you were looking for a killer who when found and tried and convicted was hanged. You usually followed the case through, beginning with the investigation, then the trial and then the grisly business of covering hanging.

Another important factor is the altered relationship with the main source of information – the police – due mainly to the changing nature of policing in Britain. This has certainly moved on since the last studies of the relations between journalists and the police were conducted, between 15 and 20 years ago (cf. Tunstall, 1971; Chibnall, 1977). 'I think the old cigarette and the pint in the pub sort of ethos is disappearing to a certain extent', commented Stewart Tendler of *The Times*, a view confirmed to us by other crime correspondents. Tendler went on to illustrate the point:

Twenty years ago the Yard did almost all the major investigations inside and outside London because very few forces had the expertise, they were all very small city, town or shire forces. And so the Scotland Yard detective would sail off with the troop of Fleet Street reporters in tow. Now that has gone completely because all forces are now capable of doing their own investigations and rarely need the Yard. So the matiness that existed in that sort of travelling circus has gone. . . . You could get the situation where the detective, his sergeant and the press corps all stayed at the same hotel, so they would have a drink during the evening and he might tell them what he had done during the day. And names were made that way, great detectives were born, or not.

The relationship between the correspondents themselves has also been affected by the differences in police activity. George Hollingberry is one who laments the changes and the consequent loss of camaraderie:

> In the early days there was a tremendous esprit de corps because suddenly you went charging out in the middle of the night on a murder enquiry in some remote county and by the time you had got your story over, phoned from a local pub, you then had to think about where you were going to stay. And very often you would find yourself, five of you, sleeping in one bed! I have even shared a bath as a bed with another reporter. . . . Some nights you would congregate in the bar in some village pub and perhaps one chap might become worse for wear and a dramatic development may suddenly happen, and I have known reporters to ring rival papers with the story which their own reporter was incapable of putting over. I don't think this sort of situation would happen now but that is what used to happen in the old days when you followed the detective with the murder bag.

Work patterns within London have also altered, with little use now made of the reporters' room at Scotland Yard (although there has been some drift back because correspondents find it more convenient as a base than their new offices in Docklands). The more senior correspondents regret the demise of this meeting place, in some cases invoking a mythical past, as, for instance, did the *Sun*'s George Hollingberry:

> I can go back to when Scotland Yard was in that lovely old building on the Embankment and we had this little green hut by the side of the building with its nicotine-stained walls and in the corner there was always a poker pool on the go, and it reminded me very much of that lovely American film *The Front Page*. It was very much like that, with all these old crime reporters playing poker and knocking back the odd nip, and suddenly the phone would go and it was wonderful to see their professionalism. Suddenly the game was abandoned and there they were on the phone, making all sorts of calls. . . . As an old-timer much of the romance has gone, I loved every minute of it and very often would get bored on holiday because I felt I was missing something and would ache to get back.

The younger correspondents, by contrast, come from a different mould. They are thought to be more critical of the police and less cohesive as a group. Talking about the press room at Scotland Yard, Stewart Tendler of *The Times* said:

I use it a bit more than I used to simply because Wapping is such a long way but there was a time when everybody spent all their times there, but I never did even when I started this job, I decided against that because I thought (a) it was too cosy, and (b) it is difficult to operate like that in the middle of everybody else, in the middle of your competitors.

A CONCLUDING REMARK

In this chapter, we have reported on our wide-ranging study of how the British national press and television cover crime and criminal justice. For present purposes, we have concentrated on an area much neglected in the recent sociology of the media, namely, the interrelations between news sources and journalists. In developing our analysis, it has become obvious that the ways in which state agencies and pressure- and interest-groups develop strategies in order to intervene in the policy process via the media are worthy of detailed examination. This process relates closely to the scope and limits of public debate and the ways in which this in turn may affect the formation of public opinion. As we have pointed out, recent research has been too centred upon the media themselves, thereby ignoring how political organisations and institutions organise in order to affect media coverage. This study of crime and criminal justice reporting has allowed us to reopen these questions in British media research and criminology.

REFERENCES

Chibnall, S. (1977) *Law-and-Order News: An Analysis of Crime Reporting in the British Press* (London: Tavistock).
Cohen, S. and Young, J. (eds) (1973), *The Manufacture of News: Deviance, Social Problems and the Mass Media* (London: Constable).
Ericson, R.V., Baranek, P. V. and Chan, J. B. L. (1989), *Negotiating Control: A Study of News Sources* (Milton Keynes, Bucks.: Open University Press).
Gans, H. J. (1979), *Deciding What's News: A Study of CBS Evening News, NBC Nightly News, Newsweek and Time* (New York: Pantheon Books).
Hall, S., Critcher, C., Jefferson, T., Clarke, J. and Roberts, B. (1978), *Policing the Crisis: Mugging, the State and Law and Order* (London: Macmillan).
Morrison, D. and Tumber, H. (1988), *Journalists at War: The Dynamics of News Reporting during the Falklands War* (London: Sage).
Report of the Working Group on the Fear of Crime (1989), chaired by Michael Grade, Home Office: Standing Conference on Crime Prevention (London: Home Office).

Schlesinger, P. (1987), *Putting 'Reality' Together: BBC News*, 2nd edn (London: Methuen).

Schlesinger, P., Murdock, G. and Elliott, P. (1983), *Televising 'Terrorism': Political Violence in Popular Culture* (London: Comedia).

Schlesinger, P. (1988), 'Die Interpretation von Gewalt', *Innovation* (Vienna), **4**(5), 435–53. Also in Italian: 'Quanto è violenta la società contemporanea? Alcuni problemi di interpretazione', in Luigi Bonanate (ed.), *Il Futuro della Pace e la Violenza del Futuro: Atti del Simposio Internazionale Città di Lugano, 18–19–20 November 1987* (Lugano: Edizioni Città di Lugano) pp. 165–80.

Schlesinger, P. (1989a), 'From production to propaganda?', *Media, Culture and Society*, **11**(3), 283–306; in Italian translation as: 'Dalla produzione alla propaganda?: Campi d'indagine e modelli interpretativi in cinque studi recenti', *Problemi dell'Informazione* (Bologna), **14**(4), 567–93.

Schlesinger, P. (1989b), 'Rethinking the sociology of journalism: source strategies and the limits of media-centrism', in Marjorie Ferguson (ed.), *Public Communication: The New Imperatives* (London: Sage) pp. 62–83; Spanish translation in: *Estudios sobre las Culturas Contemporáneas* (Colima, Mexico) (forthcoming); Italian translation in: *Problemi dell' Informazione* (Bologna: forthcoming).

Schlesinger, P., Tumber, H. and Murdock, G. (1991), 'The media politics of crime and criminal justice', *British Journal of Sociology*, **42**(3), 397–420.

Tunstall, J. (1971) *Journalists at Work: Specialist Correspondents, their News Organisations, News Sources and Competitor-Colleagues* (London: Constable).

Wolff Olins (1988), *A Force for Change* (London: Wolff Olins).

9 Women's Criminal Careers*

PAT CARLEN

INTRODUCTION

In 1985 I conducted taped interviews with 39 women between the ages of 15 and 46. Each had at least one criminal conviction, the vast majority had substantial 'form' and a disproportionate number had been convicted of a serious crime either of violence or against property. The main aims of the research were, first, to discover what the women themselves saw as being major influences upon, and turning points in, their criminal careers; and secondly, to explain both the sources of those self-perceptions and their effects. Each woman was told that I wanted her to describe her progress through law-breaking, police stations, courts and custodial institutions, and to start her narrative from the point where she thought her troubles had begun. Not surprisingly, all of the women asked me what I intended to do with the taped interviews after they had been transcribed. In reassuring them that all quotations from the transcripts would be used pseudonymously, I was also able to explain that no individual history would be used in full. I stressed that, as I was a sociologist, I would be looking mainly to social factors in investigating why their lives had gone the way they had. That in analysing the transcripts I would be trying, first, to ascertain what each individual biography had in common with the 38 others and, secondly, to describe and explain the variety of effects that these shared social factors had had on their criminal careers. In fact, what I told the women was how I hoped to translate their individual (autobiographical) oral histories into a socio-biographical analysis of women's criminal careers (see Carlen, 1988).

The remainder of this chapter will be divided into two: first, a summary of both the research findings and the arguments developed from the results of the ethnographic analyses; secondly, a discussion of the research's policy implications.

SUMMARY OF FINDINGS AND THEORETICAL PERSPECTIVE

Four major factors – poverty, being in local authority residential Care, drug (including alcohol) addiction and the quest for excitement – were explicitly identified by the young women as being prime constituents of their law-breaking and criminalisation. Ethnographic analysis of the women's oral

204

histories was, however, directed not merely at describing sequences of law-breaking and criminalisation, but also at finding out both *how* and *why* such law-breaking and criminalisation had come about. To facilitate the construction of such explanations the analyses were informed by the criminological perspective known as *control theory*.

Instead of posing the question, 'Why do people break the law?', control theory asks, 'Why do people conform?' and replies that people are more likely to conform when they perceive that they have a vested interest in so doing, when they have more to lose than to gain by law-breaking. This perspective has the virtue of explaining the law-breaking of both rich and poor, though economic factors are not posited as being the only determinants of how people calculate the rewards expected from either law-breaking or conformity. Nor need positive calculation be a prerequisite to law-breaking. A drift into crime, accompanied by the concomitant rewards of friendship, financial gain and excitement, can engender the alternative 'controls' that gradually commit the woman law-breaker to a way of life more satisfying than that offered by conventional labour and marriage markets and/or the meagre (and often uncertain) payments of the Department of Social Security. Thus the inversion of a control theory explaining why the majority of women appear to be law-abiding only partly explains why *some* women break the law in the first place. It is even less useful in explaining why a few of all women law-breakers go on to become recidivist criminals and prisoners.

Instead, therefore, of analysing only the processes that condition the conformity of women who are law-abiding,[1] the research also analysed the particular combination of circumstances at the points in their criminal careers when the 39 women felt that they had absolutely *nothing* to lose (and *maybe* something to gain) by engaging in criminal activity.

Marginalised by a combination of class position (the poverty of which denied them adequate material means for alleviating their multiple personal misfortunes such as ill-health, bereavement and isolation), gender, in some cases racism, and in all cases overcriminalisation,[2] the women frequently implied that at certain times in their lives they had had neither material nor ideological incentive to be law-abiding. Once they had broken the law, the inequalities stemming from class, gender and in some cases racism, combined to overdetermine their almost certain criminalisation. Subsequent institutionalisation, outlawing (as far as employment was concerned) and ensuing commitment to a deviant lifestyle ensured that the further they progressed in their criminal careers and the more their options narrowed, the less they had to lose by being 'nicked' and the less they had to gain by conformity.

These findings were incorporated into the formal theory of the relationships between women, gender, crime and poverty outlined below.

WOMEN, GENDER, CRIME AND POVERTY – SUMMARY OF ARGUMENTS

1. Whereas for working-class men in employment the major locus of social control is the workplace (Young, 1975), working-class women have traditionally been contained within *two* material and ideological sites of social control: the workplace and the family. Working-class women have therefore been doubly controlled. They have been expected not only to make the 'class deal' but the 'gender deal' too.
2. Most working-class women make both the class deal and the gender deal because the exploitative nature of those two deals is obscured by ideologies of familiness and consumerism working together to engender within them a commitment to, if not a belief in, the rewards of respectable working-class womanhood.
3. This commitment to the rewards of respectability is most likely to be engendered when young women are brought up in families where both psychological and material rewards are represented as emanating from either the labours or 'love' of a male breadwinner. (Even though many families do not nowadays *have* a male breadwinner, the normative heterosexuality celebrated in women's magazines, pop songs and the predominantly conservative and liberal mass media still represents male-related domesticity coupled with a wage-earning job as the twin ideals to which all (gender-) competent modern women should aspire.)
4. Under certain circumstances some women do not acquire the psychological commitments to male-related domesticity, tend not to have their class position occluded by the outward trappings or inner constraints of 'family' ideology and yet *do* acquiesce in a commitment to consumerism which is the only space within which they believe they can make their own lives.
5. The majority of women do not become embroiled in criminal careers, even if on occasion they do break the law. This under-criminalisation occurs because, while they remain within the family, they are seen to have made the gender deal and to be gender-regulated. Conversely, girls in Care, single women living alone and other 'women without men' are often seen as being gender-decontrolled. Already seen, therefore, as being *unregulated women*, they are also seen as being potential

recidivist law-breakers and the authorities act accordingly (see Carlen, 1983, pp. 66–9).

6. The early imprisonment of young women combines with prevailing economic and ideological conditions to minimalise (or in many cases, destroy) the likelihood of their having either future opportunities or inclinations to make either the class deal or the gender deal. They perceive themselves as being marginalised and, therefore, having nothing to lose, decide that law-breaking is a preferable alternative to poverty and social isolation.

7. Those women who are rendered marginal by their lack of commitment to both the class deal and the gender deal can also experience a sense of injustice as a result of two major social and political discourses: the 'Christmas card' image of family life and the private/public distinction that celebrates the myth that the governance of family and domesticity should (and indeed does) remain beyond the purview and regulation of the state.

8. The 39 women had in the main committed crime because, in addition to experiencing poverty and an excess of welfare regulation, they had also sensed that such poverty and welfare regulation violate some of the most fundamental liberal political discourses concerning welfare rights and the rights of private citizens.

9. The women's perceptions of the class and gender deals on offer to them had not been alone in atrophying their capacity to believe in and/or be regulated by either state laws or patriarchal mores. Additionally, the contemporary and competing rhetorics of social welfare and individualistic consumerism had engendered in them a strong commitment to obtaining a decent standard of living and defending their domestic and personal space by *any* means within their power.

POLICY IMPLICATIONS

When they talked with me in 1985 and 1986, 12 of the 39 women claimed that they had turned their backs on crime for good. Conversely, 12 others asserted that they were by then committed to a life of crime or, at least, the pursuance of their own particular crime-line in the future. A further 15 said that, although they desperately wanted to lead a 'normal life', they were afraid that, if they were to be 'realistic', they would have to assess their chances of being crime-free in the future as being slim. The 27 women in the two latter groups were those who, in effect, believed that their chances of ever enjoying prosperous law-abiding lives were practically nil.

Is it possible, therefore, to respond to deviant girls and criminal women without narrowing their options to such an extent that, both for material and psychological reasons, they feel that, as they are always/already outsiders, there is a certain inevitability about the continuance of their criminal and penal careers? To help answer that question, Table 9.1 summarises just *how* the combined law-breaking and criminalisation of working-class women can effect a further narrowing of already meagre life chances. I then discuss alternative ways of confronting women's crime and propose some reforms of those parts of the welfare, judicial and penal systems that presently respond so ineptly to it. Finally, and most importantly, there is a consideration of the more fundamental political and economic changes prerequisite to a rethinking of criminal justice for women within a programme of social justice in general.

NARROWING OPTIONS

In 1981 Marsha Rosenbaum wrote:

In analysing the career of the woman addict, I found her career is inverted. Heroin expands her life options in the initial stages and that is the essence of its social attraction. Yet with progressively further immersion in the heroin world, the social, psychological and physiological exigencies of heroin use create an option 'funnel' for the woman addict. ... Ultimately, the woman addict is locked into the heroin life and locked out of the conventional world. (Rosenbaum, 1981, p. 11)

Amend the above quotation by substituting 'crime' for 'heroin' and 'woman criminal' for 'woman addict', and it well describes the careers of that tiny minority of young female law-breakers who go on to become recidivist criminals. The Table 9.1 lists the interactive sequences that cumulatively facilitated the beliefs of 27 of the 39 women that they had become such outsiders that either they could not get 'back in' or that they did not want to. They also believed that, regardless of what they themselves did, their criminal record had marked them as non-employable for life; and/or that, regardless of their present good intentions, they would again get into some kind of criminal trouble once they either returned to their old haunts or became overwhelmingly depressed by the dullness of a law-abiding and poverty-stricken existence 'on the dole'. Said Cynthia:

My future's finished. I'm a criminal now and with my record – I mean I've been charged thirteen times – I can't get a job unless I say, 'Right,

TABLE 9.1 *Narrowing options: interactive sequences in the outlawing of deviant girls and law-breaking women*

Outlawing	Interactive sequences
From family	Guilt or anger about physical or sexual abuse; entry into residential care; or running away from home.
From education and employment	Truancy from school; absconding from residential care; or failure of social workers to find a school for the student.
By drugs	Attractiveness of drug-taking in the short term can lead to formation of habit, estrangement from family and non-drug users, and eventually criminal activity for the purpose of funding the drug habit. Young people in care who are discovered using drugs may be escalated into the criminal justice system more quickly than young people still living with their families. Poor women who offend are unable to pay for the private treatment which sometimes keeps better-off drug-users out of prison.
By residential Care	Loss of contact with family and non-institutional associations; identity problems stemming from constant assessment and categorisation; escalation into criminal justice system. Isolated and vulnerable upon leaving residential Care.
By sexist responses to unconventional behaviour – often pursued in quest for excitement	Early criminalisation likely if young girl engages in behaviour defined as masculine. More likely to be reconvicted if convicted at an early age and more likely to become institutionalised. Once on circuit of absconders, some young women attempt to 'pass' as male for self-protection; others tattoo themselves in order to signify either 'hardness' or 'deviant' status.
By welfare surveillance	Social work intervention in relation to adolescent female status offences,[3] official regulation of women's poverty, and the state policing of motherhood[4] can together alienate women from local authority social services and other welfare agencies, thereby increasing the likelihood of their receiving a custodial sentence if they should appear in court.
Imprisonment	Learning more crime skills; further debilitation of physically and mentally vulnerable women; loss of material goods, accommodation, children, friends, etc., can lead to institutionalisation (i.e., inability to live outside institutions).
Record	The criminal career produces the criminal record that is such a barrier to employment that some women become convinced that their only way 'back in' is through men or motherhood, a conviction that can lead to even more disastrous results than the previous criminal convictions did!

I have been in trouble' and own up. Some interviews I say, 'No, I ain't
been in trouble.' I need to marry an Arab geezer with all the money
[laughs] but that will never happen.   (Cynthia, aged 19)

Zöe detailed her experience at greater length:

The things that I was interested in when I was younger are closed to me
now because of my criminal record. I could never go back into teaching
– that option isn't open to me any more because I've got a conviction for
possession of cannabis. The best job I've ever had was working for – [a
nationally known entertainments company]. I worked in the offices doing bookings. I lied on the application form because it said, 'Do you have
any criminal convictions apart from driving offences?' and I put 'No'.
And then we had a spate of thefts there and, unbeknown to us, we were
all investigated by security – they're all ex-policemen. Well, their friends
in the police force came back and said, 'You've got a right one here –
prostitution, theft, deception, fraud, drugs, the lot!' So I was sacked.
Several years ago, when I was trying to get myself sorted out, I tried to
apply for nursing and the Director of Nursing said there was no way they
could take me on. You have to have a clear record for five years and I
don't know whether I can wait that long, just sitting on my butt doing
nothing. I had thought about trying to get back into something to do with
food but more on the business side of it. But I'd have to have a City and
Guilds qualification and I can't get a grant for that because it's not
classed as something you can get a grant for. I can't do it and stay on the
dole because it's a full-time course! I just feel that I've completely
wasted my life, just ruined it.   (Zöe, aged 28)

Zöe has seven 'O' levels and three 'A' levels. What chance for the majority
of the 39 who had no educational qualifications at all? Their only hope is to
lie when asked about their record. Most decline to, because they already
know someone who *has* lied and consequently lives in fear of being found
out. Muriel and Monica, for instance, were living in such fear. Others were
less concerned about the obduracy of the criminal record, more demoralised
by their previous recidivism and doubts about their ability to keep to the
straight and narrow when confronted once more with poverty, isolation, and
drugs.

There's women in prison today who've got young children. They say
they are going to change and start a clean slate. But, when they go back
into society, they find they've got bills, certain things that need doing and

they haven't got the money. Then, once they've been put into prison for stealing, they're going to do it again – and make it doubly worse and they'll always end up coming back into prison.   (Audrey, aged 18)

The effect of imprisonment on future decisions to commit crime was mentioned frequently by those who thought they would either choose to break the law or drift into lawbreaking again:

> I was quite worried when I had to go in but, when it was over, I felt all right. I thought, 'Well, if I come back again, at least I know what it's like.' (Sadie, aged 20)

The women who had been addicted to heroin when they were received into prison were particularly dubious about their futures:

> They always say that, if you go in prison and come off heroin, then you'll always go back on it because you've come off it without your own will. All I think to myself is that I can't wait to get out there and have a bit. Because prison's made me even worse, I think.   (Jessie, aged 20)

Sally was adamant that she would only be law-abiding if the law were to be changed in such a way that she could get as much heroin as she needed.

Most of the 12 who said they intended to continue law-breaking stated this intention baldly and with no further elaboration than the observation that 'doing cheques', shoplifting – or whatever – was their way of earning a living. Tara, though, like Cynthia (above), explained more fully her view that she could still expand her narrowing options if she committed more sophisticated crimes:

> [My parents] are in America and in the last four years the bonds have just dropped. I've become so independent that I don't even want to know them. I wanna get on with my life and get what I want. When my kids go into the nursery, I'll go out and get money without getting caught. I know myself now. Before I had Sasha I began to know myself and what I want: which is my own flat, my own car and my own identity as a woman – you know – struggling or doing whatever she wants to do. And I'm getting there.   (Tara, aged 21)

And who knows? Cynthia and Tara *may* eventually join the ranks of those unidentified law-breakers (mainly of the white-collar and corporate variety) whose anonymous existence perennially disproves the old adage that 'crime doesn't pay'. But for the rest of those 39 women the future is bleak; and, I would argue, most bleak for Daphne, Della and Bobby, the three 15-year-olds already doing time in Bullwood who gave no indication that they had any awareness whatsoever that their options were narrowing fast.

And what of the women who had already given up crime? To a woman they claimed that although prison is no picnic – and in several cases had become more difficult to take as they had got older – fear of imprisonment in itself would not have kept them out of trouble. In every case they had stayed out of prison because of what they had going for them on the outside – not because of fear of another custodial sentence. Thus Josie and Muriel could both look back with gratitude to the probation hostel that had given them the space and material help to enable them to believe that, after all the years in institutions, an alternative way of life *might* be possible.

What changes, however, could be made to ensure that fewer women get into the welfare/penal institutional complex in the first place; *and* that those who do so are not solely dependent upon 'luck' or opportunity and incentive to cut free of at least some of the *most* debilitating, disabling and outlawing effects of being women in poverty and in crime?

BROADENING OPTIONS

A major aim of the research was to provide a detailed ethnography of the perennial outlawing of a small minority of women who, once they have come to the attention of the authorities (either because of their parents' inability to care for them, or through their own deviance or law-breaking), are caught up and mangled by the regulatory machinery of the welfare and penal systems until both they themselves, and those who repeatedly judge them, have few grounds for optimism about their chances of not falling foul of the law in future.

Table 9.1 charts the major career points at which such outlawing can occur or be further endorsed (though obviously not every stage is applicable to every career discussed here). It will now be argued that the response to deviant or law-breaking women could be very different at each of these stages, so different that the options of women already in trouble might be *broadened* – rather than narrowed still further.

OUTLAWING FROM FAMILY: SUMMARY AND POLICY
IMPLICATIONS

The issue is whether government will continue to encourage the social forces that so often split, stress and isolate families, or whether it will work to create a protective and supportive framework of public policies that can cushion families against those undercutting forces and – more actively – help develop the conditions under which patterns of tolerance, reciprocity and understanding can flourish. (Currie, 1985, p. 246)

In recent years a number of criminological studies have indicated that, once women break the law, they are judged not only in terms of the seriousness of their crimes but also – and often predominantly – in terms of their conformity to idealised notions of proper femininity and women's proper place in the idealised nuclear family (cf., in Carlen, 1983). Most recently, commentators writing from a wider range of perspectives have pointed to the hypocrisy of a government that makes repeated calls for the promotion of 'family values' (whatever they might be!), at the same time not only making swingeing economic cuts that fall most heavily on already poor families, but also taking the increasingly punitive actions against unemployed young people that further add to family tensions and divisions. In referring to the 'outlawing' of increasing numbers of young and not-so-young women from 'the family', I am not, however, referring so much to the fact that some women are rejected by their already overburdened families once they have been in trouble. Rather, I am referring primarily to my arguments that, as a result of prevailing ideologies concerning the normality of the conventional nuclear family: (a) sentencers see troublesome young girls in Care as being potential recidivists because they are without family and therefore gender-decontrolled; and (b) single women are not seen as heading 'proper' families at all. A more material effect of this 'outlawing' from family is the isolation and ensuing vulnerability experienced by young women once they leave the care of the local authorities for good. What should be done?

1. *There should be adequate state financial support for all household units* – single-parent, communal, conventional nuclear, extended or whatever – regardless of whether or not they conform to the traditional and idealised concept of 'the family' (cf. Currie, 1985).
2. *Residential Care (or life 'on the run' from it) should cease to be seen as being the only alternative to 'family life' for young girls wishing to gain some independence from their families.* A network of hostels (maybe attached to schools) should be made available for the use of young persons aged 13+ wishing to be away from their families for either shorter or longer periods. (See Carlen, 1990, for detailed discussion of accommodation for women in trouble.)
3. *Sheltered housing, grants for setting up home, and a network of specifi-*

cally post-Care hostels should be established for the benefit of young persons leaving residential Care. And, as young women presently find it more difficult to get accommodation than do young men, in the short term at least, priority should be given to the provision of low-rent housing for young women either leaving Care or setting up home on their own – and without 'families'.

OUTLAWING FROM EDUCATION AND EMPLOYMENT: SUMMARY AND POLICY IMPLICATIONS

Just as it would be wrong to blame social workers *per se* for the women's alienation from welfare agencies, so too it would be wrong to attribute blame to schools and teachers for the women's lack of education. For, although some truancy may be blamed upon schools' failure to engage the interests of their pupils, the women in this study had, in the main, stayed away from school either because they had more pressing problems to deal with at home or because they were already involved with law-breaking activities which they wished to pursue during school hours. Once in residential Care several young women refused to attend the new school found for them near their children's home. Others ceased going to school simply because no new school had been found or (if they already had a record of bad behaviour) because no school in the area would take them. A few, moreover, were of the opinion that their local schools would have provided only a second-rate education in any case (though they offered little evidence to support this opinion). More made the point that, even if they *had* attended school, present unemployment rates made it unlikely that they would have ever been able to get a job commensurate with the extra burden of schooling undertaken. The view put forward most frequently was that education had not been seen as a major priority for these particular young women in Care – that they had already been seen as no-hopers. In 1985 and 1986 all but Monica, Muriel and the three 15-year-olds felt that their education and job prospects were bleak. Two reasons were given: one, that they had missed their chance educationwise and that it was by then too late to get any qualifications; two, that even though they had gained some qualifications in prison, these would be insufficient to gain them employment outside.

Two fundamental changes in education and employment policies should be made. First, and because at the present time the living conditions of some young people are *so* poverty stricken that as teenagers they are in no fit state to compete with their better-off counterparts already shooting along the examination paths to higher education, it should be an axiom of social policy that no one should ever lose for good their chances of education. Secondly, all job-training schemes should be linked to the creation of worthwhile jobs. For although the majority of the women in this study said that they 'hated' or would not do factory work or 'shit jobs', many of them described voluntary work that they had done and liked – for example, working with children, working with old people, working with community groups, and so on. As Elliott Currie has argued in the American context, 'the need for good jobs rather than just *any* job is one central theme in any employment policy that fits what we know about work and crime' (Currie, 1985, p. 267). Another would be to ensure equality of employment practice and protection for both women and men.

OUTLAWING BY DRUGS: SUMMARY AND POLICY IMPLICATIONS

At the time I met them, six women were still addicted to heroin, two (at least) still had an alcohol problem and others said that they had suffered from some kind of addiction in the past. I shall now briefly summarise the women's views both on the part drugs had played in narrowing their options and also on the shortcomings of the few and far-between facilities designed to help them.

All who had taken drugs remembered the positive aspects of their drug-usage. The 'blanking off' of extremes of misery seemed to be the most highly valued effect of heroin, whilst alcohol was lauded more for its facilitation of conviviality and an increase in social confidence. Glue alone was remembered with abhorrence – and, unlike ex-users of other drugs, none of the ex-glue-sniffers appeared to contemplate the possibility of a return to that particular habit. Other drugs were either valued for their various pleasure-inducing properties or for their capacity-increasing effects (for example, the wakefulness engendered by 'speed'). Some women had also valued the cameraderie of what they referred to as 'the whole drug scene'. Yet, for most, the glamour of the 'scene' and the positively experienced effects of the drug had been relatively short-lived. The pleasures of heroin-usage in particular had soon been outweighed by the need to 'work' non-stop (usually, in the case of these women, in law-breaking activities) in order to fund an increasingly expensive habit. Others became aware that the effects of, for instance, their glue-sniffing or drinking were making other people shun them.

Women on heroin were the most critical of the social response to their addiction. Their particular grievances concerned:

1. the fact that they had been given no drugs therapy while in prison;
2. their belief that, as heroin addicts, they would have avoided a prison sentence if they had been rich enough to register at a private fee-paying residential rehabilitation centre;
3. the fact that so few places are available on state- or charity-funded residential rehabilitation programmes;
4. the fact that the rehabilitation centres that do have free places available are often run according to a punitive ideology that some women experience as degrading them still further;
5. the fact that, whilst the pains of imprisonment had aggravated their condition, their penal confinement had also equipped them with a variety of new criminal skills and contacts wherewith they would be able to finance and feed their addictive habits in future;
6. the lack of rehabilitative facilities to help ensure that, once addicts had come off heroin, they kept off.

Although it is likely that a substantial number of heroin users do *not* fall into the arms of the law, that, in the view of at least one treatment centre, 'prison continues to be the major source for the "treatment" of the majority of drug users in this country' (Picardie and Wade, 1985, p. 8), the women whom I interviewed were derisive of the notion that imprisonment would force them to abstain from drugs. Shirley (although not an addict) had been offered heroin for the first time when she was in Holloway. Others frequently made the point that 'if you go in prison and come off heroin, then you always go back on it because you've come off it without your own will' (Jessie, aged 20). Picardie and Wade, moreover, claim that:

> the most convincing evidence that prison is bad for addicts is in the heroin overdose figures: 10 per cent of people who die from heroin overdoses do so after coming out of prison. They do not realise that their tolerance to the drug has been reduced by their forced withdrawal and go straight back to the level of dose they were taking before.   (Picardie and Wade, 1985, p. 83)

And it is not surprising that they *do* want to go back to that level of dose, given that the poor usually come out of treatment centres, hospitals or prisons to no back-up facilities whatsoever.

More fundamentally, a constant complaint was that women in particular did not (or would not) like the type of treatment offered by some of those more established and well-known treatment centres which aim to make drug users confront the state to which the drug has brought them. Women who already had low self-esteem felt that they needed to be 'buoyed up' rather than 'brought down' by treatment.

If the experiences of the women in this study are representative of other lawbreaking addicts, then it seems that, as far as women offenders who are also heroin (or other drug) addicts are concerned, changes of policy need to be made in at least four major areas. They are:

1. *Sentencing.* Drug addicts should be sent to prison only because of the seriousness of their crimes – not because the judge or magistrate erroneously believes that imprisonment in itself will 'cure' addiction.
2. *Prisons.* All imprisoned drug (including alcohol) abusers should be offered treatment/counselling whilst in prison, though it should be made clear to them that such treatment/counselling must be followed by their involvement in a continued programme of 'throughcare' once they leave prison. (If imprisonment were to be reserved for the most serious women criminals such programmes for imprisoned women drug-abusers would not be so expensive.)
3. *Throughcare for addict ex-prisoners.* Programmes of treatment for women addict ex-prisoners should be established together with a network of other support services.
4. *Treatment.* A variety of treatment models should be employed to meet the varying needs of different women. For, as the Advisory Council for the Misuse of Drugs reported in 1982:

[As] there is no typical addict, it follows that there is no single treatment or rehabilitation strategy confined to one discipline or service which will be effective for all individuals. Each individual drug misuser's problems must be assessed and the most appropriate match made to the services available. (Quoted in Picardie and Wade, 1985, p. 84).

But existing provision favours males simply because many of the few services presently available are not suitable for *women*. This is because: (a) several women addicts have been so badly abused by males that they are not prepared to join mixed 'concept' houses or other treatment programmes that cater for both men and women; (b) some women addicts are not prepared to leave their children in order to enter residential rehabilitation programmes; and (c) women with already low self-esteem are not prepared to enter into aggressive forms of treatment which they see as degrading them still further.

OUTLAWING BY RESIDENTIAL CARE: SUMMARY AND POLICY IMPLICATIONS

The research findings suggested that residential Care can itself have deleterious effects on women's subsequent careers, the major reasons being:

1. *that 'girls particularly end up being committed to Care orders because there is really no adequate provision for them within the tariff system'* (Gelsthorpe, 1983);
2. *Care's overemphasis on 'assessment'* which results in some young people believing that they are in Care as a consequence of some (unknown) individual pathology, rather than as an effect of a social situation beyond their control;
3. *Care's movement of some children and young persons from placement to placement which prevents the young people from establishing long-standing friendship ties.* This can precipitate them into a quest for excitement and friendship in circumstances of risk and danger which their sheltered life in Care has not equipped them to cope with;
4. *Care's punitive response to misbehaviour with children's homes as contrasted with 'turning a blind eye' to criminal behaviour outside the homes.* This can result in young people being escalated through the whole gamut of secure places in the Care system without anyone pointing out to them that it is their *criminal* behaviour which, if continued, will eventually land them in very serious trouble indeed. The punitive response to bad behaviour within children's homes can also result in the absconding that almost inevitably leads to law-breaking;
5. *the failure of some authorities to ensure that young people in their Care have adequate information about all aspects of sexual activity.* This lack of sex education can obviously have disastrous effects for young women – and their ensuing offspring;
6. *the failure of the Care system to prepare young people for non-institutional living.* This can result in post-Care money problems and depression of such magnitude that some young people see law-breaking and maybe a subsequent return to institutional life (but this time in a penal institution) as attractive alternatives to isolation and penury in an inner-city bedsit.

What should be done?

While it is recognised that some of the problems of some children in the care of the local authorities stem from experiences that they had *before* they were ever admitted to residential Care, it does seem that at least some aspects of Care exacerbate those problems. Certainly the research analyses suggest:

1. that young people in Care need to be provided with much greater stability of residence than had been experienced by many whom I interviewed;
2. that increased provision should be made to prepare young persons in Care for adult life, including sexual activity and non-institutional living;
3. that there should be less emphasis on assessment and categorisation of young people in children's homes;
4. that young people should be seen as being in need of care way beyond the time when their Care Order finishes. A range of services, for example, befriending schemes, residential weekends and post-Care-contact social workers, should be on offer to young people leaving Care for at least ten years after the Care Order has been lifted.

Moreover, it is also suggested that the task of those working in children's homes would be made much easier if increased state support for types of household units other than the 'family' resulted in such a multiplicity of styles of domesticity and intimacy that children's homes could be seen as being but one type amongst several styles of living – and not, as often happens now, be resented as the state's ultimate filing cabinet for un-wanted, unfortunate or delinquent children.

OUTLAWING BY SEXIST RESPONSES TO UNCONVENTIONAL BEHAVIOUR: SUMMARY AND POLICY IMPLICATIONS

The 1980s have seen the publication of a plethora of articles and research monographs on women's experiences of the courts (either as lawyers, defendants or witnesses) which report that women in the criminal justice system are discriminated against by a judicial logic shaped by outdated typifications of both femininity and women's proper place in an idealised nuclear family (see, for example, Carlen, 1983). It is therefore suggested that:

1. *There is a case for sensitising court personnel to the stereotyping that precludes consideration of contemporary women's actual gender problems* and to the courtroom practices that particularly inhibit women.

2. *There is a case for the radical rethinking of the concept of culpability in terms of what a reasonable woman (often with prior experience of her relative powerlessness in face of male violence) might be justified in doing in certain circumstances.* For example, it is often implied in rape cases that the female victim was blameworthy because she did not put up enough of a fight; or women who stab their husbands, because they know from experience that they cannot defend themselves with their bare fists, are often seen as being more culpable because they have used a weapon.

OUTLAWING FROM WELFARE BY EXCESSIVE WELFARE SURVEILLANCE: SUMMARY AND POLICY IMPLICATIONS

By the time I met them, many of the women were so antagonistic towards social workers that it was unlikely that any traditional-type social-work intervention could be effectively made into their lives in future. Even more unlikely was it that social workers themselves would be particularly sympathetic to clients who had already used many different strategies to evade supervision and who, in some cases, had even used physical violence to obstruct them in the course of their duties. Yet most of the women recognised that in addition to more realistic levels of financial support, they did need some kind of emotional/psychological or even just neighbourly practical support to help them sort out their (often extremely tangled) affairs. Others readily admitted that their troubles had become so acute that they should seek expert assistance. Still they were reluctant to turn to social workers. Those who had been in Care blamed social workers for setting them on the road to dependency, while those who had either sought welfare assistance or had it imposed on them in later life thought that there had been a gradual increase of social work control over *all* areas of their lives. What, then, could be done to help ensure that those most in need of welfare support do not become those who are also most alienated from the agencies empowered to provide it? As I have already suggested steps that could be taken to reduce the stigma, alienation and isolation of young women both in and recently out of Care, I shall here limit discussion to consideration of the difficulties confronting social workers charged with the task of supervising mothers' child-rearing practices and probation officers charged with supervising adult women offenders.

The abuse of children in Britain is fostered by a fundamentally flawed social organisation which isolates adults and children into small privatised groups wherein children have to bear alone, and for much of the time unprotected, the full brunt of the domestic violence caused by adult tensions, frustrations and misery. At the same time, the popular notion of familiness has been constituted within ideological and political discourses that promote a private/public distinction celebrating the myth that the governance of family and domesticity should (and does) remain beyond the purview and regulation of the state. Social work supervision of parenting – and mothering in particular – is therefore resented by women (and fathers) who, given prevailing ideologies about family privacy, also believe that they have a *right* to be bitter. In such a situation it seems that social workers can only be expected to supervise parents if their task is facilitated by a whole range of back-up facilities, pre-eminent among them being full-day nursery provision where offending parents could be required to attend with their pre-school children. Such provision could have the following advantages: it would enable parents to share the burden of child-rearing with both professionals and other parents; it would enable social workers to share the burden of supervision with other professionals; and it could reduce the likelihood that parents would see themselves as being locked in a personalised conflict with one individual social worker.

OUTLAWING BY IMPRISONMENT: SUMMARY AND POLICY IMPLICATIONS

The majority of imprisoned women are in gaol for relatively minor crimes. The effects of imprisonment on already-poor women's lives are such that one would expect no one in their right minds to send such minor offenders to prison 'for their own good'. Yet, on those rare occasions when sentencers do justify prison terms, this is often exactly how they explain their sentences – particularly on young girls and drug-takers. However, girls and women who are already beset by a variety of problems are further outlawed from society once they serve a term of youth custody or imprisonment. This outlawing occurs in three major ways.

1. *Prison is a school for crime.*

> I know more now than before I came into prison. I know about burglary, how to cut off burglar alarms, how to pick pockets. A girl here who's made a lot of money out of shoplifting showed me how to make a little thing out of a hairclip to take the buzzers off. And that judge says it's done me good! (Kay, aged 21)

All you learn in prison is kiting [forging cheques], smuggling [drugs] and crotching [hiding stolen goods in one's crotch]. Basically, I thought about prison, 'What a waste of human life.'   (Yvonne, aged 37)

2. *Prison debilitates.* Josie O'Dwyer (O'Dwyer and Carlen, 1985) has already given what is probably one of the most vivid accounts of the pains, tensions, debilitations, violence and degradations inherent in the disciplinary regimes of the women's prisons. Her account of women prisoners' self-mutilations, mounting tensions, sense of nothingness and, sometimes, paralysing or rampaging fear and anger were echoed by many of the 39 women. Lena explained to me why she had slashed her face:

> The other week we wasn't getting hardly any association. If you're locked in a lot, you get mad and you don't know what to do with yourself. You just laze about, go to sleep. I done my face because I was down, things on me mind. I can tell when it's coming on. I get a funny feeling in my stomach and I want to cry.   (Lena, aged 21)

Daphne, like Yasmin was, at 15 years old, already acclimatising herself to solitary confinement:

> I've got used to it, so it's alright. I don't mind being locked in. All the better! I go to sleep and I think about when I get out. I dream. I always dream about the children's homes.   (Daphne, aged 15)

3. *Imprisonment aggravates poverty and its related problems.* When already-poor women go to prison they usually lose their accommodation, what few possessions they have, and often, and most devastatingly, the custody of their children. In NACRO's study of 29 people's post-release experiences it was found that:

> People generally suffered a decline in housing standard post-release; for the women it was more severe. The majority – 81 per cent – were in secure housing before imprisonment, a figure which declined to 45 per cent post-release. . . . The women were more likely to mention money and bills related to housing as problems they faced on release. Fifteen out of 22 mentions (ie. two thirds) of such problems came from women, even though they were only one third of the sample.   (NACRO, 1986)

Anne, Sally and Hazel also spoke from experience:

> Prison leaves you really sort of bewildered. All of a sudden you're thrown out into the big wide world and, if you did have anything, you've lost it. The second time I came out I felt very strange and lonely. (Anne, aged 20)

> Say you go into Holloway and you've got three suitcases with all your possessions in – they won't keep 'em, not at all. You can only have three sets of clothes. So you lose everything. (Sally, aged 35)

> One woman I knew lost her house because social services wouldn't pay the mortgage while she was in prison. When she came out, she'd got nothing. [My young son] didn't understand why he couldn't see me while I was in prison and then it took me five years to get him home. But, as I said, social workers seem to have this attitude that, because women are in prison, they're not really bothered about their kids. (Hazel, aged 29)

SENTENCING

Seear and Player (1986) list a number of sentencing changes that could effect reduction of the women's prison population, one of the most valuable suggestions being that 'by law no woman should be sent to prison for [certain] identifiable, non-violent offences' (Seear and Player, 1986, p. 6). Additionally, they suggest that women should not be imprisoned for non-payment of fines, that only exceptionally should they be remanded in prison before trial, and that alternatives to imprisonment should be found for the mentally ill. All these proposals have been made before, and the history of the modern criminal justice system suggests that exhortation alone will not change sentencing practices rooted in a groundless faith in imprisonment as *the* magic cure for crime. Therefore, and as Seear and Player themselves recognise, statutory change is required to effect a more rational and coherent system of sentencing.

As I have travelled round talking to prison staff I have become more and more convinced that prison regimes (whether for men or women) will not be improved until prison officers are formally given a greater role in their development. As far as women's prisons are concerned, I have repeatedly heard very positive ideas for change put forward by women officers who have then told me that, under the present hierarchical and centralised staff structure, they will have little chance of having their ideas taken seriously by the powers that be. Be that as it may, it seems that, as a priority, programmes should be developed which aim to reduce the debilitating tension and anxiety suffered by women prisoners. These programmes could include at least the following: more life- and career-skill courses (as opposed to domestic and mothering courses); more opportunities for association both informally, in groups, and with people coming from outside the prison; and more effort by the Prison Department to contact volunteer professionals willing to give legal, housing, educational and other advice to prisoners – together with the necessary rule changes to allow them into the prisons. These measures should also be seen as possibly contributing to a reduction in tension and anxiety by non-pharmacological means.

Mothers in prison are a group whom the prison authorities should be particularly concerned to send out stronger both mentally and physically than when they went into prison. In this connection the Prison Department should examine the many US projects that involve having children fostered near their mothers' prisons. Additionally, all prisoners should be allowed to meet their families regularly in pleasant surroundings, as well as being able to telephone them from payphone call boxes on the reverse-charge system.

OUTLAWING BY CRIMINAL RECORD: SUMMARY AND POLICY IMPLICATIONS

Crime causes such misery that it is not surprising that the known law-breaker is regarded warily, that the ex-prisoner is shunned. Yet, before one is tempted into believing that this fear of the convict is a universal element of human nature, it should be noted that it is usually the poor and the powerless who suffer most from the stigma of having a criminal record.

Several things could be done:

1. *All prisons should have a rehabilitation officer* employed specifically to get jobs, accommodation, education courses, child-care arrangements and any other special counselling or treatment facilities required, set up for women *before* they leave prison. Such officers could build up lists of sympathetic employers, accompany women to interviews and keep in touch for as long as the ex-prisoner required them. A start in this direction has already been made by the National Association for the Care and Resettlement of Offenders (NACRO)'s Women Prisoners' Resource Centre (WPRC). But such essential work should *not* (as

in the case of WPRC) have to depend on charity funding. The rehabilitation of ex-prisoners should be seen as a state responsibility.

2. *All women serving long sentences (over one year) should be found paid employment outside the prison for at least the last six months prior to their release.*

3. *A programme of information about crime and punishment should be initiated.* This might create the more enlightened ideological climate which would most probably be a necessary prerequisite to changing the public's view of women criminals as doubly deviant – that is, as being both bad persons *and* bad women. If the public were to be more accurately appraised of the characteristics of its prison population, then it might be in a better position to make judgements about the desirability and necessity of continuing to maintain such a costly network of penal institutions.

WOMEN, GENDER, POVERTY, CRIME AND CRIMINAL JUSTICE

Three major changes are proposed.

First, changes need to be made in policies relating to housing, social security, tax, wage and pension structures and, in particular, to the wages and working conditions of the part-time, mainly female, work-force. Such policy changes should be directed at realising a situation where women would no longer be expected to be dependent upon males and a concomitant male-related domesticity.

Financial independence, though important to all women, is of especial importance to women, like the ones in this study, whose previous experiences (for example, of male violence and family lives torn apart by poverty-stricken living conditions), histories of institutionalisation or present sexual orientation make them reluctant to link their fortunes with a male in the future. Yet, despite previous bad experiences of 'family life', some women already in trouble with the law, and with a host of other problems stemming from poverty and a generalised feeling of marginalisation, are nonetheless led by existing social policies to believe that their only way 'back in' again is via men or motherhood. Once they act on such beliefs, the outcome is usually disastrous – as the women I talked with knew only too well.

The second change that could immensely benefit women (and men) would be a move towards a more community-oriented type of provision for families engaged in child-rearing – and other types of care.

Thirdly, criminologists and politicians concerned with the relationships between criminal justice and social justice need to develop more sophisticated models of culpability, responsibility and accountability. Undoubtedly some readers will be tempted to accuse the present author of profferring a deterministic explanation of the crimes of women in poverty, of attempting to absolve them from responsibility for their actions. Yet the analyses presented here claim only to indicate that, under certain relatively rare *combinations* of otherwise general economic and ideological conditions, some women are more likely than not to choose to break the law and/or be imprisoned. Such analyses do *not* assume or imply that the women involved have no choice. Yet we still need to understand the actions and ideologies of the offender and her sentencers. As Stephen Box has put it:

> A demand for justice must go beyond retribution for the offence and reparation for the victim. It has to include a demand for *understanding* the offender. It needs this not in the hope that the offender will then be excused, condoned or justified. Nor does understanding the offender necessarily shift the blame to the victim. The demand for understanding is necessary because *although people choose to act, sometimes criminally, they do not do so under conditions of their own choosing.* Their choice makes them responsible, but the conditions make the choice comprehensible. These conditions, social and economic, contribute to crime because they constrain, limit or narrow the choices available. Many of us, in similar circumstances, might choose the same course of action. (Box, 1987, p. 29, emphasis in original)

Quite so. And the question then becomes: what might encourage them (and, possibly, us) to act otherwise? Of course, Jock Young is right to point out that 'the offender should be ashamed, he/she should feel morally responsible within the limits of circumstances, and rehabilitation is truly *impossible* without this moral dimension' (Young, 1986, p. 29). But whence does morality emanate? It should be the product of a society seen to be committed to reducing inequality and of communities seen to be committed to the welfare of *all* their members. Without reciprocal commitments between those who offend, their victims and their judges, it is unlikely that those who break the law will feel shame. Shame is usually the product of the transgressor's conviction that by her actions she has diminished the stock of social good. Many of the women in this study had had very little experience either of other people's goodness or of the world's goods. It was only when some of them began to experience them that they started to believe that a life without crime might be both desirable and possible.

*   This article has been constructed from extracts from my book *Women, Crime and Poverty* (Milton Keynes, Bucks.: Open University Press, 1988).

NOTES

1.   In 1988 females were found guilty of or cautioned for only 15 per cent of all indictable offences.

2.   One of the greatest advances made by the symbolic-interactionist criminology of the 1960s was its insistence that law-breaking and criminalisation are two separate processes, each requiring an entirely different explanation. Although it was recognised that law-breaking would usually be one contributory factor in subsequent criminalisation, the most innovatory contention was that criminalisation and its effects might be major factors in subsequent law-breaking and/or further criminalisation. From this perspective, therefore, criminalisation was seen as a sequential process having both subjective and objective conditions of existence that influence the social meanings of a person's criminal career. Thus, whereas not all convicted lawbreakers suffer the stigmatising effects of conviction (for example, tax dodgers, corporate criminals and traffic offenders are seldom disgraced even though they have several convictions), some young people (especially those in residential Care) perceive themselves as having been criminalised even though they have never been found guilty of any criminal offence. In this chapter unconvicted law-breakers and law-breakers convicted without incurring stigmatisation are referred to as being *under-criminalised*. Law-breakers whose criminalisation has been out of all proportion to the seriousness of their individual offences are referred to as *over-criminalised*.

3.   'Status offences' are those offences which can only be committed by children or young people, for example, non-attendance at school; being beyond parental control.

4.   'State policing of motherhood' refers to the supervision that mothers receive from social workers. The term is not used to imply that such supervision is in itself oppressive or undesirable; it is used to indicate how such supervision often alienates the very women who may most need social work help if they should at any time fall foul of the criminal law. Young men before the courts are less likely than young women to have already alienated social workers as a result of conflicts about parenting.

REFERENCES

Box, S. (1987), *Power, Crime and Mystification* (London: Tavistock).

Carlen, P. (1983), *Women's Imprisonment* (London: Routledge & Kegan Paul)

Carlen, P. (1988), *Women, Crime and Poverty* (Milton Keynes, Bucks.: Open University Press).

Carlen, P. (1990), *Alternatives to Women's Imprisonment* (Buckingham: Open University Press).

Carlen, P. and Worrall, A. (eds) (1987), *Gender, Crime and Justice* (Milton Keynes, Bucks.: Open University Press).

Currie, E. (1985), *Confronting Crime: An American Challenge* (New York: Pantheon).

Gelsthorpe, L. (1983), *Children in Care*, evidence given to House of Commons Social Services Committee Inquiry (London: Her Majesty's Stationery Office).

National Association for the Care and Resettlement of Offenders (NACRO) (1986), *They Don't Give You a Clue* (London: NACRO).

O'Dwyer, J. and Carlen, P. (1985), 'Surviving Holloway and other women's prisons', in Carlen, P. *et al.*, *Criminal Women* (Cambridge: Polity Press).

Picardie, J. and Wade, D. (1985), *Heroin: Chasing the Dragon* (Harmondsworth, Middx: Penguin).

Rosenbaum, M. (1981), *Women on Heroin* (New Brunswick, N.J.: Rutgers University Press).

Seear, N. and Player, E. (1986), *Women in the Penal System* (London: Howard League for Penal Reform).

Young, J. (1975), 'Working-class criminology', in I. Taylor, P. Walton and J. Young (eds), *Critical Criminology* (London: Routledge & Kegan Paul).

Young, J. (1986), 'The failure of criminology: the need for a radical realism', in R. Matthews and J. Young (eds), *Confronting Crime* (London: Sage).

10 The Victims of Fraud

MICHAEL LEVI and ANDREW PITHOUSE

INTRODUCTION

On 19 June 1989 the trial of the popular comedian Ken Dodd on a series of tax-evasion charges commenced. The headlines the following day read 'Premier's Letters of Tribute to "Diddling" Doddy' (*Sun*); 'Diddy Dodger Doddy's Diddling' (*Mirror*); 'King of the Diddle Men' (*Star*); 'Diddled Men of Knotty Ash' (*Today*); and 'Diddling Dodd and 20 Bank Accounts' (*Express*). All these were on the front page. The 'quality' papers all carried the story, but as a major item on the inside page. This confirms one point – examined later – that conventional notions of media neglect of 'white-collar crime' and fraud (Box, 1983) are now *passé*, even if they were ever wholly true. (The jury later acquitted Dodd of all charges.) High-class fraudsters, as popularised by the film *Wall Street* and Tom Wolfe's best-seller *Bonfire of the Vanities*, are big news and have become part of the popular culture of crime. Their criminality (and, *a fortiori*, the criminality of alleged health and safety offences that result in deaths at sea) may not be as unambiguous, in terms of social typifications of evil, as that of the Mafia. But fraud is increasingly treated as 'real crime', in ways described elsewhere (Levi, 1987).

The object of our ESRC-funded research study was to examine critically some popular and academic assumptions about the impact of fraud on victims and the way in which fraud victims are treated by the various agencies in the criminal justice system: police, prosecutors and sentencers. These were issues upon which no hard evidence had been collected in Britain or, for that matter, elsewhere in the world. We collected a great deal of information of a statistical nature, but our study also lies within (a) the 'appreciative' tradition in sociological research, whereby the researcher – whatever his or her personal views – seeks to convey the world as experienced by the research subjects; and (b) the 'consumerist' tradition in criminal justice research, feeding back to service-providers the perceptions of them held by crime complainants. We also wanted to find out systematically about the circumstances and effects of 'rip-offs' respectively committed against intimates and against strangers, and how the courts dealt with offenders from varied social and criminal backgrounds who were convicted of 'white-collar' crimes. Finally, we aimed to examine the ways in which the television and radio media dealt with a form of crime for which traditional stereotypes of evil and dramatic physical harm – the staple diet of *Crime Watch UK* and of most news and documentary coverage of crime – were unavailable.

Fraud victims do not normally feature in crime victimisation surveys (Mayhew *et al.*, 1989), in mainstream victim support and compensation movements, or in the standard debates concerning 'what should be done for the victims' and 'what is to be done about law and order'. The principal author of this study was astonished to be informed, by a leading figure in the victim-support movement, that one reason given by the police for their inability to do more for crime victims was that they had to waste so much time dealing with fraud! (The police probably were thinking of cheque and credit-card fraud rather than high-level fraud, but if genuinely meant rather than mere excuse, this confirms survey research on some police attitudes to the deserts of fraud victims.) As Fattah (1986, p. 5) observes, most victim movements are focused around personal victims of street and household crime. The explanation he advances for the neglect by victimologists and victim activists of white-collar crimes – by which he appears to mean primarily 'business regulatory' crimes such as pollution and health and safety violations rather than business deceptions – is that they have a slow gestation period. Notwithstanding (or because of) the lack of attention they receive, the fate of (broadly defined) victims of white-collar crimes is, he states, 'even a sadder one than that of victims of conventional crime. The reason is that they lack any means of redress and usually have no recourse against the perpetrators of the abuse.'

Our research findings reveal that these allegations of media neglect and of victim powerlessness are gross oversimplifications: many frauds and alleged abuses of corporate or governmental power receive considerable coverage; and there are even victim campaigns for redress against alleged frauds – such as Barlow Clowes and McDonald Wheeler – and harmful products – such as Opren – even if these do not attain the status of (successful) general victim movements. Moreover, the relative invisibility of white-collar crime (and, *a fortiori*, fraud) victims within the 'victim movement' is more than just a question of the time taken to show damage and the obviousness of impact. In relation to 'fraud', the negative portrayal of offenders and – that ambiguous term – 'victimisation' presents difficulties, since the act itself covers such a large variety of possible victim– offender interactions. By analogy with the general comments about victim stereotypes by Christie (1986, p. 19), the ideal victim is indeed the person who did not precipitate the offence herself, had no reasonable prospect of knowing that what she was doing would harm her, and was deliberately tricked by an already wealthy person into a transaction that caused her serious harm. However, images of fraud are far more ambivalent than those of burglary, robbery or – as we write – of rape. For example, in the film *The Sting*, a dishonest, nasty, ugly racketeer is ripped off by charming, physically attractive con men who get him to bet on races that he believes to be 'fixed' to ensure that they win. So – as in *Trading Places* – we have a positive image of the white-collar offenders and a negative one of the victim(s). Consequently, it makes a great deal of difference what we construe as 'fraud' when we answer questions about its harmfulness and seriousness (see Levi, 1987, ch. 3; Grabosky *et al.*, 1987).

Popular images of what a given type of crime is like may often be mistaken (Maguire, 1982; Hough and Mayhew, 1983, 1985). Fraud is about being manipulated into believing that something is true when it is not and/ or that something is in one's own interest when it is not. This, along with jealousy/envy, is one of the great emotional themes that underlie many of our interactions with our parents, lovers and colleagues, even though we may not like to think of ourselves as deceivers. So the view of fraud as a somehow abstract, modern and, and above all, *technological* crime is a myth. Fraud has much deeper roots in the human psyche. Yet, as our research confirms, compared with such 'crimes of the powerful' as the manufacture of harmful pharmaceutical products, 'fraud' occupies a complex area in which those on modest incomes and the wealthy rip-off consumers, vendors and investors ranging from the very rich through to – less rewardingly because they have less to steal – the poor. There are a number of issues here to be analysed, few of which have received any sustained attention hitherto: who are the victims of frauds? who are the offenders? what are the popular images of victims and offenders in fraud cases? how do these images affect media and criminal justice treatment of offenders and victims? what is the impact of fraud upon the victims? how satisfied are they by the treatment they receive from justice agencies and what determines their satisfaction? Are they any observable differences in the sorts of sanctions meted out to different sorts of fraudsters? After reviewing the sources of our information, let us see what the research reveals about these and other relevant questions.

SOURCES OF EVIDENCE

The regulation of fraud is a messy activity. Governmental and quasi-governmental agencies engaged in investigating it include the police – both fraud squads and divisional CID – the Post Office, Department of Trade and Industry, HM Customs and Excise, the Inland Revenue, the Office of Fair

Trading, the Bank of England, Lloyd's, the Securities and Investments Board, and self-regulatory organisations such as the Securities Association and the Financial Intermediaries, Managers, and Brokers Regulatory Association. In addition, there is a vast array of commercial bodies – from Visa and Dun & Bradstreet to sub-gumshoe private eyes in pokey offices – whose investigation and recovery services are purchased by victims. Over 50 officials from almost all these agencies were interviewed.

Also interviewed was a sample of victims of fraud drawn from court records at the London Central Criminal Court (1984–5) and Cardiff Crown Court (1983–4) and a more *ad hoc* set of victims known to the private-sector 'police' contacts of the senior researcher, totalling 70. The former were selected so as to represent both 'repeat players' – larger commercial organisations such as insurance companies, who were generally multiple victims – and 'one-shot players' – generally private individuals such as investor-fraud victims. We were able to discuss fraud with representatives of prominent companies in the banking, credit-finance, insurance and building-society sectors. In addition, 94 private and business victims in our court sample who were not interviewed filled in postal questionnaires regarding the impact of fraud and their experience with the criminal justice system. The years were selected as the most recent two-year periods for which full records were available: examining the records was a very time-consuming process.

Interviews with non-reporting victims were harder to obtain than had been assumed prior to undertaking the research: one reason given by 'inside contacts' was that as a result of the higher media and political profile of fraud in 1986–7, there was too much hostile publicity about the non-reporting of fraud.

Finally, journalists, researchers and producers from the major radio and television programmes that routinely contain fraud items were interviewed in depth about how they construed programmes and selected items for inclusion. Unfortunately, despite our 'consumerist' suggestions that it would be important to obtain feedback on people who had come to them with complaints to see how they felt about the experience of being a 'public victim', they refused to divulge names or even to pass on our letters, pleading 'confidentiality'. Too much consistency can be a dangerous thing!

RESEARCH FINDINGS

Media representations of fraud tend to be divided into two major categories: *offender*-oriented stories, which focus upon powerful people – either those of high social standing or with 'organised-crime' connections; and *victim*-oriented stories, which focus upon weak and decent victims who, 'preferably' (in media terms) as a result of lax governmental regulation, are lured into investing in firms whose collapse leaves them destitute. The ideal story is one that combines both these elements. Unfortunately, the reality we found was considerably more prosaic. Although the term 'white-collar crime' is usually treated – at least by non-criminologists – as a synonym for fraud, most frauds taken to court would be depicted more accurately as 'blue-collar crime', being committed by people of modest social origin. On the other hand, looked at in terms of average sums involved and total costs, the major fraud victims were financial services firms and the major offenders were *white*-collar males.

Most victims whose cases were prosecuted were organisations: only 15 per cent were private individuals. The smaller frauds are typically what might be described as 'hit-and-run' thefts against banks and credit-card companies by 'blue-collar' males. The larger ones typically involve more social and commercial interaction between victims and offenders, and are carried out by white-collar males using business organisations who defraud, on average, twice as many victims as do the others. We shall now examine the data in more detail.

The Victims

The victims at both Cardiff Crown Court and the Old Bailey were typically businesses providing financial services. Private-citizen victims were a distinct minority in both places: they comprised just 36 out of 291 at Cardiff, and among this group, those that lost most did so at the hands of family and friends (or former friends!). Frauds by kith and kin constituted just three of the 36 cases, and averaged £4500 compared with £300 for the average individual victims defrauded by outsiders. At the Old Bailey, there were only ten private citizens among 116 victims: four were relieved of an average of £11,500 by 'close friends'; two lost (but later recovered) their family home from relatives who forged documents to remortgage their property without their knowledge; and the remainder lost an average of £1000 in various business encounters. In short, friends and family seem to be in a better position than strangers to defraud private citizens of large sums.

For these private victims, the victimisation experience could be likened to a (comparatively mild) sort of rape. Much of the rape literature speaks of victims' tendency to have internalised mainstream values, to the extent of blaming themselves for having placed themselves in the position to become victims. For fraud victims, particularly those who prided themselves on being 'street-wise', being 'suite-foolish' was a blow not only to their pockets but also to their self-esteem and (where others had been told about it) to their social reputation. This sense of victim culpability was not because they had been conned – as in *The Sting* – as a result of entering into dishonest transactions, but rather because they seemed conscious of the primacy of the 'let the buyer beware' principle in relation to commercial transactions. To negotiate out of this self-blame, they looked for clues to reassure themselves (and others they knew) that they had done everything that was reasonable under the circumstances to protect their property. In some (rare) cases, where they were part of a large body of creditors of crashed investment firms, the victims were able to project the blame on to the authorities who had licensed the business, thereby absolving themselves (at least consciously) of emotional and intellectual liability for their victimisation. In short, there exists some sort of built-in assumption of negligence on the part of fraud victims, which they feel obliged to rebut for their own peace of mind as well as for the sake of their social reputation as competent negotiators of the world.

In both courts, the majority of victims were commercial organisations. Those who lost most were (in descending order): banks; customers or clients in an assumed fiduciary relationship with the fraudster; employers; suppliers of goods and services; insurance companies; finance companies; building societies; retail services. Since then there has been a spate of revelations regarding rings of mortgage frauds, with multiple mortgages on the same or even a non-existent property. So building societies will have increased their market share as fraud victims, even prior to their wider involvement in the supply of financial services. Retailers suffered less because unless negligence or conspiracy is shown, many frauds in this sector make their impact not on them but on the credit-card and hire-purchase companies whose credit facilities are misused.

Banks in our sample of *court* cases lost a total of £3.2 million: £170,000 of this was stolen by 13 blue-collar fraudsters; the remainder by 23 white-collar ones. Eleven white-collar fraudsters relieved their trusting clients or customers of £1.8 million. Employers lost £1.7 million, mainly to 28 white-collar employees. Suppliers of goods and services lost £1.1 million to ten white-collar and £10,000 to three blue-collar defendants. Insurance companies lost £230,000 to nine white-collar fraudsters and £60,000 to 16 blue-collar ones.

These findings on the sectoral distribution of fraud victimisation correspond reasonably well with the survey by Levi (1988) of cases handled by fraud squads nationally in 1985 (though these exclude the normally smaller cases handled by CID officers on division as well as frauds dealt with by other public-sector agencies). That survey found that the *average* amount at risk in frauds was £2.36 million against banks, building societies, and insurance companies; £269,000 against other private sector victims; £184,500 in public sector corruption cases; £87,849 against other public sector victims. In terms of cost of fraud per business sector, this amounted to: financial services 60.56 per cent; other private-sector victims 35.05 per cent; public-sector corruption 2.64 per cent; and other public-sector victims 1.75 per cent.

The media (and political) focus upon fraud squads – particularly in London – in generating images of fraud can be misleading. For in terms of the *distribution* of cases handled by fraud squads in 1985, financial services institutions accounted for 13.5 per cent; other private-sector victims 68.6 per cent; public-sector corruption, 7.4 per cent; and other public-sector victims, 10.5 per cent. (These are data about numbers of *cases*: the typical number of *victims* per case would be greater in investment frauds against private individuals, and – though measurement is difficult – in public sector corruption.)

The origin of these data in fraud squad files, however, automatically excludes the many small frauds involving banks and hire-purchase companies that are dealt with on division, as well as all the 'black economy' frauds handled – though seldom prosecuted – by the revenue departments and the Department of Social Security. As Reiss and Biderman (1980) have also noted in the US context, the varied criteria used by different agencies to define crime and even criminal investigations *operationally* make it meaningless to aggregate data across them. If one performed this aggregation exercise with criminal fraud cases, the portrait of fraud would be skewed in the direction of over-representing both social security and banking frauds that are minor in value compared with other frauds, even if substantial in relation to property crimes generally: in 1986, the median value of non-fraud crimes (including attempts) was just over £100 for burglaries in a dwelling; under £100 for robberies, for burglaries other than in a dwelling, and for thefts even *including* car thefts, which distort the figure upwards. (Excluding attempts and cases where nothing was taken, the *average* losses were £644 for burglary dwelling; £578 for burglary other than in a dwelling; £1191 for robbery; and £150 for thefts, excluding autotheft.)

There is one sense in which looking at costs in absolute terms is misleading: the impact of fraud (and other crimes) should properly be seen in terms of the victim's *means*, net of insurance costs and benefits. In other words, a fraud of £100 upon a poor person may be more damaging than a fraud of

£10 million upon an asset-rich insurance company, though the latter *appears* to be more serious (and is significantly more likely – quite properly, for such frauds normally require more expert attention than do simpler, lower-value ones – to be a candidate for the attentions of the Serious Fraud Office launched in April 1988 under the Criminal Justice Act 1987). An alternative method is to look at how seriously the *victims* regard their loss. In our survey, 37 per cent of all victims thought that their fraud was a serious or very serious loss to themselves or to their organisation; the remainder thought the loss was either moderate or not significant at all.

Investigation and Prosecution: the Victim Experience

The questionnaire data yielded some recurrent themes among certain victim types about the police and court management of their case. To begin with, just under half the private citizens and commercial organisations discovered the fraud through their own investigations. The remainder did so through information received from banks, trading standards, commercial contacts and, in the case of private victims, through neighbours or their banks. No private victim and only 13 per cent of commercial victims were protected by insurance against loss. Once the fraud was discovered, the majority of all victims (88 per cent) notified the police themselves. In doing so, almost half discovered that the police were already involved by reason of other offences committed by the fraudsters. The idea that fraud can be prevented by victims 'spreading the word' to others at risk was *not* shared widely among our victim set. Just under half of all victims informed other organisations, trade associations, commercial contacts, friends or neighbours about the fraud.

Only a minority (12 per cent) of private victims had reported a fraud before, compared with nearly half the commercial victims. The majority considered the police to have responded appropriately to their complaint. None of the private citizens thought that the interest of the police flagged when dealing with their complaint, whereas some 17 per cent of commercial victims thought this. A third of all victims stated that the police had suggested that they – the victims – investigate further the alleged fraud that they had reported. A half of all victims stated the police gave them advice on how their case would be dealt with and the majority of these victims (83 per cent) were satisfied with the advice they received.

For most victims the main source of information and advice about their case came from the police. Only a minority (10 per cent) mentioned lawyers, colleagues or friends in this respect. Over a third actually appeared in court as witnesses. Their experiences of court differed not least because private citizens were mainly first-timers whereas 59 per cent of the commercial victims had appeared before. Most victims had a minimum of two weeks notice of their court appearance. Once at court, half the commercial victims experienced delays averaging 2–4 hours in being called. However, 15 per cent stated that their case was delayed for more than one day. Among the *private* victims, 25 per cent stated that they had been delayed more than one day. Overall, 80 per cent of victims indicated that they suffered moderate to minimal inconvenience due to the court appearance.

Before appearing in court, half the witnesses said that they were briefed by the police; a further 10 per cent by counsel; and a quarter by no one at all. Half of both private and commercial victims stated that court appearance was a difficult and uncomfortable event, but 83 per cent stated that they were not reluctant to appear. Commercial victims were more likely than private ones to be cross-examined: 82 per cent compared with half. Three-quarters of victims were able to follow the procedures and formalities of court. 88 per cent of commercial but only 57 per cent of private victims considered that the jury had understood their case.

On average, white-collar fraudsters received prison sentences of 25 months at the Old Bailey and 15 months at Cardiff Crown Court, compared with 13 months and 11 months respectively for blue-collar fraudsters. Some 56 per cent of white-collar offenders were imprisoned, compared with 75 per cent of the blue-collar ones. Prison or suspended prison sentences were typical for all fraudsters. Seventy-seven per cent of victims knew the verdict in their case and also stated that it was important for them to know the outcome. Around half of all victims thought the sentences were lenient or very lenient; the remainder considered them to be adequate. None thought the sentences too severe. Only 40 per cent of commercial and 56 per cent of private victims applied for compensation, and of those who *did* apply, only 11 per cent of commercial and 20 per cent of private victims were actually awarded compensation. Forty per cent of all victims considered that their rights had not been fully enforced, particularly in respect of compensation. But 70 per cent thought that their involvement in the case had led to others being better protected and that the law also had been upheld. Most victims believed that the necessity for honesty in commercial dealings had been strengthened by their participation in this case. Some 30 per cent of victims thought that there were no benefits at all from their involvement in the case, and of this group the private victims were twice as likely as commercial ones to perceive that there were few if any benefits from going to court.

Interviews with fraud managers from major companies in the financial services sector revealed views that matched those contained in the questionnaire survey. While most interviewees stated that they were satisfied with the service they received from the police, there were divisions over their experience of the *prosecution* process. These reactions were partly the product of initial *expectations*. Commercial victims were more likely than private ones to believe after the event that there were benefits resulting from taking fraud to court and appeared to have 'better' court experiences. This could be explained by their being 'repeat players' and having often had prior police experience. Our data support what has become conventional criminological wisdom regarding the critical role played by victims in managing their victimisation and in activating criminal justice system. Few corporate victims were insured against fraud (except in the sense that the taxpayer bears a portion of the losses, which are 'costs' offset against the burden of taxation). Therefore, as is the case with the uninsured poor and 'ordinary' crime, the financial motivation for reporting fraud was absent. Reporting was a conscious decision made after some deliberation. Neither retribution nor compensation figured significantly as motives for pursuing fraudsters. Rather, ritualistic citing of company policy and 'general deterrence' were the central rationales. General deterrence was asserted as an article of faith rather than something empirically demonstrated: however, commercial victims are not alone in this respect! What *was* proven in their minds was that the cost and effort of participating in the formal legal system was not usually borne out in just deserts for themselves or for the fraudster. Like many police, 'repeat complainants' saw themselves as an under-appreciated group desperately trying to hold the thin blue line (or perhaps black line) against 'the criminal', without real support from the archaic courts.

It is logically true that the need for support from the courts is a consequence of defective crime prevention. Although those we interviewed considered that fraud prevention was primarily the responsibility of management, when pressed they agreed that there was a collective and individual failure to prevent fraud. This was partly a question of cost and attitude towards what were seen as 'unproductive' controls (because their effectiveness could not be measured in advance) – reluctance to spend money on competent staff, or to require duplicate controls; and partly a question of corporate imagination and priorities – marketing schemes that tried to 'close' deals without sufficient verification of bona fides was one example cited. Although efforts to optimise cash flow lead to tighter managerial control over stock-ordering, borrowing and lending (including trade credit), the general management view is that business is about marketing and selling. It seems plausible that fraud prevention is seen by senior managers as negativistic and 'killjoy', out of tune with the ideologically prevalent 'can do' enterprise philosophy. Unpaid sales to credit fraudsters, or unwittingly employing fraudsters because there was insufficient time to make background checks on them, are not equated psychologically with sales not made, even though rationally they ought to be thus equated. The sale or the employment decision comes first: the perceived crime rate is not high enough to discourage risk-taking. This is an important mental obstacle to fraud prevention (Levi, 1988).

Fraud and the Media

Unlike many other sorts of criminals, the extent of media obsession with some élite *offenders* does not involve depicting (and often amplifying) any harm done to the *victims* of those élite individuals: it is their celebrity itself that is the object of fascination. In *Wall Street*, as in the real-life insider dealing activities of many of the Boesky circle, injured victims nowhere appear. Nor was there any serious attempt to indicate that major damage was caused by Keith Best, then Conservative MP for Ynys Môn, whose conviction for dishonestly making multiple share-applications led to his resignation from Parliament and (temporary) suspension from the Bar (Levi, 1989).

We did not interview the makers of programmes such as 'Dallas', 'Dynasty', 'Big Deal', 'Budgie' and 'Minder' which – though not didactic in 'The Archers' tradition – could be construed as programmes about fraud. Our respondents frequently commented upon their 'social motives' for programme-making: to inform, warn and also entertain their audiences about the dangers and benefits of particular goods and services. They spoke of the underlying recipe for successful broadcasting, which meant that they had to provide more than 'information' or some worthy bromide along the lines of 'worker education programmes' common in communist regimes. They were compelled to construct their programmes in such a way as to win and hold an audience by popular appeal, preferably by exposing the inadequate regulation (or, even better, corrupt deliberate non-regulation) of some major cause of avoidable human suffering. These programmes depend largely on the problems brought to them (a) by victims of some illegality or 'abuse of power', or (b) by officials such as trading standards personnel keen to mobilise support for a change in the law and/or commercial practice.

The selection for programming from those problems depended significantly on the production values noted above: they had to be both reasonably relevant for the audience and 'fresh'. For example, if a recent programme in the series or in a rival series had just looked into a shady timeshare holiday scheme, callers with a similar problem would be unlikely to have their case publicised, though they were often referred to other sources of help and advice. This editorial function was seen as an indefinable gift or skill, but no attempt was made to justify the *non*-replication of stories. This was taken as being self-evident. The programme researchers and other production staff had their own lists of contacts to check stories or to appear to give 'an expert opinion'. It is possible that with increasing farming-out of programmes to independent companies in the future, the values of commissioning producers will become even more critical as a reference group in determining what counts as 'a good prog': whether programme consumers will find their interests best-served thereby is a separate issue, since although there is little point in making an educational programme that no one is interested enough to watch, the feedback in the media market is imperfect, particularly regarding decisions *not* to run a given idea: the problem of 'false negatives'. Researchers and producers all complained that anything to do with fraud was time-consuming and expensive to research and difficult to make 'filmic': radio (and newspapers) actually had some advantages over television here. Devices such as the use of stylised puppets in a programme on insider dealing were praised as partial successes in the attempt to make programmes more interesting visually. With the exception of 'World in Action' (Granada TV) or the episodic programmes by 'Fulcrum' (for Channel 4) and 'The Money Programme' (BBC2), there was a tendency for programmes on fraud in the City to be undertaken by people who knew little about the world of businesses and to degenerate into an only slightly more critical version of 'Lifestyles of the Rich and Famous' (namely, here are some very rich people who live with these gorgeous women in this fantastic home we would all like to live in, but *these* very rich people have done *bad* things), sometimes accompanied by the standard, if dramatically reasonably effective, 'Roger Cook's "Checkpoint" sequence' of 'doorstepping'/ejection/fight/menacing dog/reporter retreats under hail of threats/libel writ. This point is reinforced by the all-consuming media circus coverage of the conviction, sentencing and prison experiences of the Guinness Four in September 1990.

Fraudsters

One of our criticisms of most crime studies is that they tend to be separated out into criminology – which, for present purposes, we may define as the study of offenders in their social and geographical context – and victimology – the study of the victims of crime. Although the latter is the primary orientation of our study, it is critical to understand the process by which people come to be victims in relation to a pool of potential offenders and their motivations. In the course of reviewing court files on fraud victims and the *modus operandi* of fraud, we decided that given the marginal extra effort, it might be illuminating to collect data on the backgrounds of offenders.

The way in which public and police images amplify and sometimes make worse the behaviour of their 'folk devils' is a central theme of sociological work in the 'moral panic' tradition (Cohen, 1982). (However, much more effort has been expended on examining the motives behind and mechanics of such labelling than on reviewing its impact on offending *behaviour*.) Apart from questions of political and/or economic influence over white-collar law-enforcement agencies which, even if they exercise their judgements without direct interference, means that the agencies act with low resources and a 'correctionalist' rather than 'retributivist' motivation, the traditional advantages imputed to white-collar criminals include: (a) that they are (in the West) primarily white-*colour* criminals; and (b) that they do not possess other social or physical attributes that render them vulnerable to isolation and stigmatisation.

Since our court research was completed, there has been a change of regulatory attitude which has led to the prosecution of several leading City figures, for example, in the Guinness and County NatWest cases, though – controversially – not the Al Fayeds who own Harrods (Select Committee, 1990). However, in our sample, there were *no* people who could reasonably be viewed as disgraced members of the commercial or industrial élite. There were several professionals acting criminally and a few professional criminals with a record in this line of felony. But most fraudsters were blue-collar solo offenders of very modest socio-economic status who used deception to obtain cash or goods from organisations such as banks, finance companies, government agencies and employers. They did not use their own business or profession as a tool of fraud. As for personal background, the white-collar male fraudster is typically older, employed at the time of the offence, educated to a reasonable standard and married with children. The blue-collar male fraudster is typically unemployed at the time of the offence, generally without educational qualifications and is more likely to be unmarried than his white-collar counterpart.

The most minor frauds were excluded from our sample because, unless the accused opted for trial by jury, they would have been dealt with at magistrates' court. However, bearing this in mind, blue-collar men in Cardiff faced charges averaging £1367, while their white-collar counterparts made off with £3919. At the Old Bailey the blue-collar males were charged with fraud offences averaging £3497, compared with white-collar fraudsters averaging £110,243. There is a substantial London weighting allowance in the fraud world! Those who used their occupation – usually to embezzle from their employers – stole an average of £14,000 in Cardiff cases and £128,000 at the Old Bailey. The white-collar male who used an organisation of some kind to manipulate the fraud made most of all: £19,193 in Cardiff and £283,813 in London. A minority (41 per cent) of white-collar defendants used their own businesses as the vehicle of fraud, yet on average they were able to victimise more individuals and organisations than was any other category of fraudster. Our findings coincide with those of a contemporaneous American study based on offenders dealt with in US Federal Courts (Weisburd *et al.*, 1991).

The Fraudster in Court

The length of time before cases come to court has aroused much concern in legal circles. This is partly because of the strains on the prison system caused by remands in custody. It is less common to think in terms of the gaps between offence, charge and conviction. However, we collected data on these issues. A long gap between offence and apprehension is – from the offender's viewpoint – usually a desirable thing, whatever its impact on special or general deterrence and on incapacitation. At both courts, those cases dealt with quickest were frauds undertaken by blue-collar defendants; on average the time taken from offence to sentence was 13 months. For white-collar fraudsters at both courts who used neither their occupations nor an organisation to advance their crimes, the average wait was two years three months. Those who took longest to come to trial were white-collar defendants who used an organisation to defraud: their offence–sentence gap averaged three years three months. Such frauds both take longer to detect and allow for more plausible excuses that delay prosecution. (Delays may also improve the chance of acquittal and mitigate sentence.)

Though less welcome to those offenders remanded in custody – except where they can have food and drink sent in – the period between committal and sentence was likewise divergent: at Cardiff, the blue-collar male waited 11 weeks compared with five to six months at the Old Bailey; at the other extreme, at the Old Bailey, the white-collar male waited ten and a half *months* between committal and sentence compared with a maximum of four months at Cardiff. The longer the delays, the more problems there are with witness recall or availability: some executives had emigrated by the time the case came up to trial.

A review of case records at both courts revealed that different types of fraudsters experienced consistently different types of disposal. Some of the reasons for this may be due to the following characteristics associated with the defendants. First, it is typically the case that white-collar fraudsters commit fewer non-fraud crimes (such as burglary) than do blue-collar defendants in the course of their frauds. White-collar fraudsters using an organisation to defraud committed the fewest non-fraud crimes. They also have far fewer prior convictions and prior prison sentences. Once convicted, blue-collar male fraudsters – while stealing less than their white-collar colleagues – were more likely than them to receive a prison sentence. Those who used an organisation to steal were less likely to get a prison sentence, but when they did, they received the longest sentences. This confirms findings from the United States (see Levi, 1987, ch. 7; and Weisburd *et al.*, 1991, for reviews of American studies).

THEORETICAL AND POLICY CONCLUSIONS

We have presented here a summary and interpretation of *part* of the information collected in our study. Our general conclusion is that, as in the case of other crimes such as burglary and robbery, labels such as 'white-collar crime' and 'fraud' give a misleadingly coherent appearance to extremely varied patterns of behaviour and victim impacts. Fraud victims vary from very rich to fairly poor, and their reactions to fraud do not necessarily correspond to their occupational status: perhaps because of its effect on their self-image and social reputation, some working-class victims who saw themselves as street-wise characters were far more disturbed than some wealthy persons by frauds which both could afford. Whereas organisational representatives tended to view fraud as a regrettable 'fact of life' reflecting declining social morality, private victims expressed greater concern about their own failings in being caught out, and about how foolish other people would think them if they discovered that they had been conned.

Except where a case has a high political or media profile – in which case senior officers outside the Fraud Squad display an interest and demand results – the British police tend to give priority to individuals who appear to be plainly damaged by their experiences. However, performance indicator pressures place a high personal and organisational premium on rapid case solution: to the extent that repeat victims knew their way around the system and did the right kind of investigative work prior to reporting the crime to the police, they could redress the police *attitudinal* balance which favoured prioritising the cases of private victims. The absence of non-fraud data makes it hard to tell whether British corporations enjoy the advantage found by Hagan (1988) in the processing of burglary, robbery and theft complaints in Canada, but it seems likely that any advantage British companies have in getting their offenders convicted is attributable less to systematic class bias than to the fact that they (and the police) sift out a higher proportion of the ambiguous cases before the conduct is reported and recorded as a suspected 'fraud'. We, like Weisburd *et al.* (1991) in the US, found that most of those convicted of fraud could be more accurately described as 'blue-collar criminals' than as white-collar ones. However, except where many élite personnel are convicted, samples of *convicted* offenders cannot allow us to infer that élites receive (or do not receive) special privileges: they may be treated more generously *at the pre-reporting and recording stages* because of their social position or because of the embarrassment they may cause to the organisation. So, interesting though it is that many 'blue-collar' types commit frauds, this does not mean that 'white-collar' types do not get away with it. Nevertheless, official reactions to frauds of different types do *not* fall easily into the *marxisant* framework that sees the police simply as the handmaidens of 'the' social and economic élite.

The policy implications of our study suggest that there may be greater need for counselling of fraud victims – particularly 'private' ones, though small businesses may be counted as 'private' for this purpose – than is generally recognised in victim support movements or among the police. Fraud – like most other crimes – has highly varied impacts that are not consistently predictable on the basis of the information available. But quite apart from the economic effect of fraud on business, which is greater than all other crimes combined, there is little warrant for the police or for those who determine *non*-police regulatory resources to treat fraud as a 'victimless crime'.

Economists might like to dream of some rational world in which utility curves of 'pain from crime' could intersect with those of 'police effectiveness' to produce an optimal model for police resource allocation. However, the reality is that 'law and order' movements often involve the mobilisation of images of nasty offenders and suffering victims: more abstract, collective interests tend not to generate the political pressures that have produced action plans such as the UK government's 1990 *Victim's Charter*. By contrast to the folk images of burglary which may *over*state the pain many burglaries cause to victims, we have found that, except in the context of investment frauds which leave pensioners destitute, the folk image of white-collar crime may *under*state the pain it produces by taking it for granted that, in some sense, fraud victims not only can afford but also *deserve* their losses because of their supposed 'contributory negligence'. Accepting that governments, policing and prosecution agencies have an obligation to consider more abstractly 'the public good' and that comparing *scientifically* the impact of different forms of crime may be impossible, there is a certain irony in the fact that much of the increased media and regulatory attention to 'white-collar crime' during the 1980s has occurred in precisely those areas of fraud like insider dealing and the making of multiple share-applications which – however politically 'sexy' in the context of financial services deregulation and privatisation issues and the status of offenders – probably have least effect on the emotions and/or the pockets of real individuals who cannot afford their loss.

Subject to any changes that may come about as a result of increased media reporting of fraud scandals and the 1990 CBI/Crime Concern initiative on the prevention of crime against business, there was no evidence from our survey that much information about methods of fraud or the sorts of people who commit it was getting through either to corporate or to private victims, and it seems to us that there is considerable room for improved social awareness regarding the risks of fraud. Otherwise, while Neighbourhood Watch members are being encouraged to keep up their (patchy) surveillance on strangers passing through their area, the fraudsters will be allowed unsupervised to steal the entire street.

REFERENCES

Box, S. (1983), *Power, Crime and Mystification* (London: Tavistock).

Christie, N. (1986), 'The ideal victim', in E. Fattah (ed.), *From Crime Policy to Victim Policy* (London: Macmillan).

Cohen, S. (1982), *Folk Devils and Moral Panics*, 2nd edn (London: Paladin).

Fattah, E. A. (ed.) (1986), *From Crime Policy to Victim Policy: Reorienting the Justice System* (New York: St Martin's Press).

Grabosky, P., Braithwaite, J. and Wilson, P. (1987), 'The myth of community tolerance toward white-collar crime', *Australian and New Zealand Journal of Criminology*, **20**, 33–44.

Hagan, J. (1988), *Structural Criminology* (Oxford: Polity Press).

Hough, M. and Mayhew, P. (1983), *The British Crime Survey* (London: Her Majesty's Stationery Office).

Hough, M. and Mayhew, P. (1985), *Taking Account of Crime* (London: Her Majesty's Stationery Office).

Levi, M. (1986), 'The costs of fraud', unpublished study for the Home Office.

Levi, M. (1987), *Regulating Fraud: White-Collar Crime and the Criminal Process* (London: Tavistock/Routledge).

Levi, M. (1988), *The Prevention of Fraud* (London: Home Office, Crime Prevention Unit).

Levi, M. (1989), 'Suite justice: sentencing for fraud', *Criminal Law Review*, 420–34.

Levi, M. and Pithouse, A. (forthcoming), *The Victims of Fraud* (Milton Keynes, Bucks.: Open University Press).

Maguire, M. (1982), *Burglary in a Dwelling* (Aldershot: Gower).

Mayhew, P., Elliott, D. and Dowds, L. (1989), *The 1988 British Crime Survey* (London: Her Majesty's Stationery Office).

Reiss, A. and Biderman, A. (1980), *Data Sources on White-Collar Law-Breaking* (Washington, D.C.: National Institute of Justice).

Select Committee (1990), *Department of Trade and Industry Investigations*, Report of the Select Committee on Trade and Industry (House of Commons Paper).

Weisburd, D., Wheeler, S., Waring, E. and Bode, N. (1991), *Crimes of the Middle Classes: White-Collar Offenders in the Federal Courts* (New Haven, Conn.: Yale University Press).

11 It's Not What You Do but the Way that You Do It: Tax Evasion, Tax Avoidance and the Boundaries of Deviance

DOREEN McBARNET

The publication of the official crime rates every year routinely stimulates outcry over the breakdown of law and order. Large-scale white-collar crime has increasingly become front page news. Yet law and order may be undermined just as much, and quite routinely, by activities which are quite immune from any hint – or possibility – of criminal stigma. These activities are committed by people who, far from breaking the law, go to great lengths to ensure they abide by it, yet while abiding by the law they also escape its impact. They are both immune to legal requirements and prohibitions, *and* immune to any threat of penalty or stigma. This chapter explores this paradox in the context of a study of tax evasion and tax avoidance, and argues that social control through law is challenged not just by those who abuse the law but also, and perhaps more fundamentally, by those who *use* it.

THE RESEARCH PROJECT: BEYOND WHITE COLLAR CRIME

This research project was undertaken in the wake of increasing public discussion of the 'black economy', the scandal over large-scale tax evasion among casual workers on Fleet Street and the 'lump'[1] in the contracting industry, an estimate by the Chairman of the Board of Inland Revenue of 7.5 per cent of gross domestic product (or £3–3.5 billion) being lost to the revenue through tax evasion, and the exposure of large-scale VAT fraud. The Inland Revenue had been reorganised with the aim of greater enforcement efficiency; and the Keith Committee had been set up to explore the enforcement powers of the Revenue departments. In short, the effectiveness of tax law and enforcement was being defined as a problem.

There are several standard routes for research into an area like tax. One is the criminological route: why don't people comply with the law, why do they break it? Or the enforcement agencies are studied. Those enforcing the

247

law are seen as having inadequate powers or resources, organisational pressures are seen as directing attention to some sorts of contravention of law rather than others. In studies of regulation, agencies are seen as 'captured' by those they are regulating, penalties are seen as too low to deter, establishing proof as too difficult to secure conviction, judges as too readily swayed by white-collar status. The institutional treatment of 'white-collar crime' as different from conventional crime, being dealt with by regulatory agencies rather than police, by regulatory law rather than criminal law, may be seen as undermining deterrence by removing the threat of criminal stigma. The substance of the legislation itself may be scrutinised, and seen as reflecting the interests and values of economic and political élites, because of lobbying or basic economic power. Law, class and state are seen as in alliance. Law apparently against the interests of economic élites is seen as merely symbolic; if legal control or legal regulation of white-collar activities fails, it does so because it was not, or not wholeheartedly, intended to do otherwise.

This research project set out with a different approach to the problem of legal control of white-collar activities. It suggested another model of law and another relationship for law, class and state. It treated law not merely as substance, a body of requirements and prohibitions served up on a platter to be accepted or rejected (often with the implication that for economic élites it could be accepted since it would inevitably be in their interests). Rather it approached law, *after* legislation, as a 'raw material to be worked on' (McBarnet, 1984), as something which might be used, manipulated, crafted to suit one's own interests. The approach focused less on the content of law – of legislation and case law – and more on exploring its methods, structures and ideologies, its 'facilitative form', and how it could be actively used.

From this model flowed several changes of perspective, framing theoretical issues in new ways. Law need not be a monopoly of the state (however constituted or influenced) but might be available to others to use *against* the state. Loopholes in the law might well be written into law as a matter of underhand policy, the product of symbolic law, but they might also be constructed after the event by active legal work. Legislation might be the end-product of a process of lobbying and subtler means of exercising power, but it might also be a starting point for a process of legal manipulation and creativity, *turning it*, *whatever* influences the lawmakers had sought to reflect or constrain, to the service of specific interests. In short, the primary concern of the project became the craft of law itself, the *post hoc* use and manipulation of law. The focus was on those subject to the law, on their role in actively constructing law in their own interests, and on the professional and financial advisers involved in the process. Indeed, the role of the professions as mediators working on the law for economic élites, to make it fit their interests, emerged as a key part of the research.

Our particular interest lay not in petty moonlighters (those who evade tax by failing to report income, often paid in cash) but in economic élites, on big business and on what our interviewees referred to as 'high net worth individuals' – people and organisations subject to redistributive taxes, who could afford expert professional advice and commission creative legal work; people and organisations for whom tax involved large sums of money, who had a strong economic motivation to escape it, but also (perhaps) a strong motivation to escape any risk of criminal stigma. One question for the research was whether and how both goals could be simultaneously achieved. If law was a 'material to be worked with', was it possible to use and manipulate law and legal institutions to achieve the same goals as crime – escaping legal prohibitions or requirements – without its risks of penalties or stigma? Studies of the politics and enforcement of law had shown some of the ways in which white-collar activities could escape the criminal label. What could a study focused on the 'craft of law' add?

As a result of these perspectives, the project took a rather unconventional approach. It did not look just at crime, nor even just at 'law-breaking', whether dealt with under criminal law or administrative law, as tax violations often are. Nor was it confined only to grey areas where law might or might not have been violated. We also went further and studied activities which were indisputably lawful, activities which did not merely escape investigation or labelling by enforcers, but which *could not* be defined as violations of law, which were indisputably on the right side of the boundary of deviance – yet which deliberately escaped tax payments just as surely as crime. Crime was thus set in a wider context, in which it became just one of several ways to escape social control.

Tax appealed as a good area to explore these issues – if a daunting one, in terms of its legal complexity and breadth (touched by many areas of law beyond the Finance Acts and tax cases), by its constant state of flux, by the moral ambivalence surrounding it, by its hybrid role between regulatory requirement and policy incentive, not to mention its decidedly boring image! It appealed as a good area to consider the relationship of law, class and state, since here, on the face of it at least, state interests in collecting tax and the interests of economic élites in non-payment could be at odds. It appealed because of the institutionalised recognition in tax law of a halfway house – tax avoidance – between full compliance with legal policy and the outright violation of the law represented by the category of evasion. It appealed because, along with the publicly expressed concern in the early 1980s over evasion and enforcement were other concerns over tax *avoidance* as a social problem.

Tax avoidance is neither criminal nor a regulatory offence. All the legal textbooks stress this. Yet the 1980s saw increasing discussion of an 'unacceptable' side of tax avoidance. Judges, seeking to develop a 'new approach' in the hope of controlling the unacceptable, referred to it as tax evasion. Inland Revenue and police acted together using techniques normally associated with large-scale criminal fraud to garner evidence for a case against the Rossminster operation,[2] which presented itself as selling not evasion but avoidance. The Keith Committee, in the few pages of its report devoted to tax avoidance, noted concern over 'schemes where the line between avoidance and evasion may have been crossed' (1983, p. 156). The hybrid term 'avoision' had been coined (Seldon, 1979). The relationship between tax evasion and tax avoidance thus offered a provocative case-study for exploring the boundaries between law-breaking and law-abiding activity.

Yet the area was not one which had attracted much empirical study. If tax evasion is still an under-researched area in the UK, it has at least attracted some study (see for example Cook, 1989). But the topic of tax *avoidance* was virtually virgin territory, having attracted little sociological attention and virtually no empirical research. In the United States, although there has been a recent burst of research on tax evasion and non-compliance, the issue of tax avoidance has been neglected, and this lacuna continues; for example, the major agenda for tax research set by a recent US taskforce has neglected the issue of avoidance (Roth, Scholz and Witte, 1989). The area, in short, called out for empirical and conceptual attention.

The research, conducted with Dr Graham Mansfield, was based on in-depth technical interviews with 105 accountants, city solicitors, barristers, judges, merchant bankers, insurers, Inland Revenue officers, tax consultants and scheme promoters, along with contextual interviews, participation at professional conferences, observation of key cases in court, and legal and documentary analysis. Quotations from interviews in the text are referred to by the category of the source – solicitor, officer of the Inland Revenue, and so on.

The research explored how the boundaries are drawn between criminal and non-criminal means of escaping tax. It described the 'grey areas' at the boundaries, where the boundaries are transgressed without discovery, and the blurred edges of law-abiding and law-breaking activities where the two interlink. It looked at the process of labelling activities 'evasion' or 'avoidance', showing how 'labelled' taxpayers or their advisers could take not a passive but an active role in the process, ensuring, by a range of techniques involving what we called 'non-disclosing disclosure', that even in grey areas, a criminal label was made impossible (McBarnet, 1991). The taxpayer could also seize the initiative and pre-empt labelling altogether by using the letter of the law and the institutions, forms and methods of the law to construct alternative routes for escaping tax that were immune from social control. Just as the criminal label has been seen as a construct of enforcement decisions, so legitimacy was seen as a construct of taxpayer strategy.

Tax-avoidance devices were investigated and the legal techniques on which they were based analysed. We explored the role of the professions in relation to avoidance and evasion. We studied the construction and marketing of devices designed to escape the law and showed that marketed artificial tax schemes were not confined to a few 'unacceptable' marketeers, as media coverage of and judicial approaches to the Rossminster team might suggest, but that a central role was played by City institutions and the professions. We studied the manipulation by taxpayers of the institutions of law, showed how they sought to manage what we called the 'politics of case law' (McBarnet and Mansfield, 1986), or shopped around for barristers' opinions and used them as 'fraud insurance' (McBarnet, 1991) where there were doubts about the legal status of transactions, a technique which later came to light and may have been put in doubt by the County NatWest affair.[3]

The research analysed the problems for enforcers in dealing with dynamic and creative use of law, describing the cat-and-mouse games between regulators and regulated. Recent judicial attempts at a 'new approach' were researched and analysed (Mansfield, 1989), and more fundamental contradictions, dilemmas and problems for enforcement in the deeper structures of law were explored (McBarnet, 1988; McBarnet and Whelan, 1991a). The research raised serious doubts about the feasibility of effective legal regulation of economic élites with access to sophisticated legal skills.

Some of these specific areas of empirical research and analysis have been published elsewhere, others will be. This chapter is inevitably much more narrowly focused, drawing on the larger project to explore the boundaries between deviant and legitimate behaviour, how they are managed, and to touch on some of the problems raised for social control through law.

ESCAPING TAX AND ESCAPING SOCIAL CONTROL

Faced with income or a capital gain on which a tax bill will be due, there are four possible responses. First, taxpayers can declare the deal to the Inland

Revenue and pay the bill. Secondly, they can haggle over the bill or over what might count as allowances to set against it – an option open more readily to those with large bills or complex businesses than to the mass of taxpayers whose tax is deducted at source. Thirdly, they can opt to evade tax: not declare the deal to the Revenue; keep cash under the mattress; pack it in a suitcase and smuggle it offshore; or divert it through chains of companies, trusts and middlemen, through 'black holes', as one consultant called them, such as Luxembourg or Panama, to a Swiss bank account. Fourthly, they can put lawyers, bankers, accountants, consultants to work on dreaming up a scheme which will escape tax legally, utilising the techniques not of tax evasion but of tax avoidance.

Tax evasion and tax avoidance are both designed to escape payment of tax. Both are complex terms covering a range of activities on a spectrum from the indubitably lawful to the fraudulent. Tax evasion is illegal, subject to civil or criminal penalties. It may range from failure to make a return on time through to fraudulent understatements or claims. Deliberate fraud may be dealt with through criminal prosecution. In practice, the Inland Revenue prefers to negotiate a settlement, and prosecution is rare. But it is also Revenue policy to prosecute some cases of all classes of tax law for deterrence purposes. Tax evasion with intent to defraud the Revenue is thus vulnerable to criminal prosecution and the stigma of criminal labelling. Even if dealt with under administrative rather than criminal law, evasion carries the risk of civil penalties of up to treble the amount overdue, and although these may be negotiated downward, penalties are charged (according to the Keith Report (1983), in 73 per cent of investigations by the Special Investigations Office). What is more, although the risk of being caught may be low for sophisticated evaders, the risk of prosecution if caught may be higher. Witness Lester Piggott's three-year prison sentence for income tax and VAT fraud of over £3 million.

Tax avoidance, by contrast, attracts no legal penalties, criminal or civil. Avoidance ranges through a spectrum from the 'acceptable', sometimes distinguished as 'tax planning', to the 'unacceptable', which might be challenged in the civil courts, but in neither case is it criminal or a violation of regulatory law. On the contrary, the use of legal techniques to avoid tax has been upheld repeatedly in the courts as not only lawful but as a right, an entitlement, even (in the context of company directors' obligations *vis-à-vis* shareholders) a duty. Tax evasion thus escapes tax but not the threat of social control, carrying the risk of criminal stigma or penalties; tax avoidance escapes both tax *and* any risk of stigma or legal penalty. One is law-breaking activity, one law-abiding. One is on the right side, one on the wrong side of the boundaries of deviance. Legal textbooks refer repeatedly to the 'sharp distinction' between evasion and avoidance. What is the difference between them?

The answer from the legal textbooks is that tax evasion is characterised by deceit, misrepresentation and concealment. Criminal tax evasion might involve deliberately understating profits or other income with intent to escape tax, deliberately overstating expenses, fabrication of invoices, or making false claims to allowances. It would be fraudulent to give a false description of the legal status of a payment or person; or to deliberately fail to disclose income.

Yet tax *avoidance* schemes and devices have been constructed and used routinely by large companies, banks and the stock market, by nationalised industries and 'high net worth' individuals to achieve just these ends by legal means. Such devices have involved double charging of the same interest costs twice against profits; artificial creation of losses, not actually sustained, to set against capital gains, or of expenses to set against profits; transferring allowances from a taxpayer who would be entitled to them but cannot use them to offset against tax, to a taxpayer for whom they were not intended; legal laundering of interest into tax-free capital gains, or of capital assets into revenue expenses. We have analysed elsewhere some of the techniques for achieving these ends (McBarnet, 1988; 1992). A wide range of schemes is explored in the research project as a whole. The examples detailed below may give some flavour of what can be involved.

Double-Charging Interest: the Delaware Link

In 1985, according to Revenue estimates, £700 million in double-charged interest was set against the profits of multinational companies to escape due tax, and without legislation there was not a thing the Inland Revenue could do about it. How can you quite deliberately double-charge interest, that is, charge one interest bill twice over, without risking criminal stigma? If it is done by falsifying documents to produce two bills when you have really only paid one, or by passing expenses incurred by one taxpayer and used to offset tax to another to do the same, it is illegal evasion. But it could, via the 'Delaware link' scheme, be done legally.

The trick here was clever use of jurisdictional loopholes between different countries. In this case there was a clash of legal definitions on company residency between the USA and the UK, which the scheme exploited. The US definition depended on where the company was registered. The UK test was a matter of where the company's management and control were exercised. A company could therefore be registered in the US, usually in

Delaware with its particularly favourable company laws, hence the name, but be managed from the UK and meet the requirements for residency in both countries. Being defined as resident means a company is subject to that country's tax regime. However, double-tax treaties stop double-charging of tax on the same income. In the Delaware link scheme, dual residency, immune from double tax, was none the less used for the opposite purpose, to use one set of expenses to escape tax twice.

Dual resident companies were set up and used by multinational groups specifically and deliberately to create expenses which could be claimed in both jurisdictions by borrowing money from one of the other companies in the group, thus creating interest payments as an expense. The tax-allowance value of the expenses could be used, under group relief provisions, to offset against profits in the rest of the group – but it would be used twice: once in the United States, once in the UK.

Artificiality permeated the device. The money borrowed would not necessarily be used for any commercial purpose. The dual resident company might borrow to acquire a company already owned by another member of the group. 'It would have been more palatable if it had involved real fresh investment as opposed to just shunting debt around the group to restructure it for tax avoidance' (Inland Revenue). It was important that the dual resident company did not have taxable profits itself or the interest would simply be set against those, instead of being used twice for the rest of the group, so the money to pay for the interest would be carefully injected into the dual resident company in a form which did not give rise to taxable profits. Indeed a *double* dual resident structure might be used to separate interest going out from dividends coming in.

Of course, the interest which created the double-charged expense would be paid to another company in the group and tax might be payable on it as income. Indeed, internal movements of money within a group would, without tax-avoidance devices, be likely simply to cancel each other out. In this case, however, even if tax was paid on the interest received from the dual resident company, the double-charging of the interest in the two countries meant a bonus since tax would only be paid once but expenses would be charged twice. Not content with this bonus, however, some corporate tax planners would create structures which not only allowed double charging of the interest as expense, but avoided tax altogether on the interest received as income. This might be done by using a conduit company in a tax haven. The Inland Revenue stated that it did not in practice receive tax from the interest payment income. The group might therefore achieve double tax relief on an artificial interest charge which was itself received free of tax.

Expenses were thus manufactured and double-charged to offset against tax and cut the tax bill. But the scheme was not evasion, just clever avoidance. It did not break the law; it used the law. The group complied with the rules of both UK and US tax law and in doing so quite legally charged the same expenses twice.

Manufactured Losses

Claiming losses to offset against gains is another way to cut the tax bill. Where real losses are sustained this is just as intended by legal policy. Where losses are faked, perhaps by false invoices, this would be evasion. But 'losses' which are not actually sustained can also be used to cut the tax bill via tax avoidance.

If shares rise in value, the gain, above a specified exemption level, is subject to capital gains tax. If some lose in value and some gain, the loss is offset against the gain in calculating the net gain to be taxed. One way to save tax is to sell shares at a time when they are making a loss. But this would be rather pointless; people buy shares to make gains, not losses. The investor would normally want to hold on to the shares until they rise in value, and sell them at a gain. But what if there was a tax-avoidance scheme which allowed you to have your cake and eat it, to sell your shares at a loss *and* keep them to rise in value? This is what the technique known as 'bed and breakfasting' (discussed in more detail in McBarnet, 1992) achieved. Shares showing a current loss would be sold on to a broker to crystallise the loss and produce a legal document to prove it. But they would then be repurchased the next day at virtually the same price so that they could be retained until they rose in value. By the time they were sold, the gain might in turn be cancelled out by other paper losses, current or stockpiled. The Stock Exchange's 'Black Monday' in October 1987 was seen by tax advisers as an ill wind, since mass bed and breakfasting was seen as a way of cancelling out capital gains for years to come.

There have been many attempts at using legal means to create artificial but allowable losses to reduce tax bills. A series of transactions might be set up to produce a self-cancelling effect for tax purposes, or produce a paper loss in an exempt area to offset a real gain and eliminate the tax on it without actually sustaining the loss. One which was challenged by the Inland Revenue in a celebrated case was the 'exempt debt capital loss scheme', one of many tax-avoidance schemes created and marketed in the 1970s by the Rossminster team.

The nub of the exempt debt capital loss scheme was to produce an artificial loss to offset against a real capital gain to produce a zero tax situation. One of these clients, whose case was to reach the House of Lords in 1981, was a farmer, Ramsay. Ramsay has sold land at a substantial capital gain. The Rossminster scheme created a loss of £175,000 – it could have been any figure, as required by the client – to neutralise it. The scheme required two companies and a subsidiary controlled by the taxpayer, and two companies controlled by the scheme promoters. It involved two loans, one share issue, the exercise of options on interest levels (the interest rate on one loan was changed from 11 per cent to 22 per cent, on the other from 11 per cent to zero), the sale of the 22 per cent loan to a company controlled by the scheme promoter, which then sold the loan to the subsidiary of taxpayer company B, two liquidations, loan repayments, and exchange of shares for loanstock in another promoter-controlled company. The result of all this shuffling around was that a paper gain and an equivalent paper loss were created out of nothing. As Lord Templeman put it, it was a 'circular game in which the taxpayer and a few hired performers act out a play; nothing happens save that the Houdini taxpayer appears to escape from the manacles of tax' (*W. T. Ramsay Ltd* v *Inland Revenue* [1981]).

The object of the exercise, however, was that something should happen, not in the world of real money, where the taxpayer should be no worse off for all the transactions except for the cost of the fees to the scheme's creators, but in the world of legal status. The aim was to create an unreal but legally recognised loss. The mesh of deals aimed at establishing, first, an artificial gain which would not be taxable, since the claim was that it fell into the exempt category of a debt, and, secondly, an artificial loss. This artificial loss would not simply be offset against its mirror-image artificial gain because that gain was not taxable anyway. Instead, it would be left as a free-floating loss to offset against the real gain which had brought the client to Rossminster in the first place.

Schemes to create artificial losses were themselves usually highly artificial, involving specially created companies which were never intended to trade, and based on transactions within a network of companies or trusts or banks or charities often controlled by the people selling the scheme and never intended to be more than temporary, paper-only deals. Those involved in buying and selling the scheme might then sit around a table and, wearing different hats as board members of the different companies every few minutes or every few days, sign cheques from one company to the next. Despite the large sums of money apparently being signed away, there were, other than the promoters' fees, no real costs. 'No one let go of the corner of the cheque', as one Revenue officer put it. The transactions and cheques went round in circles. But the object of the exercise was not simply to go round in circles. The objective was rather to set up a magic circle which would make a real capital gain vanish, not by fraud, not by non-disclosure of gains, not by fabrication of false invoices, but by the creation of an artificial but legally recognised loss, by legal avoidance.

EVASION AND AVOIDANCE: WHAT IS THE DIFFERENCE?

As *avoidance* a scheme may or may not succeed. Successful avoidance, accepted by the Revenue – as in the case of the Delaware link – or by the courts despite a Revenue challenge, is, by any definition, criminal or civil, a lawful method of escaping tax. The exempt debt capital loss scheme, outlined above, eventually failed in the House of Lords. The example was selected deliberately. Avoidance can fail. But so long as the companies used are properly constituted, the laws on the transactions complied with, the panoply of *legal propriety* met, the scheme is on the right side of the criminal line. It is an unsuccessful attempt at *legal avoidance* not evasion.

What then is the difference between tax evasion and tax avoidance? The simple answer may be: it's not what you do but the way that you do it. The motivation behind both approaches is the same: to escape tax. The effects are the same; public funds are depleted. In substance the activities – double-charging interest, claiming losses not actually sustained – may seem indistinguishable from false claims and declarations. In law, however, they are very different and the key difference lies in the means employed. Tax evasion methods simply ignore or break the law. Tax avoidance devices *use* the methods of law to neutralise its impact. Sometimes evasion is quite explicitly converted to avoidance; one solicitor discussed advising the use of a non-resident trust to escape tax rather than his client's proposal of a 'dummy – non-existent – relative'. By using rather than abusing the law, taxpayers can achieve precisely the same end as evasion without any of the risk of criminal stigma or regulatory penalty which evasion entails. Indeed, tax avoidance has a double purpose: escaping tax *and* doing it legally.

Thus Delaware link companies did not fraudulently present themselves as claiming interest in one country only. They claimed in both because the law of both countries allowed it. They went to great lengths to take advantage of the situation. It was very far from simply being a take-up of allowances explicitly intended for them. Nor was it simply a matter of slipping into an accidental but convenient loophole. Highly complex and artificial structures and transactions were contrived in order to exploit fully the opportunity which the gap between jurisdictions presented. The loophole was stretched far beyond its immediate scope by creative legal engineering. But no rules were broken, no transactions were hidden, no fraudulent claims or misrepresentations made. On the contrary, part of the reason for the rise in the use of the device between 1983 and 1985 (from 50 companies claiming £400 million in relief to nearly double) was the public statement by a reluctant Inland Revenue that it was, in the present state of the law, quite lawful. What the multinational companies involved were doing was not prohibited by law; on the contrary, the device was constructed *from* the law. They had not broken the law but worked creatively on its fabric and turned it to their advantage.

Likewise the artificial losses created by the exempt debt scheme involved no misrepresentation. The fictional loss claimed was not a forged or fake invoice, but a legal fiction, neatly crafted from the raw materials of law. The hallmarks of criminal evasion are misrepresentation or concealment; the hallmarks of legal avoidance are legal transformation of one thing into another: income into capital, equity into debt, and so on. Law is full of fictions – the legal distinction between companies and their owners, for example, or trusts and their beneficiaries; legally recognised fictions do not constitute fraud; only misrepresenting, forging or concealing them does. Receiving money in the name of non-existent people – the Mickey Mouses of Fleet Street – constitutes evasion; using specially created legal personae – companies or trusts – to receive money constitutes avoidance. As one Revenue officer put it: 'If it's make believe and you tell us, it's OK. It's only if you tell us it's real when it's not, that it's evasion.'

Getting the form right effectively provided what I have discussed elsewhere as 'fraud insurance' (McBarnet, 1991). Criminal acts require proof of intention – '*mens rea*' – and although in some areas of law that has proved less of a burden than it might seem, it is difficult to sustain proof of intention to break the law, when the whole strategy of avoidance is to do it legally. Often there will be counsel's opinion to back up the taxpayer's interpretation of his legal obligations, and this may be enough in itself to distinguish avoidance from evasion. Law, after all, is arguable; getting it wrong is not of itself an indication of evasion if you can provide evidence that you tried to get it right. You may, as it happened, have had to go to rather a lot of trouble to get it right. Interviewees referred to the practice of 'opinion-shopping', going to not one but a number of barristers for an authoritative opinion on the legality of a scheme until one provided the 'right' opinion – the one the customer wanted to hear. Barristers' opinions might be managed too (McBarnet, 1991). The fraud insurance supplied by 'trying to get it right' might itself be the product of a process of manipulation. Even getting the procedures *wrong* need not of itself constitute evasion unless there was intent to break the law. As one Inland Revenue officer put it: 'If it's sloppy technically it doesn't mean there was intent to evade. In fact it means there was intent to do it properly.'

So those interviewed tended to lay great stress on getting the form right, getting the procedure right, keeping precisely within the rules: 'getting funds in the right place at the right time' (City solicitor); recommending only 'technically impeccable schemes' (barrister). Some schemes were particularly admired for their 'beautiful carpentry' (barrister); or distinguished from less-marketable products by their 'technical elegance' (accountant). The Keith Committee discussed schemes which 'typically involved a complicated series of transactions prepared with full legal formalities' (1983, p. 159). Some of these schemes could involve 250 legal documents (consultant). 'Avoidance is perfectly legal,' said one Inland Revenue officer. 'I'm not against it. But if they do it they must do all the steps for real.'

This ideology of strict adherence to form, legal technicality, doing it properly, was contrasted with those who slipped over the line into the fraudulent: 'the insurance salesman, backdating documents, who has a blind spot, doesn't see the difference between right and wrong' (barrister); the standing insurance joke about backdating to beat the midnight deadline before the change of rules on controlled company pensions in 1988 – 'It's been a funny week, Tuesday the 13th, Wednesday the 13th, Thursday the 13th . . . .' Inland Revenue officers talked of the move into fraud coming where taxpayers do not go through all the proper steps but say they have. Evasion came into play when taxpayers got the form wrong and pretended they had got it right.

But drawing the line in this way left some Revenue officers bemused:

> One problem has always bothered us – the genuineness of documents. Where a scheme involves three hours of meetings with a specified order of events and cheques passing round at appropriate moments, they would be foolish if they didn't get it right and it seems an insult to their intelligence to ask for the documents. But sometimes they do forget to minute, say, a commercial motive. If we ask for the minute they'll manufacture it, and why not, they'd say, let's keep the silly Inland Revenue happy, we just forgot to minute it at the time. But the manufacture of evidence is criminal. Yet morally, if they just forgot it, is that worse than the whole business of creating a circle of artificial transactions in the first place?

The perplexity stemmed from the fact that it was the technicality and not the pervasive avoidance intent that breached the law. Getting the form right kept the device on the right side of the boundaries of deviance even where in substance, purpose and effect it did not differ from evasion. The means justified the end.

GREY AREAS AT THE BOUNDARIES

It would be quite wrong to slip into any assumption that economic élites always opt for tax *avoidance* rather than evasion. It takes only a glance at the front pages of newspapers in the last year to underline the reality of outright white-collar *crime*. And for every deviant activity that is discovered there may be many more which are not. Despite being based on interviews, which would hardly seem a medium for uncovering the 'dark figure' of evasion, this research project found instances where avoidance transgressed the boundaries into evasion, overlapped with evasion, or was interlinked with it.

In practice the line between evasion and avoidance may be hazy. 'Offshore invoicing', for example – a means of moving money out of Britain to a low-tax or no-tax jurisdiction – might range from the genuinely commercial to the fraudulent. It might involve a genuine invoice from one company to another (related) company for actual and precise services rendered at market prices. It might be an invoice from a real offshore office for vaguer management charges by staff based there. It might be an invoice issued from an office which is no more than a brass plate to show company registration. It might be an invoice on neat headed paper from a non-existent company. Where, asked the Revenue officer who gave this example, do you draw the line? The first is clearly legal but what of the others? In his terms of legitimate and non-legitimate 'make-believe', the first, entailing real expenses, is clearly legitimate; the fourth, entailing a fake invoice, clearly criminal; but what of those in between? There is a spectrum of greys at the boundaries of legality and criminality. Sometimes, as another Revenue officer observed, what begins as avoidance slips in practice through the spectrum into activities that border on or constitute evasion. An offshore company may be set up in a legally impeccable way for the initial purpose of avoidance, technically within the rules, but then become 'a vehicle for criminal extraction', for example via the issue of completely spurious invoices.

Avoidance and evasion may also interlink. The link may be distanced and indirect, akin to receiving stolen goods, perhaps unwittingly but none the less receiving the benefit of someone else's crime. Interviews suggested that this kind of interlinking can creep into bona fide avoidance schemes.

One example occurred in the context of selling-on tax-shelter leasing businesses.

In the late 1970s and early 1980s, companies making profits, and therefore incurring corporation tax bills, could reduce their tax by going into the leasing business. At the time, as an incentive to investment in equipment, the government allowed 100 per cent of the value of capital equipment to be set against profits in the first year of the purchase, thus dramatically reducing or eliminating the tax bill otherwise due. Many large companies which did not themselves want equipment but did want to wipe out their tax bills, bought equipment and leased it on to others, first of all taking advantage of their legal ownership of the equipment to take 100 per cent capital allowances to wipe out the tax due on profits in their other businesses. Capital allowances were only intended to defer tax, however. Once the 100 per cent allowances were gone, the income from the leases would be taxable. This moment was delayed by writing more and more new leases to keep up the allowances, but then a change in law removed 100 per cent capital allowances, and with them much of the tax appeal of the leasing business. The deferred tax started to catch up. If the business was sold on, its value would be reduced by the fact that tax would now be due on the income.

But what if tax were not due? If the business could be sold on to a loss-making company, it would be able to continue taking the leasing income without having to pay tax since its existing losses would wipe them out. Such a company could afford to pay higher prices for the business than the value of the leasing company otherwise (in terms of due income *less* tax) would justify. The result was a strong market for leasing companies and a tax-free escape for those companies who could no longer get tax benefits and wanted out. So far so good – for everyone except the Revenue at least, who had seen capital allowances claimed without ever getting any tax back on the resulting income. But the market was perfectly lawful.

Our interviews suggested, however, that purchasing companies paying higher prices were not always genuine loss-making companies, that the techniques employed to make above-market-price 'dicky bids', as one City solicitor termed them, slipped sometimes into evasion, as when the ultimate buyer escaped tax, not by offsetting against genuine losses but by simply 'doing a bunk out of the country'. A solicitor coming up against such offers when acting for a leasing company vendor might sniff a 'smell of fraud' about them, but would, according to this solicitor, 'need immense foresight to advise against the higher offer'. Vending companies would be likely to insist on indemnities from the purchasing company against any tax that might arise, and thus keep their own heads off the block of tax or opprobrium. But the implication is that tax avoidance might sometimes depend on *someone's* evasion.

Sometimes, what is in general an avoidance scheme depends at some point on something just a bit more akin to evasion. One key criterion used to distinguish evasion from avoidance is disclosure: if the techniques used are legal it should be possible to disclose them openly with impunity: 'you must feel you are no worse off if you have to lay all your cards on the table', as a representative of the Law Society put it.

None the less interviewees described to us examples of complex tax-avoidance schemes where the assumption was that the scheme might *not* work 'if all the cards had to be laid on the table'. One complex deal, for example, depended in part for its tax-efficiency on neglecting to disclose at the time clearance was given (Inland Revenue clearance in advance of a deal that, in the form proposed, it will not be taxable) that a third-party bid was anticipated. This was 'the sensitive bit', as the interviewee describing the deal put it, which might affect the tax consequences of the deal. Tax avoidance, then, cannot always be taken at face-value. What are apparently clever and strictly legal avoidance schemes may need careful scrutiny. It may be that, at one point or another in the complex chain of events, avoidance breaks down, with legal cleverness replaced by simply hiding key facts, and dependence on legal rules replaced by a dependence on not being caught. A complex scheme which is largely avoidance may sometimes *incorporate*, however fleetingly, elements rather more akin to the techniques of evasion.

Indeed, subtle concealment is rather more characteristic of routine dealings over tax than the disclosure distinction might suggest. In 1978 the Chancellor of the Exchequor criticised a 'new form' of tax avoidance 'accompanied by a level of secrecy which amounts almost to conspiracy to mislead'. It emerged in our interviews that the promoters of the schemes referred to here required their clients, and the professional advisers who brought them there, to sign pledges of secrecy. This was an extreme measure of concealment. Our research suggests, however, that tax is routinely escaped simply by using techniques which prevent the Revenue from realising the real nature of transactions, not just by 'ghosts' or 'moonlighters' who evade tax by failing to disclose their existence or their earnings, but by subtler methods of information control, by a range of techniques of information management, which we have termed 'non-disclosing disclosure' (detailed in McBarnet, 1991). The relevant information *is* disclosed, keeping the taxpayer on the right side of the criminal line, but it is presented in way that will not attract tax simply because it will not attract attention. Key information might be buried, noted inconspicuously in passing; hidden in a welter of irrelevancies; spread between pages 12, 119 and 164, when their tax significance depends on being related to each other. Activities might be 'redescribed' (accountant). The *method* echoes, however subtly, the techniques of concealment associated with evasion, rather than the open disclosure supposed to typify avoidance; and the maintenance of legitimacy may be more a tribute to the manipulability of the criminal boundary than to a clear distinction of approach. Providing a legal definition of the line between evasion and avoidance – disclosure – simply leads to manipulation of behaviour to fit the definition in form but not in substance.

Evasion and avoidance may interrelate in another way. The very fact that a concept of legal avoidance is officially recognised may serve to *disguise* outright evasion and perhaps even foster it. Techniques employed in legal tax avoidance are so complex, circuitous and artificial that they may accustom tax inspectors and investigators to the normality of *deviousness* and so make it harder for them to spot actual *deviance*.

MANAGING THE BOUNDARIES OF DEVIANCE

Studying the boundaries between tax evasion and tax avoidance shows, first, that the difference between deviant and legitimate behaviour may be more blurred than the legal textbook presentation of a 'sharp distinction' suggests. The Keith Committee on the enforcement powers of the Revenue departments noted concern over 'schemes where the line between avoidance and evasion may have been crossed' (1983, p. 156); and Inland Revenue officers interviewed observed that 'some of the avoidance cases now seem very near the line'. Our data suggest that sometimes the line is crossed, and that sometimes the distinction between evasion and avoidance can be very blurred indeed. Far from there being a 'sharp distinction' between evasion and avoidance, then, there is a complex interrelationship between the two in the grey area at the boundaries.

Secondly, the research shows that where clear lines are drawn to distinguish evasion from avoidance, these lines can in practice be used and managed by taxpayers and their advisers. The Keith Committee assumed as a basic principle that 'as a general rule, particular consequences should follow particular acts or omissions in every case. In this way everyone knows where they stand and compliance is likely to be improved' (1983, p. 9). But the compliance secured by clarity and certainty in enforcement may only be compliance in form rather than substance, as in disclosure which does not disclose. Policy recommendations need to take account of the scope for active manipulation by those allegedly 'subject' to the law, who are, on the contrary, often subjecting the law to their own uses. Focusing on how the boundaries of deviance are managed may also offer a new perspective on the concept of 'labelling'. The process by which people are labelled deviant or not is usually approached from the perspective of those enforcing the law. Focusing on those 'subject' to the law, and on how they can play with, or work on, the boundaries of deviance, suggests that the 'labelled' can in fact be in control of the labelling process.

Thirdly, this chapter shows that law can be not just a mechanism of social control but a mechanism for escaping it. What is being used in the management of boundaries is the law, its rules, institutions and forms. Law can be used to construct techniques which escape tax but also provide immunity from control. In defining what is a violation, law also defines what is not. In defining what is to be taxed, law also defines what is not to be taxed. In defining what is to be controlled, law also defines the limits of legal control. Boundaries mark the point for keeping out as well as for keeping in. Enforcers are not always limited by the law, but neither are those 'subject' to it. If law is a 'material to be worked on', these rules can be used and manipulated. The rules can be changed, the boundaries can be moved to catch the escapees. Loopholes can be plugged, as happened eventually with the Delaware link. But the solution is not always simple. Avoidance is dynamic and creative. If the boundaries move, so do the guidelines; and the activities may simply be adapted to the new rules. When rules were introduced to catch bed and breakfasting, by cancelling out the overnight sale and purchase against each other before calculating the tax due, the consequence was 'weekending': getting round the new rules by spreading the deals over two different stock exchange periods and using two brokers. More complex adaptations are also commonplace, and where specific devices are successfully stopped, new schemes are soon on the market aiming to replace them. Changing the rules may affect only the specific form of avoidance, not the scope for avoidance *per se*.

Of course, one way to stop manipulation of the boundaries is to remove them, or at least to refuse to map out where they are. This indeed is exactly what happened in the *Ramsay* case (and in *Furniss* v. *Dawson* which followed it). The judges reinterpreted the boundaries by looking beyond the form of the transaction to its real tax-avoidance purpose, and, despite the fact that each step in the transaction was technically correct, despite the fact that the forms employed were recognised legal forms, they refused to accept that the schemes could lawfully escape tax. What is more, instead of setting up clear precedents for the future, they explicitly stated that the law was still evolving. The result was a storm of protest, a powerful lobby, a curtailment of the new approach and a new set of guidelines. The factors involved in this process, the ambivalence of the judges, even in the new approach, and the issue of whether its demise was inevitable, are major questions tackled in the research but beyond the scope of this chapter. However, the tale, even told in brief, does indicate another level in the use of law to avoid control; in this case the ideology of the rule of law was invoked to argue against retrospective law and to argue for certainty and clarity; in short, to argue for clear boundaries. We are back full circle to clear boundaries and scope for boundary management.

This scope is not, however, equally available to all. This is partly because people dependent on payments made by others and taxed at source – most wage-earners – have little scope for juggling the declared figures. The choice then is between evasion (say, by 'moonlighting' – working for cash and not declaring it) and paying tax (which has been, in fact, already deducted). But avoidance may not be an option anyway because creative legal services do not come cheaply. Indeed, the most successful schemes are unlikely to be the popular 'mass-marketed' ones cited here (interviews suggested that it was in part the off-the-peg nature of the Ramsay scheme that provoked reaction), but the one-off, tailor-made schemes, cost-effective only for tax bills which one City solicitor, disdaining figures, described as 'more than you could possibly contemplate', evidently considering the sums beyond the sociological imagination. Even in tax *avoidance* there are strata and stratified success.

POSTSCRIPT: THE CHALLENGE FOR CONTROL

Avoidance poses a different kind of problem for control from evasion. Evasion and 'grey areas' play on problems of enforcement. The 'sensitive bit' in the 'grey' deal mentioned above would be problematic if it was discovered. Another interviewee discussed a transaction where a key factor in assessing whether or not it would succeed in escaping tax was the calculation that the Inland Revenue would not spot it. Indeed, there was concern lest the accounting practice of making provision for a tax bill which might have to be paid would 'make the Revenue wake up'. This was not seen as verging on evasion, but as 'capitalising on the real world' of, in this case, likely Revenue policing problems. The Inland Revenue faces a wide range of problems which impede enforcement, some familiar in any enforcement agency, some peculiar to white collar crime, some unique to tax. The research project describes and analyses the problems involved. In theory, however, one could conceive of an enforcers' ideal world with the requisite resources, powers and expertise to make enforcement, and with it social control of evasion and the grey areas, more effective.

Pure avoidance presents a different challenge altogether. It does not rely on concealment but on confrontation. Though, in practice, even techniques of avoidance that are assumed watertight are not 'shouted from the rooftops' (solicitor), they should escape tax and control even if they are discovered. Hence the Law Society representative's rule of thumb: 'you should feel you are no worse off if you have to lay all your cards on the table'. More tax inspectors with more motivation, training, experience, resources, might help control tax evasion and the grey areas, but would not prove the panacea for dealing with avoidance. Although discovering avoidance can itself be a problem, it is not the fundamental one. The fundamental problem is how to stop it once you've found it. How do enforcers enforce the law when the law has not been breached? How do they use strategies to secure compliance when the literal requirements of law are already being met? It may be argued that the issue is more one of prevention than *post hoc* control. Aren't laws free of loopholes possible? But this may be to take too reified a view of loopholes and of law. Tax-avoidance devices do not just depend on finding loopholes built into particular clauses of legislation; they are also complex creative constructions using basic legal forms and drawing on many statutes, cases and jurisdictions. So long as the professions – and other dealers in law – can work creatively on the fabric of law in their clients' best interests, it is difficult to see how every potential device could be foreseen and prevented.

Tax avoidance thus poses a major problem for social control, not only, in the narrow sense of this chapter, of escaping both tax and the potential penalties or stigma of evasion, but also in the wider sense of challenging the limits of civil as well as criminal law. Does this challenge to control extend beyond tax? Tax is in many ways a peculiar branch of law and some problems may be unique to it. The challenge to control posed by using rather than abusing the law, by legal avoidance, needs to be studied in other contexts, and we are already engaged in follow-up work in the area of finance.[4] However, the implication of this research, with its emphasis on the manipulability of law, and on the scope of bending it to specific interests regardless of the intentions behind it, is that economic élites with the resources to buy legal creativity can also buy immunity from law.

NOTES

1. Tax enforcement problems are created by the system of labour-only subcontracting in the construction industry, colloquially known as the 'lump'. The subcontractor does not supply any materials but only labour, with payment usually on a piecework basis. This allows workers to become self-employed and avoid Pay-As-You-Earn tax, with a real problem arising in collecting tax later if evasion practices are used. For more detail, see Smith (1986). The tax evaded was reported for the year ended 1985 at £35 million (Cook, 1989, p. 46).

2. Roy Tucker and Ronald Plummer set up an organisation specialising in creating and marketing tax-avoidance devices which attracted a good deal of adverse publicity in the late 1970s and early 1980s. See Tutt (1985) for details.

3. County NatWest Bank was investigated by the Department of Trade in 1989 for failing to disclose shareholdings. Among the resulting arrests was that of a solicitor from one of the advising firms.

4. A study of off-balance-sheet financing (McBarnet and Whelan 1991a, 1991b).

REFERENCES

Cook, D. (1989), *Rich Law, Poor Law* (Milton Keynes, Bucks.: Open University Press).

Keith Committee on the Enforcement Powers of the Revenue Departments (1983), *Report* (London: Her Majesty's Stationery Office) Cmnd. 8822.

McBarnet, D. (1984), 'Law and capital: the role of legal form and legal actors', *International Journal of the Sociology of Law*, August.

McBarnet, D. (1988), 'Law, policy and legal avoidance', *Journal of Law and Society*, 15(1) Spring; special issue edited by R. Cotterrell and B. Bercusson.

McBarnet, D. (1991), 'Whiter than white collar crime: tax, fraud insurance and the management of stigma', *British Journal of Sociology*, 42(3).

McBarnet, D. (1992), 'Legal creativity: law, capital and legal avoidance', in M. Cain and C. Harrington (eds), *Lawyers' Work* (Milton Keynes, Bucks: Open University Press).

McBarnet, D. and Mansfield, G. (1986), 'The politics of case law', paper presented at the Law and Society Association Conference, Chicago.

McBarnet, D. and Whelan, C. (1991a), 'The elusive spirit of the law: formalism and the struggle for legal control', *Modern Law Review*, 54(6).

McBarnet, D. and Whelan, C. (1991b), 'Creative compliance and the defeat of regulation: a case study in corporate finance', forthcoming.

Mansfield, G. (1989), 'The new approach to tax avoidance', *British Tax Review*, (1).

Roth, J., Scholz, J. and Witte, A. D. (1989), *Taxpayer Compliance* (Pittsburgh, Pa: University of Pennsylvania Press).

Seldon, A. (ed.) (1979), *Tax Avoision* (London: Institute of Economic Affairs).

Smith, S. (1986), *Britain's Shadow Economy* (Oxford: Clarendon Press).

Tutt, N. (1985), *The Tax Raiders* (London: Financial Training Publications).

CASES

Furniss v *Dawson* [1984] 2 WLR 226.
Ramsay, W. T. v *IRC* [1981] 2 WLR 449.

Index